The Birth of a New South

Sherman, Grady, and the Making of Atlanta

MERCER UNIVERSITY

MERCER UNIVERSITY PRESS

Endowed by

TOM WATSON BROWN
and
THE WATSON-BROWN FOUNDATION, INC.

THE BIRTH OF A NEW SOUTH

Sherman, Grady, and the Making of Atlanta

E. CULPEPPER CLARK

MERCER UNIVERSITY PRESS
Macon, Georgia
2021

MUP/ H1005

Published by Mercer University Press
1501 Mercer University Drive
Macon, Georgia 31207

25 24 23 22 21 5 4 3 2 1

Books published by Mercer University Press are printed on acid-free paper that meets the requirements of the American National Standard for Information Sciences—Permanence of Paper for Printed Library Materials.

Printed and bound in Canada.

This book is set in Adobe Caslon Pro.

Cover/jacket design by Burt&Burt.

ISBN 978-0-88146-788-8
Cataloging-in-Publication Data is available from the Library of Congress

Contents

Acknowledgments

The most collaborative project in the world is a book. It does not and cannot happen alone. Not even science achieves collaboration more completely, the result always and necessarily yielding to principals. My principals were luck of the draw. I withdrew from law school at Emory University after the fall quarter of 1965 in major part because Senator Herman Talmadge, whose son was in my class, gave a speech rebuking a close friend of mine for asking questions that impugned our South Vietnamese war policy. When the students rose in applause of Talmadge, excepting my friend and me, we walked out the back of the room and applied for graduate school—I in history and he in the Institute for Liberal Arts; thus was my journey fairly begun.

For the next nine months I plunged into subject matter, not knowing how lucky I was for visiting faculty—a professor from Duke taught "persecution and toleration in the thirteenth and fourteenth centuries." I was enthralled. Another visiting professor, then at Wyoming but later at Yale, taught "trans-Mississippi west." Yet another was an Honorary British Admiral who taught British Empire at Harvard and believed that in Africa there was White man's country and Black man's and never the twain would merge. Finally, there was Richard C. Wade, pioneering urban historian, who introduced me to a new way of thinking about urbanism and race. It led to my thesis on Henry W. Grady and changed me. To each and all, and to Harvey Young who supervised my thesis, I owe everything that follows.

But it began with family in South Georgia, Grady County to be specific. The year 1956 was pivotal though a result of everything that came before. My parents were segregationists, Methodists who never left the World Council of Churches, differences of race or color notwithstanding. My oldest brother graduated from Duke that year, and next older was under the spell of a teacher who had already embraced Martin Luther King Jr.'s cause. It helped that we were Brooklyn Dodger fans—not because Jackie Robinson was born on our Uncle Lloyd and Aunt Edna's farm, but because we hated the Yankees although we were somewhat aware and proud that the Dodgers were the most integrated team in baseball. (I did not know it then, but Andrew

Young started out preaching ten miles below the rough-board house I grew up in on the Tallahassee Highway.)

In February 1956, I was twelve years old and ran around my elementary school barefoot, shouting "Hey, Hey, Ho, Ho, Autherine's gotta go." I didn't know who she was or what it was about (Autherine Lucy was the first Black student admitted to the University of Alabama under *Brown v. Board of Education*), but I cautiously accepted the segregationist wisdom that "they," Blacks, didn't want integration any more than we did. By the end of the year, I accepted that I was a "communist" because all who believed in integration were, or so it was said in Grady County, Georgie, where I grew up. Many years later, I would write a book on the desegregation of the University of Alabama, which I published with Oxford in 1993. I recently spoke at the dedication of a historical marker to Autherine Lucy's courage. She was present, as were her children whom I got to know by writing about her journey. She changed me at a tender age in 1956, and thus yet another debt.

I went to graduate school and earned a final doctoral degree from the University of North Carolina in 1974, and I owe an especial debt to George Brown Tindall, my dissertation adviser; to Joel Williamson; and to Rodger Lotchin, another urban historian who continued to shape me. They all made this book. In 1995, I got to know Hank Klibanoff, who with Gene Roberts won a Pulitzer Prize for *The Race Beat*, a monumental accounting of press coverage of the civil rights movement.

I am grateful to many others, but librarians come first, especially Steven Brown at the University of Georgia's Hargrett Rare Books and Manuscripts Library, who knows everything; Kathy Shoemaker at Emory's Stuart Rose Library for Manuscripts and Rare Books, who helped me navigate an impenetrable access system, for an old man, at the Rose Library and remained indefatigably kind; and to Paul Crater and Sheffield Hale at the Atlanta History Center.

Then special friends! Charlotte Thomas Marshall grew up forty-five miles from me, and we met in an Athens, Georgia, gift shop some few years back. When I overheard Charlotte and her friends talking with the unmistakable accent of my native land, I introduced myself to the best Athens local historian imaginable. Her insertions and recommendations about Grady's life and course corrections for same have been invaluable. Also, former congressman John Barrow and his cousin Laura Stotler were invaluable in illumining the Barrow connection to this book. Also Peggy Galis has been an informant and cheerleader for the project.

All stories begin with immediate family. My grandchildren have watched me pile up the kitchen table with books and papers. They generally know that Grandad does weird stuff like this. Brother Charles has read and improved every sentence even as he has tasked my notion of punctuation. He is always right—sometimes. Mary, my wife of fifty-four years and a librarian, has endured yet another read-through with significant contributions, and I am forever grateful.

One for all and all for one.

Précis

Atlanta is the New South city. Rivals have emerged in recent years—Dallas, Charlotte, and others with pretensions—but Atlanta remains the epicenter. Henry W. Grady compares only with William Tecumseh Sherman in identification with what the city would become: the ultimate symbol of Civil War defeat for the South and victory for the Union. It would seal both Sherman's reputation as warlord of Union victory and Henry Grady's later fame as a national pacificator and New South builder.

This book explores the interlocking relationships of the two as they articulated the future of both a region and its empire city. The introduction grounds the book in critical race theory and its more recent articulation in Ta-Nehisi Coates's brilliant *Between the World and Me*. Part 1, The Land of Cotton, begins with the education of Henry Grady and unfolds with the imperial dominance of cotton in the nineteenth century with its global effects on all. The largest crop before the Civil War came in at just over 4,000,000 bales. It plunged to zero during the war, leading to "cotton famines" worldwide, but, by Grady's death in 1889, it had doubled pre-war numbers. The war capitalism that enslaved labor and expropriated land yielded to a post-war capitalism that moved profits away from agricultural producers and toward the manufacturing and financial centers in the North and across the waters in England and Europe. As Svenn Beckert establishes, cotton was to the nineteenth century what oil was to the twentieth. Part 1 also examines four Georgia plantations owned by the David Crenshaw Barrow family, including how they operated under slavery and emerged from it.

Part 2, The New South, begins with the Charleston earthquake of 1886, which effectively vaulted Grady to national prominence, as evidenced by the invitation to address the New England society of New York with his famous New South speech. This part also introduces criticism from Old South advocates and the debate Grady engaged with George Washington Cable in *Century Magazine* over the "Negro Problem." Most importantly, it introduces Henry Grady as an urbanist. From parks and green space to hygiene and aesthetics, he championed the modern city. He even prefigured the Centers for Disease Control that so indelibly stamp the city today. Of interest will be his championing of the arts. Grady had a grasp of aesthetics; even if Ruskin was not his inspiration, they shared an aesthetic. That Enrico Caruso paid multiple visits was evidence. Also Edwin Booth, Joseph Jefferson, Lillie Langtree, Madam Rhea, and Sarah Bernhardt were featured at Atlanta's DeGive's Opera House. Grady established an artist's colony featuring his friends Horace Bradley, James Henry Moser, and the nation's first great African American artist Henry Ossawa Tanner, along with Mary Gregory, Minnie McAffee, and Lucy May Stanton. Part 2 also introduces Grady's seizure of the Confederate narrative and its perfection through the United Daughters of the Confederacy's Mildred Lewis "Miss Millie" Rutherfordton's voluminous writings. It also examines its academic solidification at the national level through Dunning and Phillips, with eventual handoff to revisionists with Vanderbilt agrarians and Chapel Hill progressives squaring off.

Part 3, Legacy, describes how Grady inspired later New South spokesmen and women. It treats Booker T. Washington's famous speech at the Atlanta Exposition of 1895, the Atlanta race riot of 1906, the Leo Frank case, 1913–1915, the revival of the Ku Klux Klan, the second burning of Atlanta in 1917, the Red Summer of 1919, Franklin Roosevelt's move to Warm Springs, the rise to prominence of Joel Chandler Harris's son Julian and his wife Julia as they covered the Scopes trial, attacked the Klan, and received the state's first Pulitzer Prize for it. Yet the hard science of racism did not yield. Daniel Garrison Brinton, Nathaniel Southgate Shaler, and his mentor at Harvard, Louis Agassiz, put the imprimatur of nineteenth-century elite science on polygenism and racism with its belief in superior and inferior races. Charles Darwin's brilliant observations of the Fuegians on his voyage offered a path to cultural relativism, but it did not succeed, owing to his own Victorian elitism—the yin and yang of science.

Part 3 moves on to the clash between the Nashville agrarians and Chapel Hill progressives with the latter influencing Gunnar Myrdal's *An American Dilemma*. Will Alexander Percy's *Lanterns on the Levee*, Wilbur Cash's *The Mind of the South*, along with James Agee and Walker Evans's *Let Us Now Praise Famous Men*, all of whom published within a year of the others, 1941–42, and cast an important eye on life and labor in the Old and New South. Finally, Ralph McGill's towering eminence at the *Constitution* (Mr. Grady's newspaper) and Eugene Patterson's ascendance at same concludes the spreading influence of Grady's New South. Part 3 ends with Lillian Smith's demurrer against McGill's dominance and her chiding of Grady's influence. Still, Grady foreshadowed what Atlanta would become by mid-twentieth century, the self-styled "City too Busy to Hate." It would take another Georgian, also dead at age thirty-nine, to take the region and nation the rest of the way—Martin Luther King Jr.

Despite latter day aspersions about Grady's White supremacy views, Grady energized progressive thought about the future, which is a subtext of this book. The New South rose out of the Old South and cannot be explained without an understanding of race and its influence on politics, economics, and culture. Many other characters and story contributions fill out the narrative.

Introduction

They were born thirty years apart, William Tecumseh Sherman on February 8, 1820, Henry Woodfin Grady on May 24, 1850. They died just over a year apart, Grady, December 23, 1889, Sherman on February 14, 1891. They were as different as any two individuals could be. Sherman, an Ohioan, was born to one of that state's most prominent families and orphaned early; Grady was born into a loving Georgia family, but at age fourteen would lose his father to a mortal wound at Petersburg. One was edgy, almost grizzled in appearance, the Civil War's most successful field commander; the other was cherubic at birth and death, a natural orator and persuader, and as a journalist proof that the pen was all the South had left. Both had enormous energy but channeled it differently. Both would die national heroes, and before it was over both would find common cause. Together, Atlanta would be their combined Alpha and Omega.

This story begins seventy-six years ago when I was born in Grady County, Georgia, named, of course for Henry Woodfin Grady. His fame as a pacificator inspired me when I was young. His statue in the heart of Atlanta bears an inscription from his last speech: "This hour little needs the loyalty that is loyal to one section and yet holds the other in enduring suspicion and estrangement. Give us the broad and perfect loyalty that loves and trusts Georgia alike with Massachusetts—that knows no South, no North, no East, no West, but endears with equal and patriotic pride every foot of our soil, every state of our union." One eulogy etched forever another inscription: "When he died, he was loving a nation into peace."[1] As I matured, I memorized bits and pieces from his famous "New South Address," delivered before the New England Society of New York in that city, December 22, 1886, three years and one day before his death. "There was a South," he intoned, "of slavery and secession. That South is dead. There is a South of union and freedom, that South thank God, is living, breathing, growing, every day." Those words were as jarring for the Old South crowd back

[1] Graves, *Eulogy by John Temple Graves*, 592.

home that had not given up its "Lost Cause" as it was inspiring for the attending merchants, financiers, and a warlord of the Union, Sherman.

Henry Grady was the most masterful orator the South ever produced before another Georgian; also dead at age thirty-nine, Martin Luther King Jr. Like King, Grady's speaking vocabulary continued to elaborate central themes that were the glue that holds. (A good speech is given often.) Like King, Grady was a great extemporizer. With Sherman present at the 1886 speech to the New England Society of New York, Grady said that Southerners considered Sherman "an able man" though "kind of careless…about fire."[2] The audience roared. Though the great preacher T. DeWitt Talmadge proclaimed that the nation was yet to produce a "typical American," Grady demurred, saying "the first typical American, the first who comprehended within himself all the strength and gentleness, all the majesty and grace of this Republic—Abraham Lincoln."[3] The audience burst into a frenzy of sympathy. He need have gone no further, but he followed it with his usual romanticizing of a New and Old South, marching toward industrialization, diversifying agriculture, and basing race relations upon mutual respect and affection—if also premised on White supremacy. He conceded the Thirteenth Amendment completely and accepted the Fourteenth and Fifteenth Amendments as *fait accompli*, if necessarily yielding to White supremacist notions of "separate but equal" and voting restrictions based primarily on literacy. A national community embraced precisely the same view, led by liberal Republicans who believed that only the "best men," the *viri boni,* should rule. Many of these fellow travelers edited the nation's leading magazines and newspapers and formed a national thought community in support of White supremacy.

Google searches for Grady today result in many websites that depict him as a thorough-going racist not worthy of memorialization. Not without reason, many so label the whole New South movement of which he was the most prominent spokesman. Critical race theory (CRT) emerged in the mid-1980s and finds recent expression in the

---

[2] "Henry Grady's 'New South' Speech, Dec. 22, 1886." Georgia Info: An Online Georgia Almanac, georgiainfo.galileo.usg.edu/topics/history/article/late-nineteenth-century-1878-1900/henry-gradys-new-south-speech-dec.-22-1886 (accessed July 27, 2020).

[3] Ibid.

powerful and moving confession in Ta-Nehisi Coates's letter to his son, *Between the World and Me* (2015) and in *The Beautiful Struggle*, which was originally published in 2008 but gained renewed currency as a manifesto of the Black Lives Matter movement in 2015. The premise is that the terms Black and White are less "racial" descriptors than terms created to justify the subordination of Blacks to Whites. Thus, no matter one's race, ethnicity, or religious background, an individual has been classified as Black or White in the New World, thereby erasing the original diversity of those who came to these fateful shores.

Historians have not neglected the distinction that being White or Black superseded other ethnic or racial categories though they understand it from a different narrative frame. Ulrich Bonnell Phillips, a native of LaGrange, Georgia (and the nation's preeminent historian at the time of his death in 1934), wrote an essay in 1928 titled "The Central Theme of Southern History" in which he asserts that theme was a "settled determination" to maintain White supremacy. All else yielded. To be a Jew or to be German or Irish in Charleston mattered less than passing for White. Whatever one's native land or tribal arrangement in Africa meant less than being Black. Indeed, all immigrants arriving after slavery were characterized by that continuing and pervasive duality—a domination that perpetuated itself in murder (lynching), rape, incarceration, and servitude, or as Coates concludes, Blacks' fundamental loss of control over even their own bodies.

One might quarrel with or modify some of CRT's conclusions and entailments. For example, the thought that only by "race suicide" might Whites renounce their privilege, power, and property in order to make true common cause with Blacks. However, by brandishing the nation's great divide, CRT underscores its continuing influence even to the modern day. Historically Blacks demonstrated it by escapes to freedom through hopeless insurrections, migrations by underground railroads, and later by flights to the elusive "golden fields of Kansas," and even by a post-Civil War back-to-Africa movement managed exclusively by Black leadership. Then came an even greater migration of Blacks from South to North. That migration depopulated an already depressed region and deprived it of abundant labor, much of which continued to be forced labor through the convict-lease system, chain gangs, and ruinous labor contracts euphemistically called sharecropping or the crop lien system (there was almost nothing shared about it). Although there was little of promise in their new lands, at least for most it was not slavery, by whatever name, as experienced in the empire of cotton.

Coates is more nuanced than the dichotomous world he describes, and he later finds in the streets of Manhattan and Paris an interracial world, at least until he recalls what French colonizers did in Haiti—a brutal slavery. Through writing he experiences a struggle that is redemptive if not liberating, and reading him is proof of E. M. Forster's adage, "How can I know what I think until I see what I say?"

Critical race theory is but another take, if more pointed by being "essentialist," on the nation's experience from the landing of the first Africans in 1619. Sigmund Diamond, a leading sociologist and historian at Columbia (and, like Coates, from Baltimore), theorizes that what distinguished the English colonizers in the New World was how they "incentivized labor." Unlike the French and Spanish, who used native and slave labor in varying ways, the English started with a plan for indentured servitude of Whites, which encouraged artisans, tradesmen, and farmers, along with their wives and families, to apprentice for a period, usually around five years, in return for a "stake," usually fifty acres or so, and thereby a start. This pattern of servitude was "Whites only," and the English were noted also for emptying debtors' prisons, but that too was upward mobility reserved for "Whites only." Although some uncertainty existed as to which way slavery might go in the earliest years, ultimately the terms "Negro" and "slave" became a redundancy. Though Whites treated Native Americans as savages, they were not enslaved; neither were other immigrant populations with the possible exception of Chinese, known as "coolies," who came over under labor contracts little better than slavery, but still not slavery, although close enough.

But one must pause. *The Other Slavery*, by Andres Resendez, reminds us that native Indians throughout the Caribbean, South and Central Americas, up through Mexico to what would become the United States and Canada were being enslaved. Some 2.5 million were captured and sold into slavery by Spaniards, Mexicans, North Americans, and even native Indians themselves, then trafficked principally to the Caribbean islands where some of the worst slavery was exacted. Labor throughout the world was enslaved in those years for the profit of an elite few. Thus slavery was endemic although it would become identified as African and shipped to the American South. Fair enough, and even when context restores perspective, the endemic nature of slavery does not mitigate the cruelty of eighteenth-century slavery in the American South.

Critical race theorists find their intellectual underpinnings in W. E. B. Du Bois and their activist soul in Black Nationalists such as Marcus Garvey, Malcolm X, and Muhammad Ali, Black Power advocate Stokely Carmichael, and founders of CRT like Derrick Bell. Their heroines range from Phyllis Wheatley to Harriet Tubman, Sojourner Truth to Ida Wells, Zora Neale Hurston to Alice Walker, and Angela Davis to Sister Souljah. Their antithesis lies with what Coates calls the Dreamers, a term deliberately borrowed from Martin Luther King Jr.'s speech and its intended audience. The "dream" is of an integrated world premised on equality and generated by nonviolent protest; well and good enough, theorists would say, but never sufficient to "overcome." The view for CRT adherents may have been from the bottom of the well, but it is no less descriptive of an important reality of the New World: Black meant subordinate. Whether such an enlightened platform for realizable goals is the way forward is a yet unanswered question.

The national teleology is more nearly Martin Luther King Jr.'s belief in the arc of a moral universe that bends toward justice. More than myth, it is the subject of continuing debate over equality, what it means, and how it manifests itself. Embodied in eighteenth-century liberalism, it was little more than zygote. Its older liberal twins—that government should be nonobstructive and nonobtrusive—were already a given, almost noncontroversial in the relationship of colonists to king readying for a revolution. That government should also be inclusive, meaning that its laws and actions should not exclude any person by virtue of their being created equal, was embryonic. Still, the White over Black (or whatever color equation) still bedevils the landscape even as non-White Americans emerge toward a soon-to-be majority. It certainly agitates current politics.

Liberalism as Sustainable Struggle

When Martin Luther King Jr. read C. Vann Woodward's *The Strange Career of Jim Crow*, his soul leapt. It constituted proof that segregation was not born fully formed at the end of slavery. Its path may have been tortuous and tortured, but it also involved contingencies and alternatives. Segregation was not a necessary outcome and could in the same manner be altered, changed, overcome by struggle. Moreover, although drowned out by the guns of war when released in 1944, Gunner Myrdal's *American Dilemma* offered proof that freedom and equality were contested struggles in the American mind but ever-bending toward justice. Ten years later, the findings in *An American Dilemma* would buttress the Supreme Court's finding in *Brown v. Board of Education of Topeka* that separation was an inherent denial of equality, thereby giving the American stamp to freedom's struggle.

A year before *Brown*, the NAACP meeting in St. Louis proclaimed 1963 to be the due date for burning the mortgage of segregation. It turned out exactly that way as George Wallace surrendered the schoolhouse door at the University of Alabama in Tuscaloosa on June 11 of that year, and thus did Alabama become the last state to yield on the principle of separate but equal. That same evening John F. Kennedy took to the airwaves to say that the struggle for civil rights was no longer a legal but a moral issue. Following closely were the Civil Rights Act in 1964 and the Voting Rights Act in 1965, thereby implementing the essential terms of the Fourteenth and Fifteenth Amendments, all seeming to confirm the Myrdalian trajectory.

George Wallace, though, defined the trajectory of American conservatism and therefore its politics. From that door he gained four runs at the presidency. In the first year, 1964, he did surprisingly well in the Wisconsin, Indiana, and Maryland Democratic primaries. Despite Johnson's dramatic victory that year, losing only five Deep South states, Wallace had created his own White Nationalist constituency. Wallace Democrats would become Reagan Democrats by 1980. Wallace ran as an independent in 1968 and again did surprisingly well in the Midwest, California, and the South. The right wing of the Republican Party had, in the 1950s, taken over the racialist views of Southern Democrats, but its bullet-riddled body raised insurmountable questions, and George

McGovern became the Democrat's failed antiwar liberal candidate, despite his heroics as a bomber pilot in WWII. Nixon would march on to his failed presidency with the support of a solid South, measured in White flight, the Republican Party evolving to accept the Dixiecrat mantel in a new solid South. Wallace would enter only three Democratic primaries in 1976, but it was an anemic bid. Wallace conservatism—built on race, Christianity, and nationalism (albeit Southern and White)—would trump even Nixon's Southern strategy and lead to a handoff to Reagan in 1980. White Protestant conservatism would dominate the rest of the century and well into the twenty-first, Clinton notwithstanding.

Did it call for *The Fire Next Time*, book title for two essays written by James Baldwin and published in 1963? The first of his essays is a letter to his nephew, completely pre-figuring and no doubt inspiring Coates's letter to his own son, in which he despairs of current race relations. Baldwin sees in modern Christianity a stultifying religion powerless to overcome the evils of racial subordination. Forty-five years later Coates finds little difference. Both call for a revolution of thought that would turn race relations on its head, thereby ending the White over Black hegemony.

If America attains a revolution of thought that complete, it will be a culmination of all that went before, leaving historians to discover the threads of race in America as it weaves a tapestry against a background presumption of equality as ideal. What did Jefferson mean when he declared "all men are created equal," when he transparently did not believe it? Scholars have written tomes about that subject, ranging from the young Jefferson believing it mostly in his French Enlightenment way of thinking, then winding up as "master of the mountain" with a belief that only the truly "free" could be equal, meaning debt-free and White. Thus, if one were in debt to another or enslaved to another, one was not sufficiently free to exercise the ballot. Then Lincoln, who began as a colonizer, meaning ship "them" back to Africa, wound up through the trials of fire believing that Blacks should be considered equal before the law; however the circumstances of slavery had compromised their level of attainment.

Perhaps the Jefferson Memorial explains it. Ironically, R. Derek Black—the son of Ku Klux Klan Grand Wizard Stephen Donald Black and godson of David Duke, the Klan's latest personification—explains it best. Reared as a White Nationalist, R. Derek Black, by his late twenties, had abandoned his father's and godfather's tenets.

He reminded a reporter from the *New York Times* that Jefferson is not the icon of equality for which the Virginian is enshrined. His evidence is in the memorial itself: a line from Jefferson's autobiography, etched in the Jefferson Memorial, which reads "Nothing is more certainly written in the book of fate than that these people [African Americans] are to be free...," but where the inscription leaves off, Jefferson continued, "nor is it less certain that the two races, equally free, cannot live in the same government. Nature, habit, opinion has drawn indelible lines of distinction between them."[4] Thus, did Jefferson the equalitarian foreshadow separatism as embodied in the growing "back-to-Africa" movement for freed slaves and later for segregation. As this book will show, the architect of final victory in Civil War, Sherman, and Henry W. Grady would echo Jefferson's misgivings about equality down through the next century and a half. It will also show how what they said and did portended the possibility of a new order that, although fraught by White nationalism, may yet be issuing forth.

In August 2017, White nationalism reasserted itself in Charlottesville, Virginia, as marching and marauding White supremacists and neo-Nazis in a "Unite the Right" rally militantly asserted themselves against the removal of a statue of Robert E. Lee. They marched in brown shirts, gave Hitler salutes, and shouted "Jews will not replace us." They were met by America's better side with counter-demonstrators who opposed White gutter hatred as a reincarnate evil. Then a deranged White supremacist drove his car into a crowd of protestors, killing thirty-two-year-old Heather Heyer and injuring some nineteen others, many critically.

As this book will illustrate, there is never a first time. Just less than fifty years before, a similar gathering of neo-Nazis and White supremacists appeared outside Madison Square Garden where George Wallace and his running mate, General Curtis LeMay, were to receive the American Independent Party's (AIP) nomination for president and

[4] Richard E. Dixon, "Jefferson and Slavery," Thomas Jefferson Heritage Society, https://www.tjheritage.org/jefferson-and-slavery (accessed July 28, 2020).

vice president. (The AIP would revert to the American Party label that year, the original name of the Know Nothing Party, a nativist faction of the 1850s.) The neo-Nazis and White supremacists were there in support of the Wallace campaign. Counter-protesters gathered at the Garden also, and a melee erupted. Fortunately, enough police were on hand to prevent a tragedy such as occurred in Charlottesville. As the reader will observe and historians have found, there is little new under the sun when it comes to nativist violence or progressivists' embrace of *e pluribus unum*. It is the yin and yang of American history.

Ironically, a former Georgia governor, Roy Barnes, stepped forth and denounced the crime of Charlottesville. Perhaps it was not so ironic in that he had already sealed his fate for a second term by removing the Confederate battle flag from the state's banner in 2001. (The Battle Flag became a part of the state flag in 1956 when the state's senators, Herman Talmadge and Richard Russell, signed the Southern Manifesto, pledging massive resistance to the *Brown* decision that ended separate but equal in education.)

In the same article, Barnes went on to say that the Civil War was about slavery and that to ignore its brutal reality with appeals to kindness and generosity was "Gone-with-the-Wind" disingenuous; he said that a thoughtful approach to monument removal should move forward. He called for meaningful discourse that would lead to the removal of memorials, including road names, from state grounds and offices. This book will reveal how many times the South has risen again and its dominance in conservative, and especially Republican politics—Barnes's defeat being but one of many examples, his exemplary truth-telling notwithstanding, despite the fact that truth should always march on. Barnes became the last Democratic governor in Georgia, and Confederate battle flags abound, especially in the rural fields of my native state.

At the end of *Raintree County*, both book and movie, the hero is asked after a long and brutal search, "Did you find the raintree?" His answer: "No, but the search was worth it." The hero of a bewilderingly tragic tale, played by Montgomery Cliff, at the end wanders exhaustedly into the woods, only to fall asleep unknowingly under the sheltering arms of the raintree, revealed as the camera swoops up to an aerial view. So, in looking back at Grady and Sherman, I try to locate their place in the struggle for a New South, not only how and under what circumstances they entered it, but also to whom and how they handed it off—the chain of struggle. Neither will be justified by their times, but I trust explained. The search continues.

Part 1

Land of Cotton
The Education of Henry Grady

Although too young to enlist in the Confederate army, Henry Grady did become captain of the Georgia Rangers, "an organization in which Athens boys between the ages of twelve and sixteen drilled daily with mimic weapons." James Barrow, second son of the illustrious David Crenshaw Barrow family, was home on leave from a serious wound and would drill the young would-be recruits. Later, he suffered a sudden and sad death at the battle of Olustee. Grady's father's death in the same year, 1864, and the fact that the University of Georgia served as a Confederate hospital and a corral for some 600 Union prisoners immersed Grady in talk of war. As a boy would, he engaged men of both sides, Union (prisoners) and Confederates, and always left them with some food or small cash. At war's end, Federal troops occupied the town. Although the university could not reopen immediately, two faculty members set up a small male private school that Grady attended. Accordingly, he entered the university as a sophomore when it reopened in January 1866.

Grady was a good student but not studious. As a boy he was leader of the pack, and Joel Chandler Harris observed, "It is probable that his record as a boxer, wrestler, sprinter, and an all-around athlete is more voluminous than his record of scholarship."[1] Still, he excelled in languages, literature, and history but not so well in math and science (although his math teacher Williams Rutherford was his favorite). Grady was an avid reader. Dickens and Bret Harte were favorites and later Victor Hugo, but he read any and all. He did not read *Uncle Tom's Cabin*, but after the war he saw a play based on it and was highly critical of what he considered its exaggerations. He was a born orator and, as

---

[1] Joel Chandler Harris, *Life of Henry W. Grady*, 21.

noted, excelled at it. Walking across campus in his first year, he overheard an upper classman comment on his "keen originality" as a debater. It made a profound impression on him as to the "value of being original in thought and expression."[2] He was a natural leader and liked by all. In years later staffers at the *Constitution* would call him the most brilliant conversationalist they ever enjoyed.

Grady joined Chi Phi fraternity. Some said its sophomoric zeal stayed with him the rest of his life. Others in the fraternity were Walter Barnard Hill, destined to become a transformative president of the university in 1900, and Nathaniel Harris, a major figure in the founding of Georgia Tech and a true reform governor of Georgia who pledged state support for public education; however, the cotton collapse of 1917 ended that discussion. Grady joined the Phi Kappa literary society and successfully took on the older Demosthenian Society in debate. He was Phi Kappa's commencement orator in 1869. When the university declared there could be no political themes at commencement, owing to the takeover of state government through Radical Reconstruction and the presence of federal troops in Athens, Grady chose as his theme "Castles in the Air," which proved to be as airy as its title suggested—a leitmotif on the importance of "dreamers."

Why Grady took another year at the University of Virginia is not altogether clear because many reasons were given. It was the South's "queen" university with by far the best faculty and a reputation for turning out leaders. He wanted to be near his childhood sweetheart, Julia King, who was studying in Philadelphia, so off he went to study modern languages and literature. He was also determined to be its top orator and dedicated himself to that end. All his letters home turn to that ambition, and he sought to be the Washington Society's top debater. It turned out to be an elected position, and he lost by seven votes. In a slough of despondency, he went with friends to Richmond and for the only time in his life got drunk. (He was a virtual teetotaler for life, and in a famous 1887 campaign in Atlanta, he stood for Prohibition, only to lose out to his friend and co-owner of the *Atlanta Constitution*, Evan Howell.) Grady pled with his mother for another year at Virginia, but financially strapped, she simply could not relent.

---

[2] Nixon, *Henry W. Grady*, 39.

He might have read for a career in law but chose journalism because he had already showed a penchant for writing. Still licking his wounds, he penned a letter to William Arnold Hemphill, who had superintended the Methodist Sunday school Grady attended in Athens. Now Hemphill was sole owner of the *Atlanta Constitution*, which had been established in June 1868 to oppose Radical Reconstruction. Carey Wentworth Styles was a short time part owner and editor but departed before the year was out. (At the suggestion of President Andrew Johnson, who had just survived an impeachment vote, the paper took the name of a pre-war Democratic daily in Washington, the *Constitution*.) Grady's letter showed deft humor and remarkable descriptive powers as he wrote about everything from Virginia women to his disappointment at not being named final orator. The *Constitution* published the letter over his pseudonym King Hans, coined from his own name and that of his sweetheart, Julia King. The *Constitution*'s new editor, Isaac W. Avery, immediately wrote Grady requesting more submissions, and thus his career was fairly launched. (Avery would go on to be executive assistant to Governor Alfred H. Colquitt in 1880 and a year later publish a serviceable history of the state of Georgia.[3])

Grady's stint with the *Constitution* would not last long as he soon made his way to Rome, Georgia, sixty miles west and slightly north of Atlanta. His uncle and guardian, Henry Gartrell, lived in Rome and for a brief time edited the *Rome Southerner*. Gartrell was successful in business and served a term as mayor of Rome on the eve of Civil War. Connections were not enough, and Grady would fail on the *Rome Courier* and later the *Rome Daily Commercial*, thereby exhausting his mother's estate in Athens by 1872. These failures are often attributed to Grady's profligate ways, but are more likely a consequence of his news-comes-first mentality, which spared no expense. It eventually made him a great journalist, but in the meagre days of Reconstruction, not an affordable one.

One must remember that Grady was only twenty when he went to Rome, yet he was already political. He believed completely that Reconstruction was inherently radical, that its proponents were venal and corrupt, and he intended to enforce Black rule under the Fourteenth and

[3] Parks, *Joseph E. Brown*, 513.

Fifteenth Amendments, a rule that would be ruinous in its ignorance, venality, and corruption. The arch-villain was Rufus Bullock, a New Yorker by birth who mastered the new telegraphic technology and moved to Augusta, Georgia, before the war to serve as an express agent. He opposed secession but became a lieutenant colonel in the Confederacy in charge of the government's and military's telegraphy in the Southeast. At war's end, he turned Republican and favored the three war amendments. He was not alone. Joseph E. Brown, Civil War governor of Georgia and thorn in Jeff Davis's side, also turned Republican, as did James Longstreet, another Georgian and Lee's Old Warhorse, and numerous others who saw Yankee capitalism as the future reality.

Telegraphy was the future also. It linked railroads by communication to commodities and thereby became the engine of nineteenth-century capitalism. In 1859 the Adams Express Company was headquartered in Augusta, Georgia, when Rufus Bullock arrived. During the Civil War, it became the Southern Express Company. A young Andrew Carnegie began as a telegrapher with close ties to Thomas A. Scott of the Pennsylvania Railroad, who after the war would build a vast inland empire of railroads from New York to Charlotte and on to Atlanta and beyond to New Orleans and, by way of the Texas & Pacific, a southern and third continental railroad to California. Through it all, Scott bought Southern legislators and journalists to further his vast designs, the *Atlanta Constitution* not excepted. Atlanta was a beneficiary as Air Line railroads moved commerce inland and away from ports.[4]

Grady's idol was Benjamin Harvey Hill, who, along with Robert Toombs and Howell Cobb, rallied Democrats to oppose the so-called Radical Republicans. When Republicans called a convention for December 9, 1867, to organize a new constitution for the state, Conservatives gathered a sundry group of Democrats, Whigs, Know-Nothings, and other White factions in Macon on December 5 and elected Hill president. Later, over the Christmas holidays, Grady visited in the Hill home in LaGrange, Georgia; Hill's son (also named Benjamin Harvey Hill) was a fraternity brother. Grady was impressed with the father's

[4] See Nelson, *Iron Confederacies.*

"playfulness and gentle nature."[5]

Hill would impress again. As Radical or Congressional Reconstruction supplanted Presidential Reconstruction under Andrew Johnson, Georgia Conservatives, under the leadership of the aforementioned Hill, Cobb, and Toombs, gathered in Atlanta the day after the seating of Reconstruction governor Rufus B. Bullock on July 22, 1868. Known thereafter as the "Bush Arbor Meeting," because a great bush arbor shaded the speakers and shielded them from the heat. The eighteen-year-old Grady had traveled the seventy miles from Athens to take in the largest political gathering in the state's history, some 10,000 in all. He commented on the worthiness of Toombs and Cobb, but it was Hill who held him enthralled. "I don't think I was ever so much impressed by any human being as Mr. Hill that day." Not the public equal of Toombs and Cobb, Hill "but in fervid eloquence, in the stirring invective and appeal demanded just then to arouse the people to a true understanding of the situation, walked like a god for hours at heights to which the others did not soar."[6] That was not the last time Grady attested to Hill as inspiration. What the assembled Democrats shared that day was a belief that Negroes were incapable of governing and therefore should not be elected or serve if elected. They could or should be free, but government was for Whites only. Indeed, the last Reconstruction legislature in Georgia found Conservative Whites allying with similarly inclined Scalawags to expel all Black elected representatives under the foul notion that the "right to vote" did not include a "right to govern." That simple if conflicted notion explains the mindset of those who would redeem the South from Reconstruction.

Rome left Grady with one other taint, Ku Kluxism. Although formally banned by its organizers in 1869, the Klan never went away, and Rome was a seat of its more vigorous activity. Governor Bullock attempted to use its continued presence to get Grant's support to continue military Reconstruction, or "prolongation" as critics called it. Hearings on the Klan in Washington and around the South tried to

---

[5] Nixon, *Henry W. Grady*, 50.

[6] HWG, *Atlanta Constitution*, August 20, 1882; Nixon, *Henry W. Grady*, 51–52. See also W. Bragg, "Reconstruction in Georgia," *New Georgia Encyclopedia*, www.georgiaencyclopedia.org/articles/history-archaeology/reconstruction-georgia.

run it to ground, but to little avail. Three outbreaks in Floyd County (Rome) in late 1870 and early 1871, the last being on the night of February 6, occasioned a tit for tat. Grady's successor at the *Courier*, B. F. Sawyer, accused Grady of being at "the tail end of the Ku Klux" parade. Grady had insinuated much the same about Sawyer. Whatever, Grady's name did wind up on a list for the Joint Committee of Congress then investigating the Klan. When it met in Atlanta, it did not call Grady and no further evidence attaches Grady in any way to the Klan. That said, Grady acknowledged its existence and said that its reputation hurt the South in national elections, but he left an opening: "If an inexorable necessity calls for Klan action, act promptly, with decision, and do nothing more than is absolutely necessary."[7] It was a quizzical expression but common among professional Southerners who distanced themselves from the Klan without rejecting the need for it.

Grady likely knew more about the Klan than he admitted. He had already established a close friendship with Charles Henry Smith, a former mayor of Rome, Confederate officer, and retired lawyer who wrote under the pen name "Bill Arp." For his commentary, Smith adopted a "Cracker dialect" and wrote as a humorist and satirist. He was also a leader of the Klan in Rome and environs. Without doubt, Grady knew what was going on, and, with Smith as a friend, he had an impeccable source as to crimes against Blacks in that turbulent part of Georgia, especially those who had supported the Union.[8] As with Joel Chandler Harris, Smith as Bill Arp was Grady's other "find" for the *Constitution* from his Rome days. In the 1890s, after Grady's death, Smith's racism became more pronounced. He died in 1903 at age 77.[9]

The Klan also attached itself to Grady's hero Benjamin Hill. One historian said that two prominent railroad directors who opposed the influence of Tom Scott's Pennsylvania Railroad, Benjamin Hill and North Carolina's Josiah Turner, became in 1868 "public intellectuals" for the Klan.[10] If true, it belied Hill's larger reputation as an antebellum Unionist who opposed secession and was by 1869 a New Departure

[7] Nixon, *Henry W. Grady*, 82–93; H. Davis, *Henry Grady's New South*, 32–33.

[8] Dixon, "To Laugh in One Hand."

[9] Parker, *Alias Bill Arp*, 27–29.

[10] Nelson, *Iron Confederacies*, 5.

Democrat. Anticipating Grady's later theme of an economic New South, Hill told a gathering of UGA alumni in 1871 that they should acknowledge "the superiority of Yankee civilization" and called upon all Southerners "to support railroad and factory growth, and the education of labor (black as well as white) as the route to regional prosperity."[11]

Grady had much more on his mind in 1871—marrying Julia King. The daughter of an Athens homeopathic physician and a mayor of the town, Julia King was twelve years old when Grady first proposed (he was fourteen). He told the story *ad nauseam* that when he proposed, she was to give her assent the next day by wearing a yellow dress and waving a handkerchief. His twist was the "desperation" with which she waved.[12] Surely Julia, or Jule as he affectionately called her, endured the subsequent tellings. Theirs was a happy marriage, filled with cheer and devotion to their children, Henry King Grady (later changing King to Woodfin) and Augusta King Grady. His great joy was in walking "Gussie" to school on his way to work. In his diary he referred to them as his "babies." He adored his children and made them first, whatever else was on his mind.

The year 1872 was career-shaping. His newspaper ventures in Rome failed for the last time, but, undaunted, he wound up in the capital city with the *Atlanta Herald*. Grady's education was only beginning. His departure from the *Rome Commercial* trailed clouds of debt as a farewell column alluded but Grady never admitted. His first reach was to find sufficient capital to acquire an interest in the *Constitution*, but overtures to the fire-eating secessionist and unpardoned Rebel, Robert Toombs, proved unsuccessful. While in Atlanta for that purpose, he encountered the man who would complete his education. Georgia-born but South Carolina–bred Robert Augustus Alston had been present for the firing on Fort Sumter and escorted Jefferson Davis through Georgia to his final capture. A lieutenant colonel in John Hunt Morgan's militia, he followed its celebrated if oft futile trail throughout the war.

Mary Boykin Chestnut found Alston "a brilliant creature, truly,

---

[11] Foner, *Reconstruction*, 418.

[12] H. Davis, *Henry Grady's New South*, 33.

and no doubt a fair specimen of the western daredevils who rally around John Morgan." Alston was a glib but captivating talker and a best friend of her husband—although Colonel James Chestnut Jr. (later one of the South's youngest generals) on another occasion warned Mary to keep Alston at arms' length, and she promised "to be coldly polite." Still, she could not resist, "utterly forgetting he was under ban." When reproached by her husband saying, "so this is your style of being coldly polite," she thought to herself, "Indeed, I forgot all about what they said of him while he was here. The lies they tell on him never once crossed my mind. He is a great deal cleverer and I daresay just as good as those who malign him."[13] "Bob" Alston met and surpassed the bar of gentility and was handsome as well. People were always glad to see him coming. When Joel Chandler Harris first encountered Robert Toombs at the Kimball House, he did not know who he was but marveled at his garrulousness. Harris said to himself, "This man is surely related to Bob Alston of the *Atlanta Herald*, for it is not possible that Providence has endowed two families with such sublime gifts of gab."[14]

Grady and Alston had met in 1869 when Alston and Alston's favorite uncle, Tom Howard, came to Rome for a gathering on best practices in agriculture. Also present was the nineteen-year-old editor/owner of the *Rome Daily Commercial*. Grady did not find much in Howard's pitch for going slow on recommended reforms, and in a rather supercilious manner said so in the paper's next edition. Alston replied angrily and echoed his uncle, comparing Grady to a "monkey who runs riot over a powder magazine with a red hot poker in his hand." That said, the youthful Grady impressed Alston. (This particular meeting of the state Agricultural Society also put Grady back in touch with members of the Barrow family, Athenians who figured importantly in Grady's life and labors. David Crenshaw Barrow Sr. had re-formed the Agricultural Society at war's end.)

Grady's first ten years in newspapering seemed filled with accidental meetings and impetuous decisions, most of which were serendipitous. Grady was on his way from Athens to Rome in 1872 when he stopped off at Atlanta's Kimball House and bumped into Alston.

---

[13] Woodward, *Mary Chesnut's Civil War*, 430, 472–73.

[14] Julia Harris, *Joel Chandler Harris*, 11.

Grady had just been rebuffed on a deal to purchase a half interest in the *Constitution* with backing from Robert Toombs, or "Burly Bob" as Grady called him. Alston was on the verge of letting his part ownership at the *Atlanta Herald* go as well. Grady explained, "In an hour after I met Alston, the trade was closed. No papers were drawn up that night, and the details were fixed over a bowl of oysters…." The two men shared a room that night and, in the darkness, Alston asked Grady if there was insanity in his family. Grady answered, "None at all, why do you ask?" Alston replied, "Well I've been thinking over the *Herald* trade for a week. You've known of it a few hours. Now I know that a man that's quicker on a trade than I am must be crazy, and I was afraid I'd gone into partnership with a lunatic!"[15]

The terms vary among accounts, but it appears that Grady had sold his interest in the *Daily Commercial* for $1500 and financed the rest on a loan from the Citizens Bank, secured by his mother. His total investment came to $5000.[16] The loan from the Citizens Bank would be the *Herald*'s undoing as the *Herald* pilloried bank owner Joseph E. Brown. Brown did not suffer grievances lightly, but there is always more to the story.

Grady was made managing editor, which given his previous failures was suspect, and Alexander St. Clair-Abrams as editor wrote most of the political columns. The team of Abrams, Alston, and Grady was combustible, starting with Abrams but not ending there. Abrams, said to be a Creole, apprenticed with James Gordon Bennett's *New York Herald* and took on his mentor's zest for spicy, flash-and-dash stories—

[15] *Atlanta Constitution*, April 18, 1880; Garrett, *Atlanta and Environs*, 2:5; Hain, *Murder in the State Capitol*, 124–25.

[16] A letter from Grady to his mother and sister on Kimball House letterhead October 1, 1872, the date of the purchase, confirms the broad outline of the agreement, if not precise details: "I have this day bought the *Atlanta Daily Herald.* It is a good paper & I feel I will do well. Col. Robt A. Alston one of the leading men of Georgia is my partner." He wrote that he paid $1,800 in cash (Henry W. Grady Papers, box 1, folder 1, Rose Manuscript and Rare Books Library, Emory University; hereafter cited as "Rose Library, Emory"). His mother did not secure the additional loan with the Citizens Bank until February 18, 1874, mortgaging her property to support a $2000 note to Alston and Grady (ibid., box 1, folder 7).

human interest compounded daily. Such stories guaranteed the creation of readership and enemies. As Joel Chandler Harris described the threesome at the *Atlanta Herald*, "It would be difficult to get together three more impulsive and enterprising partners. Little attention was paid to the business office."[17]

Described by Grady as "a brisk young fellow full of bustle and excitement, spiced with a flavor, and suggesting a Frenchman from the clubs," Abrams flung the doors open and announced himself. "He planted himself behind one side of a hastily made counter, cocked his hat on one side, gave his goatee a nervous stroking, whistled a strain of the *Marseillaise*, and announced that the *Atlanta Daily Herald* was ready for business."[18] Abrams was also prone to duels, which Alston condoned, given his South Carolina heritage. One near-fatal encounter occurred when Carey Wentworth Styles, former editor of the *Constitution* and then editor of South Georgia's *Albany News*, accused Abrams of having Negro blood. Intervention prevented the fatal encounter, but Grady had fanned these flames by publishing Styles's accusation.[19] Alston's biographer counted, in all, five iterations of ownership and management in the *Herald*'s three-and-a-half-year life.[20] Grady spent all but two months in the various configurations and remained close to Alston. Isaac W. Avery literally crossed the street from the *Constitution* and stayed with the *Herald* from April 1874 to April 1875 and provided ballast. When Alston bought him out, Grady and Alston remained until the paper ceased publication in February 1876.

The paper ceased not only because of the enemies its owners made but also because of the want of management, made most conspicuous when, for reasons unknown, trains to Macon (due south) and Opelika, Alabama (southwest), stopped deliveries of the *Herald*. Consequently, the aforementioned would-be-duelist and editor, Abrams, with acquiescence from Alston and Grady, decided to hire an engine with mail car to make the daily trips, each of which cost $150 a day. It was impossible to make back that kind of expense. Moreover, they offered

---

[17] Joel Chandler Harris, *Life of Henry W. Grady*, 25.

[18] *Atlanta Constitution*, April 18, 1880; Garrett, *Atlanta and Environs*, 2:4–6.

[19] Hain, *Murder in the State Capitol*, 131.

[20] Ibid., fn 11, 125.

prizes that if collected piled up another $7500 in obligations.[21]

Alston had his own impulsive side, which, in 1875, had led to a challenge to duel with Edward Young Clarke, who always went by his initials E. Y. and was now latest editor of the *Constitution*. They made it to their rendezvous, just across the line into Alabama from West Point, Georgia. Somehow Alabama officials had been tipped off and knew just where to find Alston and his two seconds, thereby foiling the attempt. This farcical aside raised questions about Alston's own impetuosity, and Grady's last biographer described Alston's behavior a "humiliation."[22] Nonetheless, Grady himself stood by his man and wrote a long piece about Alston's desire not to die from violence, a column written the day after Alston met a violent death in March 1879.[23]

Grady had a knack for finding the best in those whose excesses could be at times exasperating if not embarrassing. He considered Abrams "the best journalist, pure and simple, Georgia ever had." Abrams "wrote and edited as if he were running the *London Times*, and the result was a perfect piece of journalism." While his journalism may have appeared "cold and unsympathetic," Abrams was nonetheless "tender, easily affected, full of good impulses." Grady concluded, "We have never had a writer of purer English on the Georgia press." Of his time on the *Herald*, Grady said, "I don't think I was ever happier than during the few years [1872–1876] we scuffled along in that old building. It was hard work, of course, full of desperate chances—but we were young, sanguine and fond of the profession."[24]

There was a last straw, not that the *Herald* needed much to break its back given its impecunious ways. The enmity between former Confederate Governor Joseph E. Brown (who, as readers will remember, financed Grady's loan) and the editors of the *Herald* was palpable. By the *Herald*'s accounts, Brown could do no good. Not only had Brown obstructed the Confederate war effort, but after the war he turned busi-

---

[21] Ibid., 137.

[22] H. Davis, *Henry Grady's New South*, 35.

[23] Hain, *Murder in the State Capitol*, 144; *Atlanta Constitution*, March 12, 1879.

[24] *Atlanta Constitution*, April 18, 1880; Garrett, *Atlanta and Environs*, 2:5; Hain, *Murder in the State Capitol*, 127.

ness capitalist and Republican, while sidling up to Reconstruction governor Rufus Bullock. Then when Brown stepped down from what seemed like a certain sinecure as chief justice of the State Supreme Court, provided him by Bullock, there was further perfidy. Brown stepped down in order to lease without appropriate monetary consideration the state-owned Western & Atlantic, a railroad the *Herald* estimated had cost millions in state money—some estimates range as high as $10 to $11 million. The lease enabled Brown to corner the market on coal for manufacturing and heating, effectively giving preferred treatment to his own Dade Coal Mining Company in North Georgia. The surprise is that Brown did not drop the hammer at that moment. He bided his time. He was known for "getting even."

One of Grady's first ventures for the *Atlanta Constitution* in 1869, even before heading to Rome, was to join a Georgia press excursion on the Western & Atlantic. When the proprietors of the *Constitution* learned that Governor Bullock was to be aboard, they were only too happy to send their cub reporter in their place. Grady wrote a scathing report indicating that Bullock had done all he could to bribe the Georgia press. The train was loaded with all the emoluments to impress reporters, including champagne and cigars. Grady consistently filled his reports with human interest stories and sights along the way, until the end. Then Grady took aim at Bullock, charging him with "bribery" and "bartering patronage" in order to garner press support. Even Grady's editors stood back for a moment, but they soon joined the chorus resulting in a lawsuit for libel, which Bullock later dropped owing to his growing disfavor. Joel Chandler Harris was along for this ride for the *Savannah Morning News*. Grady took an instant liking to him, and thus began what Harris's daughter-in-law Julia described as "their long and delightful association which was fruitful for such rich results to Georgia journalism and letters...."[25]

At the *Herald*, Grady simply took up where, in truth, he had never left off, criticizing any and all associated with Radical Reconstruction in Georgia and that included former governor Brown. Again, the surprise is that Brown withstood it as long as he did, for he held the note

[25] Nixon, *Henry W. Grady*, 71–73; Grady Scrapbooks, Rose Library, Emory; Harris, *Joel Chandler Harris*, passim.

through his Citizen's Bank on Grady's interest in the *Herald*. When Brown "called" the loan, the already weakened *Herald* could not survive and accordingly was put up for sheriff's sale on February 6, 1876. Over the next two months, Grady and Alston attempted two other ventures, the *Atlanta Courier* then the *Sunday Telegram*, a weekly that offered a sprightly summary of news from other papers. Both failed.

Of more interest, Grady's hero Benjamin Harvey Hill was implicated in Bullock's and Brown's Reconstruction politics and at a table set in Atlanta by Bullock that included Brown; General Columbus Delano, then secretary of the interior; and Simon Cameron, secretary of war for Lincoln until essentially disgraced after a year and later Senate politico during. Hill accepted the invitation at great political cost. In a later lengthy interview with Joel Harris, published by the *New York Sun* for which Harris was a correspondent, Hill exonerated himself and was featured as having rescued Georgia from the dastardly acts of Reconstruction.[26] Journalist as mediator: Grady did it many times.

Another truth is that the table was not set by Bullock, but by Tom Scott, magnate of the Pennsylvania Railroad and master manipulator of Southern politics and journalism. The fete for Cameron and Delano was set to confirm railway redemption, not Southern Redemption, although it contributed to both. Over yet another oyster dinner at the Kimball House, for which it was famous, Scott mastered an arrangement between Hill and former governor Joseph E. Brown to allow for Scott's mastery of the former state-owned Western & Atlantic, which now escheated to Scott, with Hill, Brown, and other figureheads managing its local operations, but subservient to Scott.[27] In the new order, capital as ever trumped politics.

Three announced failures in a span of five months and out of money from his father's estate, Grady's head should have been hanging. Instead he claimed to have started life "ready-made," only to have "speedily un-made himself and was now hopefully rambling along the road to regeneration."[28] His assessment was at once clear-eyed and optimistic. Over the next four years, he would demonstrate not only this

---

[26] Harris, *Joel Chandler Harris,* 14–34.

[27] Nelson, *Iron Confederacies,* 163.

[28] HWG, *Atlanta Constitution,* August 15, 1880; Nixon, *Henry W. Grady,* 123.

irrepressible side but his determination as a journalist. First, he borrowed fifty dollars and headed to New York, where he made his way to the *New York Herald* (no doubt influenced by his admiration for Abrams). On presenting himself, James Gordon Bennett was nowhere to be found, so Grady found the managing editor, Thomas B. Connery, "the *alter ego* of young Jim Bennett," and "absolute arbiter" when Bennett was away, as he frequently was. Grady came right to point and proposed that he be named Georgia correspondent for the *Herald*.

Connery had an imposing reputation—many thought him "the best newspaperman in America." He gave Grady some paper, told him to write a trial article on political conditions in Georgia, then left the building for an hour. On return, he found Grady leaning back in his chair with feet on desk. "What's the matter?" asked Connery. "Nothing," replied Grady, "except I'm through."[29] Grady spent an anxious night at the Astor House, nearly out of money, worried about whether the 2000-word article would be published. It was, and an anxious Grady appeared much too early the next morning and waited for Connery, who told the young man he would be named Georgia correspondent and paid at space rates.

Eventually, Grady would negotiate similar arrangements with the *Chicago Inter-Ocean*, the *Louisville Courier-Journal*, *Detroit Free Press*, *New York World*, and the *Springfield Republican*. However, at space rates, Grady's writing was not likely to be financially sustainable. In July 1876, he made a total of $22, and he made less in August and September. On his way back from covering election riots in South Carolina in October, he called at the office of the *Augusta Constitutionalist* and received an offer to be its editor. He promptly accepted and asked only that he be allowed to return home before taking over.

In typical Grady fashion, he packed and with overcoat on arm headed to catch the next train back to Augusta—only to meet Evan P. Howell, who asked where he was going. When told, Howell, who only the day before had bought half interest in the *Constitution*, asked why Grady didn't work for the Atlanta paper. Somewhat sheepishly, Grady said the paper would not have him for all the trouble the *Herald* had given the *Constitution*. Howell said he controlled the matter now; if

[29] Nixon, *Henry W. Grady*, 123–24.

Grady would show up at 10:00 the next morning, he would match the *Constitutionalist*'s offer of $100 a month.

The truth is, Howell had been looking for Henry Grady. Howell and his partner, W. A. Hemphill, saw something special in Grady, and they were right.[30] Within days, Grady would be working on the biggest story of the last half of the nineteenth century—the contested election of 1876. The election, pitting Rutherford B. Hayes, the Republican, against Samuel Tilden, the Democrat, was a virtual tie, with Tilden holding an electoral vote majority and a clear lead in the popular vote, but three states—South Carolina, Louisiana, and Florida—were contested. The Oregon territory also had one electoral vote. If the elections had been "Whites only," there would have been no question of Tilden's election, but enough of Reconstruction held over to make it close. The *New York Herald* was desperate to send its correspondent for the final count in Florida.[31] Grady's employers at the *Constitution* also saw it as a historic opportunity and sent him to Tallahassee.

As Grady always did, he was off on the next train and found himself in the company of federal soldiers and General Lew Wallace, who was a Republican observer. Wallace, who was inexplicably "out of action" at Shiloh, when he was supposed to come up on Sherman's right, was also soon to become author of *Ben Hur* (1880). He and Grady began a long friendship. The Republican-controlled panel ruled all Florida electors for Hayes, thereby making him the next president, but Grady had a problem: telegraphic communication was down in Tallahassee. He commandeered a buggy and, with new friend Lew Wallace, headed for the nearest telegraph office. Arriving ahead of the other reporters, Grady occupied the wire for a complete story. When he ran out of content, he started tapping in text from a spelling book in order to keep other reporters at bay. Lew Wallace could only admire such cunning.[32]

The Democratic observer was former governor of Georgia Joseph E. Brown, the man who controlled the Citizens Bank note that killed

---

[30] Howell also accepted Grady's suggestion that he hire Joel Chandler Harris.
[31] Florida would also hold the balance in a presidential election in 2000.
[32] Ibid., 133–36; Hoogenboom, *Rutherford B. Hayes*, 276–77.

the *Atlanta Herald.* Surprisingly, Grady came away liking him, a surprising turn given earlier developments. Grady and other *Herald* editors had lambasted Brown for complicit relations with railroads and the convict-lease system. Grady was remarkably flexible in judgment when new facts and conditions emerged, and his evolving opinion of Brown was a good example.[33] On Grady's turnabout with respect to Brown, Harris himself said, "In such a contest as this [the Florida vote count], Senator Brown was absolutely master of the situation, and Mr. Grady took great delight in studying his methods, and in describing them afterwards."[34]

Hayes won the electoral vote 185 to 184. In the end, although surely a stolen election, it became known as the Compromise of 1877, with Southern Democrats acquiescing in Hayes's election in return for the removal of federal troops from Southern states, South Carolina and Louisiana being the last two. Grady stayed with the coverage through 1878 and won plaudits for it. He was also pioneering a new technique in journalism, the interview. Mrs. Thomas "Stonewall" Jackson; Jefferson Davis; Confederate generals Longstreet, Gordon, and Toombs; along with William Tecumseh Sherman, all came to life through Grady's pen. He went entirely to space rates (column inch), even for the *Constitution*, and his fortunes began to improve. Grady's style and instinct for stories at last made space rates work.

Grady turned to human interest stories with uneven results. He took up the cause of a fourteen-year-old girl named Sallie, who had been imprisoned for vagrancy and forced to work alongside male convicts. He sainted her, raised money, found a room in a charity home, and got her a job. The judge who had sentenced her contradicted Grady's account and said Sallie was sixteen and a prostitute; Sallie soon proved the judge right.

Grady was entering a period of, if not ennui, then uncertainty. He understood his brilliance, but felt rudderless. He gave a masterful

---

[33] Brown, who was also criticized for obstructing Jefferson Davis's war effort by, among other things, reclassifying government jobs to frustrate the draft, made at least one friend out of it, Joel Chandler Harris, who took advantage of the provision. And, Grady had just landed Harris a job with the *Constitution* (Trudeau, *Southern Storm*, 4).

[34] Joel Chandler Harris, *Life of Henry W. Grady*, 29.

speech at Emory College, where students there still had something of the pre-war generation's rowdy edge, hissing and hooting down speakers, yet he held them enthralled for two hours. He would not give another speech of consequence for eight years. Grady could have made large fees as a speaker but was getting more comfortable from income earned as a writer. The *Herald* was gone and with it attacks on the men who would become the Bourbon Triumvirate—John Brown Gordon, Joseph E. Brown, and Alfred Colquitt. The *Herald* had taken them to task for everything from profiteering through the convict-lease system to getting sweetheart deals with railroads, thereby converting the public trust into a trough. Yet Grady had seen another side of Brown in Tallahassee and began to soften his stance. Moreover, Evan Howell encouraged him to write about railroads, which he took up with zest. Drawing an advance from the business office, he set out on a journey that took him to more than a dozen states and threw him in the company of H. Victor Newcomb, soon to become president of the Louisville and Nashville Railroad.[35] The question should soon arise: was Grady too enthralled with railroads? But there was an intervention.

Murder in the Capitol

Tragedy struck in a way that called into question Grady's former commitment to his friends at the *Herald* and especially to the man he called his best friend, Bob Alston. While Grady hobnobbed with the captains of railroading, Alston, as chairman of the general assembly's joint committee on the penitentiary system, had become frustrated by abuses among those who profited from leased convict labor. His report named names and cited worst cases. Some powerful men who leased the convict labor, such as Joe Brown and John B. Gordon, could lift their skirts above the mud, but their overseers in these crimes could not. By 1887 Gordon, then governor, got credit for turning on the system, even inconveniencing his neighbor, Senator Brown, whose coal mines had increased their use of convict labor over time. By then Alston was eight years in his grave, a victim, his biographer believes, of his vehement protest of the system.

[35] H. Davis, *Henry Grady's New South*, 41.

Edwin Cox, Alston's neighbor in the Kirkwood subdivision of Atlanta, was a sub-lessee of prisoners on John B. Gordon's plantation in Taylor County, about eighty miles south of Atlanta. Gordon granted his good friend Alston power of attorney over his Atlanta interests, and when he asked Alston to sell Gordon's interest in the convict leasing company, Alston in turn told Cox that as a sub-lessee, he would no longer have access to the labor of sixty convicts. On March 11, 1879, an infuriated Cox accosted Alston in an Atlanta barbershop. Although Alston and Cox had been friends, matters devolved quickly on the day of the confrontation. Cox challenged Alston, instructed Alson to arm himself, then purchased a .41 caliber "Swamp Angel" revolver and purposed to kill Alston. Alston tried to defuse the situation, even approaching Governor Colquitt to intervene (the governor was surprisingly casual and did not act promptly), but Cox would not be appeased. At about 3:30, both Alston and Cox went to the Treasurer's Office in the capitol (which was then in the Kimball House hotel) where they quarreled. Alston shot first with a borrowed gun, wounding Cox in the upper lip and hand. Cox missed his first shot, but then fired into Alston's temple, killing him. He was pronounced dead at 6:40 p.m., March 11, 1879.[36]

Although convicted of premeditated murder and given a life sentence that was affirmed by the Supreme Court, Cox served only three years in Senator Joseph E. Brown's Dade County Coal Mines. Though Black prisoners convicted of petty crimes such as vagrancy slaved in the mines for years, Cox was given light duty running the farm that fed its convict labor. This disparity could indicate only complicity in a corrupt and venal system; no one exposed it at the time, and revenge crimes between Whites were frequently given a pass. In 1882, newly elected governor Alexander Stephens, former Confederate States vice-president, pardoned Cox. During his first months in office, Stephens handed out a spate of pardons, nine for capital offenses—a not uncommon practice at the time. But where was Grady, Alston's best friend?

He was wailing and importuning any within earshot of his best-loved friend's virtues. Charles Henry Smith, as Bill Arp, wrote in the

---

[36] Garrett, *Atlanta and Environs*, 1:958–59. For the tension between Gordon and Cox, see Eckert, *John Brown Gordon*, 264–65.

Constitution,

> Some years ago I happened in Atlanta the day that Cox killed Alston—Alston who was Grady's friend, and Grady loved him like a brother. The town was wild. There was hurrying to and fro as the excitement intensified, and Grady was by turns the center of every crowd. Horror-stricken, shocked and grieved, he told and retold the sad news in all its tragic details, seeking and courting sympathy from every listener, and every little while Howell would call him gently away and say: "Can't you go to the office now? This thing must be written up you know." All the evening Howell watched and waited, and every time he urged Grady to go he said, "I will; please wait just a moment. I promise you I will go directly; there is time enough." As fresh listeners would join the crowd Grady would tell it all again, and grieve again, and so the night came on, and eight o'clock and nine o'clock and ten, and the paper must go to press at three. Finally, Howell became desperate, and seizing him by the arm he forced him bodily to the building and up the stairs to his room and begged him to write.

Grady wrote a "brilliant narrative…and clothed it all in such pathetic, passionate language that seemed to have been written with the tears that fell upon his pen." He denied rumors that Alston had been involved in two previous duels and described him as the most genial person he knew.[37] Grady repeated the story often of how Alston "did not want to die with his boots on," that he lived in dread of a violent death. Perhaps it was his father's violent death in a revenge killing and Alston's own reputation for dueling that cast the shadow, as evidenced in his "near duel" with E. Y. Clarke, former editor of the *Constitution*. In all, Grady wrote five and half columns on Alston's death, providing full details of the altercation, but never mentioning the convict-lease system as a potential motive. He also underscored a common view of Alston: that his ebullience was born of a certain boyishness, a childlike enthusiasm that marked his enjoyment of politics and journalism. As Grady put it, "He was just emerging from his boyhood when he died,"

---

[37] Hain, *Murder in the State Capitol*, 203–204; Dugat, *Life of Henry W. Grady*, 41–42.

this although Alston was well into his forty-seventh year at his death.[38] On arriving home after midnight, Grady confided in his diary that it had been "a murder most foul," and the next day in another entry he declared Alston his "most devoted friend."[39] He made no further entries on the subject, but then Grady was a desultory diarist at best and "confide" may be too strong a word for the type of entries he made, as most were perfunctory.

Ironically, Grady avoided associating Alston's murder with his withering criticism of the convict-lease system and with those most prominently associated with it, the Bourbon Triumvirate itself—Joseph E. Brown, John B. Gordon, and Alfred H. Colquitt.[40] More compelling is the straightforward explanation by Gordon's biographer that Cox was angered over the loss of some sixty convict lessees from the pending sale of Gordon's Taylor County farm.[41] Be that as it may, the further irony is that Cox, Alston, and the triumvirate were friends and neighbors in the Kirkwood section of Atlanta, then considered a distant residential suburb, now home to the Carter Presidential Center. Moreover, Grady was soon to become the Warwick (i.e., kingmaker) of Georgia politics, effectively managing the campaigns throughout the 1880s of Brown, Colquitt, and Gordon, otherwise known as the "Atlanta Ring" All the while, Alston had been moving toward the Independent Democrats, led by Dr. William H. Felton and his wife, Rebecca Latimer Felton, whose case against the Bourbon Triumvirate was linked in no small part to the abusive convict-lease system that enriched them. Grady had himself joined the hue and cry against Joseph E. Brown, when allied with Alston on the *Atlanta Herald*. Now he was silent, even as his closest friend may well have lost his life to that same system.

---

[38] Scrapbook by Martha Gartrell Nicholson, Grady's aunt, Hargrett Rare Books and Manuscript Library, University of Georgia (hereafter cited as "Hargrett Library, UGA").

[39] Henry Woodfin Grady Papers (hereafter cited as Grady Papers), box 2, folder 12, Hargrett Library, UGA.

[40] A recent biographer of Alston makes a case that Gordon and Colquitt bribed Edward Cox to kill Alston (Hain, *Murder in the State Capitol*, 223–25).

[41] Eckert, *John Brown Gordon*, 264–65.

Railroads and the Triumvirate

Grady was already in the embrace of railroads and what they meant for Atlanta's fortunes—inseparable. On joining the *Constitution* in 1876, Grady had been placed in charge of its weekly edition. Sometime later, he complained to W. A. Hemphill about having gotten "it up to booming" and was ready to move on to the daily. He got his wish—and soon more.[42] The ties to railroads would lead to personal fortune. In the year following Alston's death, Grady traveled with H. Victor Newcomb, president of the Louisville and Nashville (L&N), to over a dozen states, ending up in New York, where Newcomb introduced Grady to Cyrus W. Field at the Stock Exchange. Field is most famous for his association with laying the Atlantic Cable, one effect of which was tying American cotton markets directly to London, thereby eliminating factors and middlemen. Field instantly took a liking to Grady and, upon request, loaned Grady $20,000 for a one-fourth interest in the *Constitution*. The terms called for Grady to repay the loan in one year at 6 percent interest.[43] Grady paid it off within two years. Newcomb is said to have offered guidance in stock speculation, leading to the suspicion that Newcomb may have provided more direct payments although there is no record of direct payments in Grady's personal account books. Grady's personal income certainly could not have paid off the loan.

There were rumors that Field's main interest was in garnering support for his brother's candidacy for the Democratic presidential nomination. The brother, Stephen J. Field, was a justice of the U.S. Supreme Court and held what today would be regarded as libertarian views, then just commonly conservative. He voted in the majority of *Plessy v. Ferguson* that held "separate but equal" to be constitutional and was the first justice to introduce the idea that corporations should have the

[42] Grady to Hemphill (no date), "I have worked at the Weekly till got it up to 'booming.' Now trust me for one thing further' *try this*" (William Arnold Hemphill Papers, Atlanta History Center).

[43] May 8, 1880, promissory note to Field payable semiannually at 6 percent. Left as collateral 200 shares of Constitution Publishing Co. stock par value at $100 each. Due May 8, 1881 (H. W. Grady Papers, box 1, folder 1, Rose Library, Emory).

standing of "persons" before the law. The *Constitution* supported Field's candidacy, and Evan Howell, as a convention delegate, supported Field until there remained no hope. Grady heaped lavish commentary on the candidate; still, no direct evidence supports a quid pro quo.[44] However, it was more evidence of the link between telegraphy and railroads and their combined influence on journalism in the last half of the nineteenth century. On the date of Grady's purchase of his interest in the *Constitution*, May 8, 1880, he was sixteen days short of turning thirty. (Another May 8 in 1945 famously marked the end of the war in Europe.)

There was more to the meeting in New York City than arranging a loan for Grady. A deal was cooking in Georgia that Newcomb believed would be a game changer for the Louisville and Nashville's fortunes in that state. Senator John Brown Gordon needed money and wanted to step away from his seat in the Senate with only months left in his second term in order to get it. Gordon's biographer and another contemporary of Grady's said that it was Gordon who introduced Grady to Field.[45] If true, Gordon may well have been in New York when the deal was brokered. Whether that's true is less important than the fact that Newcomb wanted to oblige Gordon by arranging a position for him as chief counsel for the L&N at a hefty annual salary of $20,000—another account says $14,000. Newcomb was trying to make another arrangement from Georgia sources for the remaining $6,000. Cheap![46] He further wanted former governor Brown to succeed Gordon by gubernatorial appointment. Brown's filling that slot would have two effects: one, it would appeal to his ego, and two, it would remove him from operations of the Western and Atlantic (the rail link between Chattanooga and Atlanta), which Brown served as president. Already Newcomb had moved to acquire a majority of W&A stock, but by charter, the original lessees of the state-bid still governed the road; so the law foiled Newcomb's bid to control the railroad outright, but not his and the L&N's influence over it.

---

[44] H. Davis, *Henry Grady's New South*, 41.

[45] Eckert, *John Brown Gordon*, 225; Joel Chandler Harris, *Life of Henry W. Grady*; Marion J. Verdery, "Memorial of Henry W. Grady," for the New York Southern Society, 77.

[46] Garrett, *Atlanta and Environs*, 2:1–3.

Enter Henry Grady. Perhaps one now knows the reason Newcomb spent so much flattering attention on the soon-to-be managing editor of the *Constitution*. Grady signed the note with Field on May 8 in New York, dropped by Washington, D.C. on the way back, and was in Athens by May 10, where he carelessly spilled the beans to friends he assumed to be confidants. Grady even devised a secret code, so that the colluders could communicate by telegraph in confidence. Those who learned about "something being up" through Grady's indiscreet revelations in Athens likely passed it off, as did Rebecca Latimer Felton, no friend of Grady, as his "careless handling of facts."

Be that as it may, the game was on and it was serious. Grady telegraphed Brown in Nashville, who was there for a Confederate veterans' gathering in honor of Joseph E. Johnston, and in code told Brown what Newcomb wanted to accomplish with Gordon and that Newcomb also wanted Brown to participate in Gordon's salary with a contribution through the W&A of some three to five thousand dollars of the twenty total—thus the "20,000 figure." One coded message to Brown from Grady May 18, said, "I advise you break engagement Nashville & leave tonight without fail. Come to St. James Hotel (New York)." And the next day: "Jones [Newcomb] extremely anxious for personal interview with Smith [Brown] & cannot leave NYork. He asks Smith [Brown] name earliest possible day when he can come. Here everything all right. Best feeling but interview essential soon as possible. What earliest day Smith [Brown] can come?" Moreover, Brown turned cranky at the suggestion he step away from the Western & Atlantic or that it provide a portion of the salary. He declared any remuneration for Gordon to be a board decision, not his alone, but he felt certain he could assure three thousand dollars. Still, Brown wanted the Senate seat badly and became a player.[47] Whether such an elaborate ruse was necessary, it became framework for "the deal."

Governor Colquitt, who almost certainly knew of the deal as early as May 10 or even earlier, still took some persuading from Grady.

---

[47] The "code" in Grady's hand is in box 3, folder 8 of the John Brown Gordon Papers at Hargrett Library, UGA. Among other terms it stipulates that Newcomb is "Jones," "Smith" for Brown, "Williams" for Gordon, and "Jim" for Colquitt. Whether such an elaborate ruse was necessary, it became "code" for the deal.

Colquitt wanted Gordon to hold off on the Senate resignation for reasons of the governor's own vulnerability should the seat appear stolen. Yet Gordon would not be denied and submitted his resignation on May 19, thereby setting in motion the chain of events envisioned by the conspirators.[48] In the end, Gordon could plausibly deny knowing anything beyond his own desire to resign for a more lucrative job. (He claimed two offers, one of which, in Oregon, he had accepted before the L&N made its bid.) Brown, despite some hell-raising from his usual detractors, completed Gordon's term and was re-elected in November to another. Colquitt, relying in part on Gordon's and Brown's popularity in the northern part of the state, but more on Grady's management of his campaign, won election to a second term as governor and subsequently to the Senate himself. In the end, it was Grady who would receive most of the credit as mastermind. He would ever after be known as the Warwick of Georgia politics and would prove it repeatedly over the final decade allotted to him. Within days of the deal he turned thirty.[49]

John Brown Gordon's biographer thinks Grady's biographer, Raymond Nixon, got it right when he summed it up this way: "Undoubtedly there were understandings of the kind that friends reach every day in business and politics, but on the basis of the available evidence the transaction must be described as a 'deal not a steal.'"[50] Money was flowing rather freely. Grady himself was a beneficiary. From May 8, 1880, until he made his first payment on the note to Field, he had borrowed $36,000: the Field note ($20,000) plus a new house the Gradys moved into at 353 Peachtree Street. Evidence indicates that he may have made $12,000 off his stock speculations with Newcomb, for he paid that amount on his house, leaving a $4,000 debt and borrowed $10,000 to make his first payment to Field. Moreover, in this same time, Grady felt obliged to cover a $10,000 loss Evan Howell's brother incurred on Grady's suggestion that he buy L&N stock. Grady's records reflect his paying at least $6,000 of that amount.

Thus, in a year and a half, Grady incurred $46,000 in obligations.

---

[48] Ibid.

[49] Garrett, *Atlanta and Environs*, 2:1–3; Nixon, *Henry W. Grady*, 170–86; H. Davis, *Henry Grady's New South*, 65–70; Eckert, *John Brown Gordon*, 214–31; Parks, *Joseph E. Brown*, 574–80.

[50] Nixon, *Henry W. Grady*, 172; Garrett, *Atlanta and Environs*, 2:2.

His earnings during this same time frame would not have come to more than $30,000 assuming the rise of $12,000 from L&N in stock and his own earnings from the *Constitution*, which at a maximum draw from salary and dividends would not have been greater than $18,000.[51] Even conceding fragmentary records, what is known could only indicate Grady had access to other sources of income, one of which may well have been payment for the time he spent with Newcomb, who had wanted Grady to be his private secretary, a position Grady declined.

Grady's first biographer, Raymond Nixon, offered a defense against Grady's profiting from the relationship with Newcomb by indicating that the *Constitution* sided with the railway mogul E. W. Cole of Nashville in his battle with the L&N in summer 1881. Cole was organizing routes to the west and south, which competed with the L&N's interests. Still, the abandonment, if such it were, may have owed more to Cole's Georgia connections, which included the powerful Lemuel P. Grant of Atlanta, Edward Porter Alexander of Savannah, and General Gordon, which collided with Scott's Pennsylvania RR and the L&N. Railroading in the South was still chaotic with state-owned railroads and smaller feeder lines competing with the emerging trunk lines. Grady no doubt profited from his relationship with Newcomb, but even Newcomb had a short tenure as head of the L&N. Still Grady remained connected, if not imbedded, with Southern railroading. It was important for inland Atlanta's future—and likely for his own profit.

One of the reasons Grady never accumulated great wealth was that he distanced himself from it. None of the railroad deals he encouraged and promoted found him as a direct participant or beneficiary. He had long championed a route to the coalfields and mineral-rich resources of northern Alabama and on beyond to the Mississippi. He lobbied tirelessly for a charter for what was to be called the Georgia Western. Here his ambitions for Atlanta squared with ex-Senator Gordon's interest in getting rich. The charter Grady sought became Gordon's one and only successful foray into business. Within a year of his resignation from the Senate, the state of Georgia authorized the charter. Gordon, in turn, purchased it for $50,000. Gordon organized it as the Georgia

---

[51] Grady account book, Rose Library, Emory.

Pacific Railroad and tirelessly worked New York and Europe for the necessary capital in stocks and bonds. He succeeded and within three years completed the railroad and realized nearly a million dollars in personal wealth, which was huge for the day, but didn't place him among the financially elite.

So Gordon plunged headlong into Florida as the next El Dorado. In February 1883, he obtained a bill of incorporation from the Florida Legislature for the International Railroad and Steamship Company of Florida. He dreamed of a route from the Georgia line to Key West and beyond through steamship connections to the Caribbean, Mexico, and Central and South America. He did not want for vision; what he lacked was money, and when he at last got enough for the first leg to Tampa, a loan for $236,000, it proved a chimera. The Chicago and New York financier John Randolph Dos Passos agreed to lend the money in return for half the profits on this first leg. Then, as suddenly, Dos Passos reneged without explanation. Thus did the father of one of America's future literary greats, John Roderigo Dos Passos, inspire and dash hopes as his son would later do for those who leaned left in American letters, only the father did it more quickly.[52]

Gordon's failures as a businessman and, for that matter, as an agriculturalist did not render him poor although he never achieved the prosperity he so desperately sought. Still, he built the magnificent Sutherland, a manor-style house in the Kirkwood section of Atlanta. It was set on 200 acres, and there he entertained grandly. Though a reputation as a military hero and statesman was not enough for Gordon, it was for Georgians. Grady would use that popularity over and again to sustain the Bourbon Triumvirate and with it the Atlanta Ring, and what a feat it was. Grady had put it together in a week's time while traveling back from New York to Atlanta in May 1880. But Grady had much more on his mind. He had $20,000 in his pocket and was now to be a part owner and equal in the *Atlanta Constitution* with Evan P.

[52] Eckert, *John Brown Gordon*, 266. Eckert does not acknowledge John Randolph and John Roderigo Dos Passos as father and son but neither did the senior Dos Passos, at least for a time. John Roderigo's mother was not his father's wife. Though the two would marry after the death of John Randolph's first wife, the father didn't acknowledge the son until two years later, when John Roderigo was 16.

Howell and W. A. Hemphill. With the title of managing editor, he no sooner had swung down to the terminal platform in Atlanta than he set out to re-make the *Constitution* into a paper of record and consequence for the South and Nation.

Grady as Journalist

From May to September, Grady accomplished his goal. Everything from type to layout gave the *Constitution* the look it bore for the rest of the decade. Where and how the columns were to appear, news first, editorials on page 4, all had his attention. He was never particularly interested in editorials (though he was a fine editorialist); Joel Chandler Harris was lead editorialist. Grady's main interest was on what today would be called "trends" in business and agriculture and always on railroads as the new engines of capital. Human interest stories remained popular, and with Harris and Arp on hand, he had plenty of that. He could even write fanciful character sketches himself. He just did not want to localize the paper. At DeGive's Opera House in Atlanta he got to know stage favorites: Edwin Booth (brother of Lincoln's assassin), Joseph Jefferson, Lillie Langtry, and Madame Rhea. When rumors spread about Sarah Bernhardt's private life, Grady quickly defended her, writing that "outside of her love affairs it is claimed that Sarah's life is full of charm, charity and goodness." Besides, he concluded, "it might be well to remember that it was a Magdalene on whom the Master poured the balm of forgiveness and mercy."[53]

Democratic politics remained an obsession. He was at the Cincinnati Convention that same summer, and though his favored candidate Thomas Francis Bayard of Delaware lost to former Union hero at Gettysburg, Winfield Scott Hancock, he did not despair and moved on to spotlight railroads, industrialization, diversified agriculture, state politics, and a pending Cotton States Exposition. The *Constitution* staff, from compositors, printers, delivery boys, writers, editors, and managers, all caught the spirit. Grady was everywhere. What Joel Chandler Harris saw in his early career as lackadaisical was now a whirl of invention. Even at the *Constitution*, as Harris put it, "One day he would fill

[53] Joel Chandler Harris, *Life of Henry W. Grady*, 310; Nixon, *Henry W. Grady*, 184.

several columns of the paper with his bright things, and then for several days, he would stand around in the sunshine talking to his friends and entertaining them with his racy sayings." "Charming as his pen was, it could bear no reasonable comparison with his tongue."[54] Still, with Gordon to shore up, Colquitt to elect, and Brown to re-elect, no moss gathered where Grady trod.

In this time and under these circumstances, Grady declared himself. In 1882, a petition circulated and garnered the signatures of 1,200 Atlantans who wanted Grady to run as congressman-at-large for Georgia.[55] Grady toyed with the idea for three days, then wrote at length,

> When I was eighteen years of age I adopted journalism as my profession. After thirteen years of service, in which I have had various fortunes, I can say I have never seen a day that I have regretted my choice. On the contrary, I have seen the field of journalism so enlarged, its possibilities so widened, and its influence so extended that I have come to believe earnestly that no man—no matter his calling, his elevation or his opportunity—can equal in dignity, honor and usefulness the journalist who comprehends his position, fairly measures his duties and gives himself entirely and unselfishly to his work.

Grady then laid it bare. "But journalism is a jealous profession, and demands the fullest allegiance of those who seek its honors or its emoluments. Least of all things can it be made the aid of the demagogue, or the handmaid of the politician." Given all that has gone before, could this be true? Could he who made the Atlanta Ring not be the handmaiden of the politician? Grady's "out" on this question was his personal refusal of office or money for positions he took in the *Constitution.* Yet to be the Warwick of Georgia politics, to promote the fortunes of railroads with loans to be paid, how inured was he? Could one be in the world, but not of it?

The answer is both personal and professional. Though Grady lived comfortably, able to support his family from his own resources and give to various other individuals and causes, he left no substantial fortune to

---

[54] Ibid.

[55] Grady scrapbook, prepared by his aunt Martha Gartrell Nicholson, Grady Papers, Hargrett Library, UGA. I counted 310 petitioners from the record in scrapbook, but it may not have included all.

support his family after his death. Thus, royalties from the memorial volume of his life, times, writings, and speeches assembled and edited by Joel Chandler Harris went to Grady's wife, Julia. He sat among and addressed the mighty. He assembled Georgia politics, policies, and politicians throughout the pivotal decade of the eighties. His vision of a New South was built on four cornerstones: slavery was over and secession renounced; the future lay in industrialization; the end of one-crop agriculture (diversification); with White supremacy and one-party politics as the solution to race relations. Though embraced in its time, Grady's vision would devolve into the radical racism that followed in the next three decades. His early death saved him those spectacles and nightmares. Still, he was a chrysalis of what the South would become fifty years after his death.

Because of slavery's rigid hierarchical system, the South came to journalism and its democratic implications fifty years later than the rest of the nation. In the 1830s, James Gordon Bennett of the *New York Herald* (whose son Grady had wanted to meet on his trip to New York in 1876) was the embodiment of what historians would call "personal journalism," which meant the politics of a paper involved active engagement with politicians, for and against. Bennett lived in the era of Andrew Jackson and his robust populism. It led to grievous politics in the financial system, i.e., Jackson's specie circular and hostility to a central bank, resulting in the first "worst" depression before the second and truly worst one in the 1930s.

We should not view Grady's robust engagement as retrograde, rather as catching up to the wilds and wiles of democratic politics. That he eschewed political office did not mean that he did not aspire to influence. Influence was his currency, and he spent it freely. Moreover, in the era of the eighties, Confederate generals commanded attention but not a national audience. Grady and like-minded New Southers linked with liberal Republican counterparts in the aforementioned national community of thought. Journalists such as Grady, Dawson, Edmonds, Watterson, and Tomkins were the voices of a New South. There did come a moment in Grady's last year that he was boomed as successor to Colquitt in the Senate. He accepted, but Gordon, of all people who owed Grady most, sabotaged it.[56]

In that abundant year for Grady's fortune, 1880, Grady took time to reminisce. From the June 15 *Constitution*, he noted the construction going on in Atlanta, including the roof that now capped his new residence going up on Peachtree. The library building was to be "one of the most ornate structures in the city." He listed the Methodist Church on Forsyth, the Fair Street public school, "the mammoth Moore & Marsh emporium on Pryor," the Air-Line Railroad shops, and a host of new residences. The wounds of war were scarcely visible, except on the outskirts where aging breastworks were popping up flowers and weeds. By the end of the eighties, they too would be hard to detect.[57] However, the demolition of one building got more attention, for it housed the *New Era* and the *Atlanta Herald* and reminded him of the great names in Atlanta post-war journalism and his heady days with the *Herald* and Bob Alston. Grady then roamed back over where they all were now, some still living and plying their profession elsewhere, some dead, Alston murdered only the year before. "Ah! well," Grady sighed, "we must all go as the old house is going (*New Era* building), and we may be thankful if there is someone to sit by the way in the sunshine and give us even a passing regret, as the gaunt workmen of Death remove us from the face of the earth."[58]

Sherman and Grady

On another trip to New York in late 1880, Grady interviewed Sherman. The general had visited Atlanta the year before and the *Constitution* welcomed him on behalf of "a people brave enough to bury their hatreds in the ruins his hands have made, and wise enough to turn their passion toward recuperation rather than revenge." The interview a year later changed the tone considerably. Grady wrote:

> I doubt there was a more conscientious soldier in the Northern army than General Sherman. There is no sentimentalism about him. To his notion war meant cruelty—it meant death—destruction—and the sooner this was realized the sooner there was a

[56] Hain, *Murder in the State Capitol*, 221; Eckert, *John Brown Gordon*, 295.
[57] *Atlanta Constitution*, June 15, 1880.
[58] Ibid., April 18, 1880.

> chance for peace. The heaviest, sharpest and most decisive blows, he contended, were the most merciful, and the real scourge, he held, was he who connived at prolonging the war with its inevitable desolation, by glossing its horrors over with a show of pity. This was his argument, severe and savage—but perhaps logical and just.[59]

Sherman never put it better although he said the same often. It was in the same year as the interview with Grady that Sherman made his famous "war is hell" pronouncement. He was at an encampment of the Grand Army of the Republic in Columbus, Ohio. President and former Union general Rutherford B. Hayes, an Ohioan, spoke first, but the audience reserved its shouts for Sherman. By then rain was pelting the veterans, but they wanted Uncle Billy. He did not disappoint, telling the crowd, "We are to each other all in all as man and wife, and every soldier here today knows that Uncle Billy loves him as his own flesh and blood." He did not have to tell them about war. "You all know this is not soldiering here. There is many a boy here to-day who looks on war as all glory, but, boys, it is all hell." Then as an afterthought he said, "I look upon war with horror, but if it has to come, I am here."[60] Had anyone else likened their relationship as "man and wife," the comparison would have sounded ridiculous, but coming from Uncle Billy, it was perfectly reasonable and received in the way he intended. Sherman believed that only "hard war" could have ended the slavocracy of the South. He was not alone. Talking with Otto von Bismarck thirteen years after the war, Grant said the Civil War had to be "terrible." "There had to be an end to slavery. We were fighting an enemy with whom we could not make peace. We had to destroy him. No treaty was possible—only by destruction."[61]

Grady continually improved the technique of the journalistic interview. His reliable reporting on Sherman revealed his ability to penetrate the man rather than the hatred his name generated in the American South, especially in Georgia and the Carolinas. Grady had other things in mind in meeting with Sherman. He had been in New York both before and after the fall elections, and he spent the entire winter

---

59 Ibid., January 1, 1881.

60 O'Connell, *Fierce Patriot*, 325–26.

61 Grant, *Memoirs*, end of chapter 15; Perret, *Ulysses S. Grant*, 452.

and much of the spring there with his wife Julia, their seven-year-old son Henry, five-year-old daughter Augusta (Gussie), his mother and her sister Mattie (Martha)—in all five and a half months. He was proselytizing for the Cotton States Exposition that Atlanta planned for fall 1881. It was an ambitious undertaking. Such an exposition needed investors, and a share of stock could be had for $100. To that end, Sherman himself contributed $2000, an important statement of his belief that Atlanta was emerging phoenix-like from the ashes he had left behind. Without ashes there would have been no phoenix metaphor to describe both Atlanta's reemergence and Grady's extraordinary role in promoting it—a symbolic commitment that Grady and Sherman would reenact several times over the decade left to each. Grady touted Sherman's generous gift as the "lead" subscription.

The exposition was not Sherman's first trip back to Atlanta. That occurred in March 1879 as part of an overall tour of Southern battlefields he had commanded. When Sherman arrived after a detour through Rome, Georgia, he registered at the Kimball house. His aide, John E. Toutillet, and daughters Lizzie and Elly accompanied him. A large contingent of Atlanta's finest greeted him, including Mayor James M. Calhoun, whose father met Sherman as mayor of Atlanta when Sherman entered it as conqueror. On that fateful day, September 5, 1864, the father requested that Sherman not follow through on his order to expel the city's entire population. Sherman refused, and the expulsion ordered commenced on September 10. As Sherman said to the mayor, "War is cruelty, and you cannot refine it.... You might as well appeal against the thunderstorm as against these terrible hardships of war."[62] Still, for the present occasion, all was sweetness and light as most citizens, who hated his name, buried their animosity with jocular remarks. His reception delighted Sherman.[63]

For this exposition Grady was the promoter, not altogether the originator. What Grady knew was that the South no longer had the capital to "bring mills to the cotton," a sensible solution to growth through manufacturing and thus employment for those marginalized

[62] Chernow, *Grant*, 442, citing Bruce Catton, *Never Call Retreat*, 398.

[63] Clipping, "Sherman's Two Visits," in Grady scrapbook, prepared by Martha G. Nicholson, Grady Papers, Hargrett Library, UGA; see also Marszalek, "Celebration in Dixie," 368–83.

by the upheaval of the previous "war capitalism" that had brought the South both expropriated land by force and labor by enslavement. What the postbellum South needed was Northern capital to replace the extraordinary fortunes plantation cotton had generated in the first six decades of the nineteenth century. Grady decided to stay in New York both to help the South obtain capital and to look after his own stock speculation with Victor Newcomb's counsel; Grady hoped that speculation would bring him financial independence.

The real organizers of the exposition were the men now taking Atlanta in hand—Alfred H. Colquitt; Joseph E. Brown; the former apostate Rufus Bullock; Samuel M. Inman, an Atlanta cotton broker; and Inman's younger brother, John, who had made a fortune on moving from Tennessee to New York. Grady was especially taken by Samuel Inman, whom he had gotten to know in the Colquitt campaign for governor. He had come to regard Inman as "Atlanta's ideal citizen" and the type of man who could rescue the South from its industrial, commercial, and financial malaise.

The exposition was the idea of Edward Atkinson of Boston and New York, who, having advanced the idea, was invited to Atlanta by Hannibal I. Kimball to promote it. It was greeted with great enthusiasm, and what started with a singular focus on cotton soon included many other states, their commodities and industries. The single exhibition hall modeled as a Cotton Factory expanded to twenty-seven other buildings on nine acres of landscaped walks and exhibits. Located two miles west of town in Oglethorpe Park, the exposition emphasized Atlanta's suburban opportunities. (Today, Oglethorpe looks tucked into Atlanta, but then it was distant.) Trains of the Western & Atlantic ran every fifteen minutes. The incorporation completed, the original subscription set at $100,000 more than doubled.[64] The exposition, which ran from October 5 to December 31, 1881, was a huge success. Kimball's work was key, and he was made president and director-general.

The numbers were impressive—1,113 exhibits, of which the

[64] See subscription list in Samuel Martin Inman scrapbook, Atlanta History Center. Constitution Publishing Company put up $500, well short of Sherman's $2,000. Whether Sherman's contribution was personal or from other sources is not known.

Southern states contributed more than half, along with six foreign nations to make it truly international. Cotton from four nations grew in patches around the halls. Gross receipts were $262,513 and total disbursements $258,475. Average daily attendance was 3,816 for the seventy-six days it was open (it did not open on Sundays). The largest number on any one day was 10,293 on December 7, Planters' Day—not bad for a city of only 38,000 inhabitants. The major exhibit building remained in operation as the Exposition Cotton Mills from 1882 to 1969. Perhaps most remarkable is that the directors did not hold their first planning meeting until May 3, 1881. Most exhibitions of this nature required a minimum of five years in preparation.[65]

Estimates suggest that Atlanta reaped $2,000,000 from visitors. Several merchants said reported each made $30,000, a huge sum in that day for less than three months of effort. Manufacturers sold implements and left with an appreciation for cotton, which had already doubled twice in production totals since the previous high in 1861. Cotton was back and still king. As Faulkner would have said, "It all began 10,000 years ago," and indeed it had, but the dramatic turn of cotton toward its imperial status in the nineteenth century was more recent.

King Cotton

Sven Beckert's book *Empire of Cotton* tells the story of how cotton was for the nineteenth century what oil was for the twentieth—the global commodity. Beckert divides the transformation into two eras, one of "war capitalism," based on the violent expropriation of land and enslavement of labor, which transmogrifies into "industrial capitalism," when the "state" replaces violence with other means of enforcement (e.g., contract wages and penal codes, in order to acquire labor—often slavery by other means). Sitting atop the pyramid of cotton was manufacturing and capital, separate and apart from cotton's production but key to it. By the nineteenth century, the leading manufacturers and agents of capital formation dwelled well beyond the region where the

[65] H. Davis, *Henry Grady's New South*, 169–73; H. K. Newman, "Cotton Expositions in Atlanta," *New Georgia Encyclopedia*, www.georgiaencyclopedia.org/articles/history-archaeology/cotton-expositions-atlanta.

staple grew. Great Britain and Europe dominated.[66]

When compared with oil, the American South was to become the Saudi Arabia for cotton. Before the 1780s, cotton in the Americas meant the West Indies, Saint-Domingues (Haiti) for example, not North America. Between 1783 and 1808, twenty-five years, 170,000 slaves were kidnapped and brought to the United States and accounted for one-third of all Blacks who had arrived on these shores since 1619. By 1860 cotton "catapulted the United States onto center stage of the world economy."[67] It was 61 percent of the value of all U.S. products. By 1861, Great Britain was by far the world leader in manufacturing cotton and was dangerously dependent on raw cotton from North America. Exports from North America accounted for 77 percent of the 800 million pounds of cotton consumed by Britain and 90 percent of the 192 million in France. Beckert writes, "Poet John Greenleaf Whittier called it [cotton] the 'Haschish of the West,' a drug that was creating powerful hallucinatory dreams of territorial expansion, of judges who decide that 'right is wrong,' of heaven as 'a snug plantation' with 'angel negro overseers.'"

Then war came and supply dried up. "Consequently, exports to Europe fell from 3.8 million bales in 1860," Beckert explains, "to virtually nothing in 1862." Cotton famines followed and riots erupted at the end of the cotton chain in Europe. There is considerable evidence that Southern planters sought to induce the famine out of a belief that their "collective monopoly" on supply would lead European powers to their side. To defuse the situation, the Federal government urged Britain and others to open other supply markets in Egypt, Asia, the West Indies, and Anatolia.[68] With considerable if imperfect results, they did try those options, but the question remained: would cotton's El Dorado reappear? Many thought gang labor was cotton's *sine qua non*; the infamous Black Codes that followed Confederate defeat attempted to provide that labor, and unreconstructed Rebels and their state governments took advantage of perceived leniency by Lincoln and actual

---

[66] Beckert, *Empire of Cotton.*

[67] Ibid., 243–44; see also Baptist, *Half Has Never Been Told*, 40, for an evaluation of volume versus productivity through the remainder of nineteenth century

[68] Beckert, *Empire of Cotton*, 246, 261–65; Baptist, *Half Has Never Been Told*, 398.

license by his successor, Andrew Johnson. Still, gang labor under old planter dominion did not last long.

There soon devolved the rueful mix of tenancy and the crop lien system, the scourge of the American South—or was it? Gang labor on plantations disappeared as owners of large plantations chopped up their tracts into many small farms. It's true that crops had to be "shared" with commission merchants at ruinous interest rates in order to obtain supplies and other essentials for farming and subsistence, but these were arrangements worked out with families (whereas slaves were bought and sold as individuals). As unjust as the new system was, a modicum of family life emerged within the Black community. By 1900, three-fourths of Black farmers were sharecroppers or renters, rent being fixed-sum payments and usually more deleterious. "Such arrangements," noted Richard White, "represented a compromise between planters' desire to bind labor to land and the freed people's desire for their own land and autonomy."[69] Yet, as the planter disappeared, the state stepped in to force labor through contracts for essentials based on "shares," which meant the only cash crop, cotton, became the currency. As Edward Baptist put it, "For sharecroppers, however, there was no scale, no chalk, and no whip at the end of the day. And that was no small thing."[70]

Sherman's Field Order No. 15, which promised that abandoned or confiscated land in the Sea Islands would go to former slaves, was a hoax. Thus the forty thousand slaves who occupied Sea Island lands, including Sapelo off the Georgia coast, and hoped that it would be a starting point to independence, were soon abandoned. As early as August 16, 1865, president Andrew Johnson signaled that original owners would re-possess their land, thereby dispossessing thousands of Black families who had taken Sherman at his word. (Sherman said Secretary of War Stanton had made him do it to begin with and that he personally was not enthusiastic for it.) Thus was land distribution to former slaves replaced, not by ownership but by "contract labor"[71] negotiated

---

[69] R. White, *Republic*, 78–80.

[70] Baptist, *Half Has Never Been Told*, 408.

[71] Contract labor was invented a century earlier as the Spanish wrestled with monarchial opposition to slavery, which infested not only the Americas but also much of the rest of the world at a time (mid sixteenth century) when the Spaniards

by landowners with former slaves; thus slavery by another name. Even Oliver O. Howard, the Christian general who headed the Freedmen's Bureau, was on board. Republicans had embraced "contract freedom like a secular gospel." Bureau agents represented "freedom as a series of contracts" for labor and marriage. It was not land for labor, but it was marginally better than slavery because it was "negotiated"—even if with a former master.[72]

If Republicans needed a sign of where Johnson would take them, it was painfully clear in his reversal of Sherman's Field Order No. 15. Born in poverty, taught to read and write by his wife, this tailor's apprentice became a tailor himself. He was also a garrulous debater and successful as a Democrat in Tennessee politics. As a unionist and Democratic senator, he was the only Southern congressman to stay in office following secession. Accordingly, he appealed to Republicans who were supporting Lincoln under the banner of a National Union Party. Given his humble beginnings and meager accomplishments, he was surprisingly successful in politics, holding office in Tennessee as alderman, governor, and U.S. Senator. In the executive office, he proved to be testy and irascible, even after becoming president on Lincoln's assassination.

Two things marked him: he detested the planter class and despised Negroes. Thus his reversal of Sherman's Special Field Order No.15 was ironic only in his giving 500,000 acres back to planters, not in his taking it away from former slaves. President Johnson supported neither the Fourteen nor the Fifteenth amendments; thus Radicals in Congress

---

could truthfully say the sun never set on their empire. When the Spanish monarchy abolished slavery in 1542, the pushback in the New World resulted in contract labor, which allowed conquistadors and colonists on their encomienda to continue native Indian slavery on a planetary scale. Prince Philip, later Philip II, "the Prudent," of Spain devolved a system of "compensated but compulsory work" that foreshadowed the type of contract labor that followed African American slavery in the United States. The compensation was little more than provisions of the same shelter, food, and clothing that accompanied slavery, but it was in the form of compensation—and thereby not slavery. Thus, from the mid sixteenth century, contract labor was anticipated as a substitute for slavery (Resendez, *Other Slavery*, 71; see also Williamson, *After Slavery*, 32–44; E. Clark, *Francis Warrington Dawson*, 198–99).

[72] Ibid., 45–46. See also Chernow, *Grant*, 471.

would take Reconstruction away from the president and make it congressional. Johnson also thought Negroes, even if emancipated, were destined to be subservient to Whites and never to rise above penury. With such White supremacist views and a disturbing personality, he was destined to become America's worst president although the current sitting executive, Donald J. Trump, may edge him out for similar personality disorders and xenophobic views. Historian Annette Gordon-Reed, winner of both the Pulitzer and Bancroft prizes, summed Johnson up this way: "Black empowerment and participation in the American system was a nightmare scenario for Andrew Johnson. 'This is,' he said, 'a country for white men, and by God, as long as I am President, it shall be a government for white men.'"[73]

The turn from landholding to contract labor for former slaves put a terrible squeeze on subsistence farming, meaning crop diversification and animal husbandry essential to feeding a family both became more difficult. All small farmers fell into the trap of raising a crop for cash, cotton, then buying meats, fruits, vegetables, and cornmeal from the same commission merchants who had taken the lion's share of their cotton crop.[74] Moreover, and most ominously, beginning with the Black Codes, not only did the state criminalize "vagrancy" (defined as being unemployed) but it also treated misdemeanor or trivial offenses committed by Black people as felonies punishable with harsh sentences, fines, and horrific physical cruelty. Thus the penal system led to convict labor—slavery again by another name. The convict-lease system remained in effect until 1908 in Georgia and was replaced by equally punitive "chain-gangs." The penal system, Southern and national, remains a grievous injustice unto this day, and the inequitable treatment of African Americans within that system has never been rectified.

Ironically, the South recovered to pre-war cotton production levels by 1870 and by 1877 obtained pre-war market share with Great Britain. By 1891, sharecroppers, family farmers, and planters had doubled production over 1861.[75] Climate and soil were still key, but new labor arrangements did not spell the end of production as volume, but

---

[73] Gordon-Reed, *Andrew Johnson*, 112.

[74] Beckert, *Empire of Cotton*, 286.

[75] Ibid., 292.

productivity itself declined dramatically. In the latter half of the nineteenth century and well into the twentieth, cotton picked by hand fell from well over 200 pounds per day in the late 1850s by enslaved labor to only 100 to 120 pounds in the 1930s despite improvements in technique and machinery.[76] Other forces would later allow a return to larger farms (and some would remain after secession and Reconstruction), but it was not the same. A bale on a five-acre plot was worth as much as a bale off of a plantation, or nearly so. Moreover, business practices changed. Gone were factors and eventually commission merchants. Fertilizer improved lands, and the old cotton belts in Southern states moved north and west of their former boundaries. Cotton was still king.

So vast was cotton's empire that the above is but a sketch of its contours. Virtually untouched were its manufacturing, technological, and capital dimensions and implications. Globally, the American South remained a matter of land and labor. However much emancipation changed those components, the region continued as a source of cotton and resisted the cold and distant forces of capitalism and any implications it might have had for social forces

In that context, Grady tried mightily to change the conversation. The Atlanta Cotton Exposition was a part of it, and Edward Atkinson was a party to it. Atkinson was the beau ideal of a liberal reformer, or what in that day was referred to as classical liberalism—free trade, limited government, and the notion that left alone any man could succeed. Jefferson was their hero, not Washington and certainly not Hamilton. A Free Labor Republican, Atkinson rode off to war and soon found himself part of the Port Royal experiment. The Port Royal Sound between Charleston and Savannah was the site of the movie *Glory*, which told the story of the 54th Massachusetts all-colored regiment, although the featured attack on Fort Wagner occurred on Folly Island just south of Charleston. It was one of the first areas seized by Union forces and, inheriting a large Negro population, they set about finding ways to employ freedmen (and women). Thus it was on the sea island of Edisto

[76] Baptist, *Half Has Never Been Told*, 410.

that Atkinson instituted wage (contract) labor in agricultural production, largely rice and cotton, with results that encouraged him.[77] He was among a group of New Englanders who thought—wrongly—that their skill and energy would make contract labor more productive than slave labor and "25% cheaper."[78] Still, Atkinson himself was sanguine about his prospects for making it work.

Richard White, in his close examination of the Gilded Age, 1865–1896, writes, "Republicans embraced contract freedom like a secular gospel." Some ex-slaves and formerly manumitted Blacks embraced it also. It was extolled for "the right to sell their labor, the right to be paid for their work, the right to move from job to job, and the guarantee of the sanctity of our family." Still, opportunities for abuse were numerous, and contracts weren't much different from slavery as the old masters demanded from former slaves whatever they could get. The truth is, almost all physical labor in the nineteenth and well into the twentieth century amounted to enslavement with derogatory designations for those so employed, such as "darkies," "white trash," and "lint-heads."[79] From textile mills to coal mines, labor faced grim realities of low wages and sweat-shop conditions. As Grady said often, the South needed to attract Northern capital. As Baptist explains, "Despite constant attempts to industrialize, the South could only offer natural resources and poverty-stricken laborers. It did not have enough local capital, whether of the financial or the well-educated human kind, and it could not develop it."[80]

When Grady got to know Atkinson, he was a highly successful cotton manufacturer in Boston, a titan in insurance, and head of the National Association of Cotton Manufacturers. Like all liberal Republicans, he was partial to journalists. The 1872 gathering of reformers in Cincinnati to nominate a candidate to oppose President Grant, whose corrupt administration was a stench to their nostrils, was called the "journalism convention" because so many journalists attended. As Henry Watterson of the *Louisville Courier-Journal*, who was the first of the New South prophets, averred, "One might have mistaken it for an

[77] Beckert, *Empire of Cotton*, 282.

[78] Baptist, *Half Has Never Been Told*, 399.

[79] R. White, *Republic*, 45–48. See also Isenberg, *White Trash*.

[80] Baptist, *Half Has Never Been Told*, 410.

annual meeting of the Associated Press."[81] This group was the same fraternity of like-minded reformers to which Grady adhered, but as we shall see, was not always in lock-step; for example, Grady was a tariffs advocate, Atkinson, punctiliously liberal, was not.

Atkinson came to Atlanta in summer 1880 to press for an exposition advocating for cotton production and manufacturing although at that time he did not have in mind the South for manufacturing—cultivating to manufacturing standards, buying farm implements, and using best labor practices for production, yes; manufacturing, no. So, when the organizers got going, Grady got going too, not only to promote but also to articulate a theme on cotton and agriculture, not altogether consistent with his new-found friend Atkinson's theme. Grady wanted cotton and its mills joined at the hip in the South.

When Grady returned from New York in late spring 1881, he began a major piece on cotton culture and the South. Associates always said Grady he was a voracious reader. As a boy, he read Blackstone's Commentaries, not because he wanted to be a lawyer but because he wanted to know how lawyers thought.[82] Notwithstanding Sven Beckert's magnum opus on cotton, banks, and governments, cotton culture had always been a much-studied subject. Grady had access to many reports and summaries of cotton production. The result was an essay for *Harper's Magazine*, October 1881, titled "Cotton and Its Kingdom," which opened with lines remarkably sage for a thirty-one-year-old: "It has long been the fortune of the South," he wrote, "to deal with special problems—slavery, secession, reconstruction.... In the cultivation and handling...of the world's greatest staple, cotton, she is grappling with a matter that involves essentially her own welfare, and is of the greatest interest to the general public." Grady delved deeper, writing, "After sixteen years of trial, everything is yet indeterminate. And whether this staple is cultivated in the South as a profit or a passion and whether it is to bring the South to independence or to beggary are matters yet to be settled."[83]

What did he mean by "a passion?" The business of cotton was

---

[81] Wall, *Henry Watterson*, 102.

[82] Joel Chandler Harris, *Life of Henry W. Grady*, 44.

[83] Ibid., 202–203.

competitive and required back-breaking labor. Did their dexterous-though-arthritic hands develop a twisted affection or passion for cotton's demands? (This writer remembers some among the generation of his grandparents who spoke almost wistfully of the land they planted in cotton and the picking thereof. Autherine Lucy, the first African American to attempt desegregation at the University of Alabama, described how she would compete against a sibling, cousin, or her own mother to see who could pick the most cotton—she disappointedly lost to her mother by a long shot. Still it was a test of who was best, which can always be a measure of self-respect. Lucy's parents owned their own land, which made a difference too.)

Grady did the numbers, "It was 1830 before the American crop reached 1,000,000 bales, and the highest point ever reached in the days of slavery was a trifle above 4,000,000 bales." As of 1880–1881, he reported, the crop was "about 2,000,000 in excess of this." Grady believed that "a crop of 8,000,000 bales is among the certainties of the next few years."[84] (And so it turned out.) He attributed the increase in acreage to the use of fertilizers that expanded cotton's kingdom into the interiors and uplands of the South. Still, the number of laborers involved in cotton production more than doubled enslaved labor before the war, a statistic that demonstrates the decline in productivity per person and a trap for the Southern yeoman.

The Barrows of Grady County

The Barrow family of Georgia, principally of Athens and environs, plays a role in Grady's life and legacy. In the year Grady was born, 1850, David Crenshaw Barrow, one of the largest landowners in Oglethorpe County (4,500 acres), neighboring Clarke County and Athens, acquired the largest plantation in what would become Grady County. Located in the Blowing Cave District of Northeast Decatur County, it bordered North Florida, just above Tallahassee. (The acquisition came from bounties Barrow collected from service in the Second Seminole War.) Over the 1850s, Barrow would come to enslave ninety people to

---

[84] Ibid.

work the plantation.[85] Its overseer was George H. Davis, a benign figure among the type usually accustomed to brutality. Davis managed the plantation from 1855 to 1865. His correspondence with David C. Barrow showed him to be literate and conversant on issues of the day. In a letter of November 16, 1860, he observes, "I believe all Has given up that Lincoln is elected and there is a good Deal of confusion among the people." Davis wanted to know what Barrow thought, and in a later letter of December 14, 1860, Davis mirrored Barrow's strong views in favor of secession.[86]

The plantation illustrated the progress of cotton. Although not virgin land, the acreage selected was still pioneering country, thus confirming cotton's claim on new lands to the south and west. The farm also underscored cotton's continuing profitability in the run up to Civil War. The land was located above the Pelham escarpment that ran from Cordele to Bainbridge in Georgia, a sharp rise in topography that gave way to a plateau of gently rolling farmland. It was ideal. Although working through factors and general commission merchants in Savannah, the Barrow plantation shipped its cotton by the Flint River in Bainbridge to Apalachicola, Florida on the Gulf, from whence it made its way to manufactories in the North and in Europe.

David Crenshaw Barrow (1815–1899) was an ardent secessionist. He got what he wanted, but his family would pay dearly in blood and treasure. Born and reared in Milledgeville, he was twelve years old when his father died, and he was sent to the esteemed Carlisle Beaman's School for Boys in Sparta, near the capital city of Milledgeville, and county seat of Hancock, home to great planters and great wealth. (It is now the state's poorest county.) A guardian later got him admitted to the Phillips Academy, Andover, and he matriculated at Harvard but did not graduate because he was expelled for disciplinary reasons.[87] He returned home in 1835 and joined the Macon Volunteers

[85] Barrow used the terms "black folks" or "servants" instead of "slaves"; it was a common preference in that era among people wanting to lift their petticoats above the muck of slavery (Coulter, *Lost Generation*, 14).

[86] David Crenshaw Barrow Papers, box 8, folders 3 and 4, Hargrett Library, UGA.

[87] University of Georgia, "Alumni Record," June 1970, 15, Hargrett Library, UGA.

for the Indian Wars against the Seminoles.

It was during this time, 1836–1838, during the Second Seminole War (1835–1842), that Barrow and William H. McKinley, his future brother-in-law, discovered the Blowing Cave area of Southwest Georgia. Twelve years later Barrow acquired it.[88] Still later, as the Civil War drew to a close, Barrow was generous with refugees who had fled to Athens, where he had become a trustee of the University of Georgia, the gateway for many of his own children. As a planter, he knew how prostrate agriculture was at the end of the war and set about organizing a re-formed State Agricultural Society, modeled after one in Iowa.

His exit from Harvard requires further context. The nation's first Whiskey Rebellion was put down by George Washington in 1794, the only commander-in-chief in U.S. history to take command in the field and at the head of a 13,000-member army, larger than any he commanded in the Revolution. The object was distillers in Western Pennsylvania who refused to pay an excise tax assessed by Alexander Hamilton to pay for the Revolution.

David Crenshaw Barrow became embroiled in another Whiskey Rebellion forty years later at Harvard. In the early nineteenth century, Harvard and numerous other colleges suffered a number of riots and rebellions; the most serious at Harvard occurred in Barrow's sophomore year. The fracture lines were students against faculty, Southron students against New Englanders, and tight identification by class year. They acted out with major eruptions in 1818 and 1823 with numerous other smaller riots along the way. The rebellions were fueled by booze and Boston brothels—unruly by any standard. The freshman class in 1832 ordered six gallons of whiskey and rum for one event. A major eruption happened in Barrow's sophomore year, 1834. It became known as the Dunkin Rebellion. It started innocently enough. Profes-

[88] Service as a private gave him the title of "Colonel," an honorific accorded to many a Southern planter. He was engaged in the longest-running battle of the Second Seminole War against Chief Osceola's band in Citrus County, Florida, April 2–18, 1836, between present-day Gainesville and Tampa. McKinley was not listed on the roster for the fight in Citrus County but may have been present because the roster was compiled many years later from contemporary newspaper accounts, which were not always accurate.

sor Christopher Dunkin, a Greek scholar, got into an unpleasant exchange with a freshman student who refused his command to "recite" and "write" in Greek. Henry David Thoreau, a freshman that year, said that at Harvard the three Rs stood for "rote-learning, regimentation, and rowdyism"—indeed.

When the freshman student was sent home, the freshman and sophomore classes exploded. In a letter home that wound up in the Houghton Library at Harvard, David Crenshaw Barrow admitted to being part of the gang that raided and destroyed Dunkin's classroom, smashing windows and breaking furniture. Although Barrow's hiding out in Andover, where he had gone to Phillips Academy as a boy, was an indication he may not have been identified as part of the raid, still his situation was tenuous. Indiscriminate expulsion had resulted from previous riots. Because of the disciplinary bent of relatively new president Josiah Quincy, the sophomore class got dismissed for an "indefinite period"; the dismissal was later rescinded, but Barrow eventually joined the exodus South of forty-four Southern students. The graduating class of 1836 was roughly a third its beginning number. So it may be, as former congressman John Barrow said in a nod to recent presidential candidate Mitt Romney's ideas on immigration policy, that David Crenshaw Barrow "self-deported" rather than being "kicked out."[89]

Ironically, David C. Barrow was leasing the Taylor mansion in Athens when Henry Grady's father purchased it along with 300 acres of nearby land in 1863—now the Buena Vista area of Athens. Because of the lease, the Grady family did not move in until 1865, the year after Grady's father's death. Major William Sammons Grady had been mortally wounded at the Battle of the Crater near Petersburg on July 30, 1864. He was at the lead of the 25th North Carolina Regiment and received five hits from shot and shell—no evidence exists that he was

---

[89] David Crenshaw Barrow to Precious Patience Barrow, June 12, 1884, Houghton Library, Harvard, and typescript from John Barrow. See also McCaughey, "The Usable Past." John Barrow a descendant of David C. Barrow and the last White Democratic Congressman in Georgia as of 2014 (and indeed in the South),

over the explosion that created the Crater.[90] He died of those wounds three months later. At war's end, Barrow's third son, Thomas Augustine (1843–1897), having engaged in major battles throughout the conflict, returned and almost immediately moved to the plantation in South Georgia to take charge of affairs. He would remain there until his death in 1897. "Bud Tom," as he was known in the family, had been posted to North Florida, Quincy, in late 1863, where his brother James was adjutant to Howell Cobb. So he was already familiar with the plantation just above the Florida line.

The Barrow family was dedicated to education and the best practices of scientific agriculture as understood in that day, so Thomas Barrow appeared alongside his father at the State Agricultural Society meeting in Rome, Georgia, a meeting Grady did much to promote. Thomas Barrow regularly attended all annual gatherings and promoted society activities in Thomas and Decatur counties. (Of the five Barrow sons who obtained University of Georgia degrees, Tom may have come closest to not graduating; the faculty's corresponding secretary felt obliged to write Col. D. C. Barrow of his son's "greatly neglecting his College duties." He corrected sufficiently to obtain his degree in 1862 after enlisting and marching off to war in 1861.[91]

Though a negligent student, Thomas Barrow took matters in hand on arriving in South Georgia. No effort was made to maintain slave or gang labor. By January 1866 he was negotiating contracts for labor and immediately hired a workforce of twenty-nine freedmen. He promised them the standard one-third of the crop from the land they tilled and additionally rented fields to four men. Sharecropping was the most common arrangement (renting was less so), but the terms sharecropper and tenant farmer became virtually indistinguishable. A visitor in June of that year described the former plantation as "clean as a well-tilled garden, the fences in good repair, the stock in good care." He described

---

[90] *Cold Mountain*, by Charles Frazier, begins with the Crater and is set in that part of western North Carolina from whence the Grady family issued, a fiercely Confederate area.

[91] Boney, *Pictorial History of the University of Georgia*, 35. The university expedited graduations in the same way during World War II, generously waiving requirements and extending credits to allow both for graduation and recruitment in 1942.

the workers, who were mostly former slaves on the plantation, as diligent and looking forward to "their share of the crop." The reader will note an apparent two-thirds reduction from the number of slaves antebellum, but that reduction probably indicates that, under slavery, numbers reflected entire families whereas the sharecropping numbers indicate individuals (heads of families) performing the labor. The total number of Blacks on the various farms may have been roughly the same as on the former plantation.[92]

Farming remained a struggle, and Thomas Barrow's correspondence with his father was apologetic. In 1870, discouraged by poor results, he declared "enough to make Job curse god and die."[93] Yet his father could be a pain. "Family legend has it that the first David Barrow was a *rather* formidable man who inspired a degree of terror among his children." The senior Barrow also despised Henry Grady's New South, but he subscribed to the *Constitution* to "keep up with what the scoundrel Grady was up to." He is said to have read it in the barn to keep his "grandchildren from hearing him cussing." Fortunately, his offspring did not share his view of Grady.[94] One descendant, Congressman John Barrow, speculates that it was the tension between New South industrialization and David Crenshaw Barrow's passion for Jeffersonian farming. That is likely a correct reading. It is also known that William Grady, Henry Grady's father and a successful merchant in Athens, was dour and not well liked, so Barrow's dislike of the younger Grady might be traced to his dislike of the elder.

It's important to note that Thomas Barrow provided and funded a school on his farm for Black children; he did so in part because of the dwindling number of schools developed by the Freedmen's Bureau and in part due to his religious convictions. He also diligently inquired about teachers for these students.[95] In March 1870, he wrote his father

---

[92] Waldorf, *Genesis of Grady County*, 137; Thomas Augustine Barrow to David Crenshaw Barrow, January 5 and 22, 1866, David Crenshaw Barrow Papers, box 7, folder 5, Hargrett Library, UGA; *Augusta Daily Constitutionalist*, June 15, 1866.

[93] Thomas Augustine Barrow to David Crenshaw Barrow, March 17, 1870, David Crenshaw Barrow Papers, box 7, folder 5, Hargrett Library, UGA.

[94] University of Georgia, "Alumni Record," June 1970, 15.

[95] Waldorf, *Genesis of Grady County*, 153.

to inquire about a Miss Mary Sanders, "the suitable person recommended to you as a teacher for the darkies here."[96]

As the number of schools for Black children declined in Georgia, the Georgia Department of Education Annual Report for 1876 continued to list a school for Black children on the Barrow farm. Along with the Poplar Springs School, it remained the largest school for Black children at the time of Grady County's formation in 1906.

By 1889, Thomas Barrow had become a pastor, serving first a Baptist church in Bainbridge and then one in Pelham, Georgia. The Pelham charge included the communities of Hopeful to the west and Meigs to the east.[97] Barrow continued farming his family's land even after being ordained and moving to Pelham.[98] Christian charity seldom trumped racism, but the school for Black children on the Barrow farm is evidence that it did have some ameliorating effects.[99]

David C. Barrow Sr. had been lucky in marriage. His first to Sarah Eliza Pope gave him the Oglethorpe plantation. His second to Priscilla Sawyer, whose brother was a wealthy soap manufacturer in Northampton, Massachusetts, and had acquired landholdings on the north end of Sapelo Island (in McIntosh County), gave him his fourth plantation. It was located in the Hog Hammock District (also known as Hugg Hummock). Barrow was already related to the Spaldings of Sapelo, who, in 1802, had carved out the original landholdings on the south end of the Island and developed tabby construction, so prevalent in the sea islands. Sapelo is eleven miles long and remains approachable only by boat. It is home to a community of former slaves whose West African culture is called Gullah-Geechee, an adaptation of Christianity. In

---

[96] Thomas A. Barrow to D. C. Barrow, March 1870, David Crenshaw Barrow Papers, box 8, folder 1, Hargrett Library, UGA.

[97] *Bainbridge Democrat*, 1891; Mitchell County Sketches, 536, undated, as cited in Sullivan, *Early Days on the Georgia Tidewater*.

[98] Ibid.

[99] Indeed, David Barrow Sr.'s second wife, Priscilla Sawyer (formerly a governess for the Barrow children), gave two acres for what became the St. Paul's Church and School for Coloreds. Ten years after Tom Barrow's death, it was listed on the first map of what was then Grady County. St. Paul's is still in service as a Missionary Baptist Church on Harrell Road, formerly the Atkinson Trace, in Grady County.

1910 they numbered 539, by 1970 it had declined to 175 and now numbers around 50.

The original Thomas Spalding, 1774–1851, who bought the island in 1802 was an important figure in Georgia politics and governance. He was a member of the assembly that wrote the state's constitution in 1798 and would eventually become a U. S. representative to Congress. Educated in the common schools of Georgia and Florida, he finished at a private school in Massachusetts. He also took a tour of England and France before returning to Sapelo in 1803. At times he owned as many as 400 slaves, but the number dwindled to 200 by 1850. He was an ardent supporter of slavery and was present for the 1850 convention in Milledgeville that opposed any act that would end it.

Thomas Spalding Sr. died in 1851 in Darien, Georgia, at Ashantilly, the home of son Charles. Ashantilly had been built in 1820 by Thomas Sr. and named for the ancestral home in Scotland. Two generations later, Thomas Spalding II married Sarah Barrow McKinley, D. C. Barrow's granddaughter. They lived on Sapelo near the Long Tabby House. At that time, Ashantilly produced primarily cane syrup and cotton, but when Sea Island cotton produced low dividends, Spalding II and his younger brother Bourke, switched to cattle, a bellwether for agricultural diversification.[100]

It is not altogether clear how much of D. C. Barrow's landholdings on Sapelo were driven by ownership of land or mortgages, which can come to same. The historian of McIntosh County and Sapelo, Buddy Sullivan, produced evidence that would indicate ownership. He notes that the mortgages on all the properties owned by Barrow family members on the South End were canceled in 1878 by signature of D. C. Barrow.[101] Further, Sullivan argues that the postbellum history of Sapelo revolved around Thomas Spalding II; his younger brother, Bourke Spalding; and their brother-in-law Archibald C. McKinley. Note that A. C. McKinley's father, William H., accompanied D. C. Barrow through South Georgia during the Second Seminole War, a journey that eventuated in Barrow's acquisition of the Blowing Cave Plantation.

---

[100] National Register of Historic Places.

[101] Sullivan, *Early Days on the Georgia Tidewater*, 369.

The Barrows, McKinleys, and Spaldings of Baldwin and McIntosh counties were related by friendship and marriage. Bourke Spalding, who managed the South End of the Island, married D. C. Barrow's daughter Ella Patience. A letter from D. C. Barrow to Bourke Spalding, January 16, 1879, reveals Barrow to be as heavily involved in management by correspondence as he was with his son in Southwest Georgia.[102] Sullivan also notes that the Barrow family acquired son-in-law Bourke Spalding's Riverside assets at some point, probably on his death in 1884.[103] Moreover, D. C. Barrow returned with his daughter Ella and her son to the Island in 1891 for a three- to four-year residence.[104] Finally, when Detroit automobile magnate Howard E. Coffin purchased the entire island in 1912, it was through the labors of David C. Barrow Jr., then chancellor of the University of Georgia, representing the purchaser and clearing all titles, "making it possible to consummate the sale." All of which would indicate ownership on D. C. Barrow's part if primarily absentee.[105] The Spalding brothers, Bourke and Thomas II, died within less than a year of each other; Bourke died in 1884 by accidental discharge of his gun while hunting, and Thomas II died in 1885 on his way back from Atlanta to Darien. He was found at 1:30 a.m. in a Macon railroad yard, nearly decapitated, after a train backed over his body. Whether his death was murder, suicide, or accident remains unknown.

All four Barrow plantations (Oglethorpe, Baldwin, McIntosh, and Decatur counties) moved quickly from slavery to freedom. Writing for *Scribner's Monthly* in 1881, David Crenshaw Barrow Jr. observed, "The confident prophecies of the croakers that Southern plantations would go to waste, and that nothing but ruin lay before us, have proved the merest bosh. The enormous increase in the cotton crop of the South alone shows that the colored people, as free laborers, have done well...." Noting that "worthless labor" could not have produced such results, he continued, "In Georgia, the negro has adapted himself to his new circumstances, and freedom fits him as if it had been cut out and made

---

[102] Ibid., 401–402.

[103] Ibid., 389.

[104] Ibid.

[105] Ibid., 606.

for him."[106] Tom Barrow, who converted to contract labor immediately upon emancipation, no doubt agreed. In May 1866, he wrote his father that upon his return from nearby Americus, Georgia, where he had visited his grandmother, he "found all the negro's [*sic*] working well and *very* satisfied. am strict with them and they are beginning to see it is to their benefit as well as mine."[107]

The younger David Barrow in his *Scribner's* article did not attribute the 20 percent increase in cotton production by 1880 over 1860 to free labor alone but to "other causes," no doubt to improved agricultural practices such as his brother's experimentation with phosphates as fertilizer in South Georgia.[108] Still there was no complaint from Barrows about free labor. Or as Grady put it in his New South speech, "We have learned that the free negro counts more than he did as a slave."

Many landowners readily abused contract labor, but Barrow apparently did not. Edward Ayers, in his monumental study of slavery and freedom in the Valley of Virginia, illustrated the trade-off vividly. Ayers shows that in the county of Augusta, Virginia (Staunton), many former masters negotiated with their former slaves brutal contracts that provided neither sufficient provisions nor income, resulting in laborers' near-starvation.[109] The freed people struggled at the margins, making ends meet with few dollars and even less food. The world of the working poor, Black and White, in the latter half of the nineteenth century and well into the twentieth was little short of desperate.

The freedman as laborer could not be separated from freedman as second-class citizen. Less than ten miles north of the Barrow Plantation lay the town of Camilla, where on Saturday, September 19, 1868, a massacre occurred. Blacks along with a few Whites set out on a march that day from Albany to Camilla to encourage voting. The crowd was estimated as high as 300 with a bandwagon in the lead. Alerted, some one hundred armed Whites awaited them. A shoot-out followed that resulted in as many as fifteen deaths among the marchers with another

[106] Barrow, "A Georgia Plantation," **[page or in whole?]**.

[107] Thomas A. Barrow to D. C. Barrow, David Crenshaw Barrow Papers, box 7, folder 1, Hargrett Library, UGA.

[108] Barrow, "A Georgia Plantation," 830; T. A. Barrow to D. C. Barrow, April 8, 1867, Barrow papers, Hargett Library, UGA.

[109] Ayers, *Thin Light of Freedom*, 357–60.

thirty to forty wounded. Only six of the attackers received wounds. As the marchers scattered to get back to Albany, marauding Whites chased them down. The outrage stirred the national press and resulted in a return to military Reconstruction in Georgia, from which it had only recently emerged.[110]

On January 1, 1906, the former Barrow plantation was incorporated into a new county formed from Decatur and Thomas counties and named Grady County by earnest petition of its citizens. On that same day, David Crenshaw Barrow Jr. was named chancellor of the University of Georgia. For the next nineteen years he helped define the modern university, including the formation of a journalism school named for Henry Woodfin Grady. Thomas Augustine Barrow should have lived long enough to witness both the formation of the county named for Grady and the elevation of his little brother as chancellor of the university he nearly flunked out of. He died in 1897 at age fifty-three and is buried in the Pelham, Georgia, cemetery, just over the line from Grady into Mitchell County, and not far from the Blowing Cave plantation. The town was named for "The Gallant Pelham," who with Thomas Barrow served the guns at Fredericksburg and other engagements before Major John Pelham was cut down at Kelly's Ford in the lead of a cavalry charge.

Another gallant soldier cut down in battle was Thomas Barrow's brother James. He had resigned from West Point, sharing the passionate views of his father for secession. His conduct demerits at the academy distressed his father but never resulted in expulsion—although they came close. (Remember David Sr. was kicked out of Harvard for

---

[110] The author found no mention of the massacre in the Barrow Papers although through Thomas Barrow, the family would have certainly known (L. W. Formwalt, "Camilla Massacre," *New Georgia Encyclopedia*, www.georgiaencyclopedia.org/articles/history-archaeology/camilla-massacre; Waldorf, *Genesis of Grady County*, 156; see also R. White, *Republic*, 98). Racial equity in Camilla is still unrealized. Seventy percent of the population of 5,300 are Black, but in 2018 the police force was still all White, as were most of the city's positions, assigned by a White city manager, not its Black mayor. Even the city's cemetery only recently removed a fence demarcating White from Black burials. Jim Crow segregation has its ways of persisting (Richard Halicks, "Racially Segregated Cemetery: Fence of Segregation in Cemetery Removed," *Atlanta Journal-Constitution*, January 21, 2018, B1).

unruly conduct.) Entering the Confederate army as a second lieutenant, Jim soon became adjutant to Howell Cobb of Athens, who would become provisional president of the Confederate Congress, then eventually a major general. At Yorktown, James Barrow, alongside his brother Tom, was seriously wounded in the thigh on April 16, 1862, at fighting around Dam No. 1 as McClellan began his campaign to take Richmond by way of the peninsula. After spending almost six months convalescing in Athens, James arrived back in Northern Virginia too late to join the fight at Antietam although he did observe Lee's retreating army.[111]

James Barrow, with the rest of his family had a relatively enlightened, at least charitable, view of Negroes. In going off to war, he requested of his father a "servant" by the name of Clark but got another named Riley. Riley was still with Jim when he was posted to Quincy, Florida. In July 1863, Captain Barrow described Riley as having earned considerable "social status," as he was "a frequent attendant at Negro weddings and occasions." In Quincy, Riley fell in love and wished to marry, but his love was to be sold, thus separating them. James requested of his father sufficient money to purchase her, thereby preventing the sale in progress, so that Riley and she could be together as husband and wife. There is no direct evidence that the father supplied the money, but there is evidence that Riley did marry and remained with Jim Barrow until Barrow's death.[112]

It was Howell Cobb's re-posting to the Middle District of North Florida in November 1862, that brought James to Quincy, primarily on a recruiting mission. Succeeding in that, he proved his West Point credentials by being a superb drill master, winning the total admiration of Cobb. While in Quincy he was introduced to the beautiful Rhoda Elizabeth Waller Kilcrease, whose first husband in an arranged marriage had by will left her with the largest plantation in Florida, near the Georgia line and thus near the Barrow plantation. (Brother Tom Barrow was also there, following his presence at Fredericksburg with T. R. R. Cobb's Legion. Major General Howell Cobb's younger brother Thomas Reade Rootes Cobb would be killed at Fredericksburg, having

---

[111] Coulter, *Lost Generation*, 73–76.

[112] Ibid., 89. Two letters from James Barrow to his father address same story.

just attained the rank of Brigadier General. Like James Barrow, his was a wound to the thigh, but from an exploding shell that tore open his femoral artery and he quickly bled to death, like Albert Sidney Johnson at Shiloh.)

It was not common landholdings that introduced Jim and Rhoda. James was extraordinarily handsome, and the two fell deeply in love and planned to marry. As Union forces threatened North Florida, James convinced Rhoda, or "Bessie" as she was known, to take her son and join his family in Athens. Then on February 20, 1864, just over the Georgia-Florida line near Ocean Pond, the Battle of Olustee erupted between approximately 5,000 Confederates and 5,500 Union troops, including a sizable contingent of Black troops, some from the famed 54th Massachusetts. The Union move into north Florida was designed in part to recruit more former slaves into Union army ranks.

Had James remained an adjutant to Howell Cobb, he almost certainly would not have been present for the battle, but his success in recruiting and drilling what became the 64th Georgia Volunteers led to a promotion to lieutenant colonel and thereby separation from Cobb's staff. At Olustee Lt. Colonel Barrow, commanding at the point of attack, took a bullet to the heart. (Both the colonel and major of the 64th Georgia had been sidelined by wounds, so James took up the flag and led.) Rhoda's favorite brother, Albert Waller, for whom her son was named, died not twenty feet from where Barrow had stood. She received letters about both deaths while still in Athens planning for her wedding. On the day of battle, the Barrows had held a grand reception to introduce her to Athens.

Brigadier General Alfred Colquitt would assume the sobriquet "Hero of Olustee" for having brought reinforcements from Charleston to North Florida to make good that state's defense. Later as governor of Georgia he would become part of the Bourbon Triumvirate that Grady formed. Rhoda's bachelor son Albert Gilchrist (the Kilcrease name being changed to its proper spelling by request of his father) would go on to become governor of Florida in 1909 and make his mother first lady, thereby fulfilling his father's pledge to make her first lady of Florida, although the father thought it would be by his election until his heart failed him. Rhoda lost five brothers to the war, and the Barrow family lost one son with two others seriously wounded. She never lost her love for Jim, and although she remarried in 1870 to a Gibbes from Columbia, South Carolina, she always told her Gibbes children they would have been sons and daughters of James Barrow had he lived. She lived to age eighty-six, still cherishing the memory of her true love.[113]

Corn versus Cotton

As Andrew Lytle reminded readers in *I'll Take My Stand*, a farm is a place to raise corn, not money. In the years remaining to Barrow and Grady, they struggled mightily with the issues of cotton as "money," and corn as "subsistence." Grady knew what farmers (i.e., croppers or tenants) were up against—*credit.* Capitalism was always going to mean that farmers would take the hindmost to factors, merchants, manufacturers, and financiers. Money flows up, not down.

Grady put it this way for the South:

> Whether its culture shall result in a host of croppers without money or credit, appealing to the granaries of the West against famine, paying toll to usurers at home, and mortgaging their crops to speculators abroad even before it is planted—a planting oligarchy of money-lenders, who have usurped the land through foreclosures, and hold the ever-growing margin between a grasping lender and an enforced borrower—or a self-respecting race of small farmers, cultivating their own lands, living upon their own resources, controlling their crops until they are sold, and independent alike of usurers and brokers—which of these shall be the outcome of cotton culture the future must determine.[114]

It may have been a bit overwrought, but history confirms its point. Subsistence farmers often came to enjoy, even love, what they had, but growth requires money for land, labor, and supplies; thus the bind. Grady goes on to describe the collapse of plantations, but he took solace in "the era of small farms." He touted "the eagerness" of Negroes "who

---

[113] Coulter, *Lost Generation*, 87–103; Kirkland, *Rhoda.* These two accounts differ on one point: Coulter believes that Rhoda was on her way back from Athens when she received the letters. Coulter's account makes extensive use of Barrow correspondence thereby adding considerable archival value.

[114] Joel Chandler Harris, *Life of Henry W. Grady*, 262–63.

bought in Georgia alone 6,850 farms in three years." More striking was "the earth-hunger of the poorer class of the whites," who in Mississippi netted "a gain of forty thousand small farms of less than one hundred acres in three years." The gain in Georgia from 1868 to 1873 was 32,824—all from slicing up the big plantations like the Barrow land at Blowing Cave in Decatur County.[115] Still, former slaves owned as much as a fourth of the land they formerly farmed, or as Booker T. Washington claimed, putting a better face on it, as much as Belgium and Holland together.

In Georgia, Black farmers may have owned less land. Historian Richard White said, "the average Black farmer (in Georgia) controlled only 10 percent of the land his average white neighbor did, and it was worth 10 percent as much."[116] That said, land hunger among Blacks remained, and it was answered, even if not sufficiently. There was a standing army of Black laborers who farmed their own land. Blacks aspired against a system that seldom relented. Whatever their purchase, they did not succeed as hoped, yet still those with land persevered.

In the Cotton States, Grady wrote, there reappeared "the planter princes of the old time, still lords of acres, though not of slaves." They were consolidating plantations, "aggregating perhaps 50,000 acres." There were names: "The Capeheart estate on Albemarle Sound for one, and not one-third of them are owned by the men who held them at the end of the war," and they were passing them "into the hands of commission merchants." Moreover, unlike plantations of old, consolidation did not mean small farms were being owned by the "many" but the "few," another handoff to commission merchants. Thus did credit flow to provisions and fertilizer, not to land, which is a security as long as the debt is unpaid, not vice versa. Much needed was "a proper system of credit," but it was nowhere in sight.[117]

Here Grady pivots to "crop diversification," his panacea. "The South must prepare to raise her own provisions," he wrote, "compost her fertilizers, cure her own hay, and breed her own stock." It is pre-

[115] Ibid., 265–66.

[116] R. White, *Republic*, 227.

[117] Joel Chandler Harris, *Life of Henry W. Grady*, 266–67.

cisely akin to the "alternative sources of energy" argument in the twentieth century. It was a beautiful argument, had perfect symmetry, made complete sense, but follow the money. Still, for the next decade Grady would carry the torch for a new agriculture, based on common sense, smaller margins, but more certain success—unless one already owed their soul to the company store. In that same decade, the 1880s, acreage devoted to cotton hovered at just over 40 percent. In 1870 it had stood at 30 percent.

Most interesting is how Grady attached his diversification narrative to the "least among us" to establish its value—the "corn-raiser," "the steadfast figure, undisturbed by change of relation or condition," this is "Cuffee, the darky farmer."[118] In Grady's day "Cuffee" was a common way of denoting Blacks in general. Grady's tale bears repeating:

> There is no more interesting study in our agriculture than this same dusky, good-natured fellow—humble, patient, shrewd—as he drives into town with his mixed team and his one bag of cotton, on which, drawn by a sympathetic sense of ownership, his whole family is clustered. Living simply and frugally, supplementing his humble meal with a 'possum caught in the night hunt, or a rabbit shot with the old army musket that he captured from some deserted battlefield, and allowing no idlers in the family save the youngsters who "'tend de free school," he defies alike the usurer and the landshark.... He is not ambitious, however, to own large tracts of land, preferring the few acres that he has constantly under eye, and to every foot of which he feels a rude attachment.[119]

This "attachment," however, is clearly not to cotton but to the land itself. "Although [the fictional Cuffee] spends the most of his life in cotton fields," Grady continues, "it does not enter into his social life, catch his sentiment, or furnish the occasion for any of his pleasures"—cotton plays no role and is not celebrated in any of the harvest "frolics"

---

[118] In Ghana, the Ivory Coast, and other parts of West Africa, children are still named for the day of the week or month they are born, their birth order, or other significant information. Cuffy or Kofi, variously spelled as in Grady's "Cuffee," stands for Friday. Kofi Atta Annan, former U.N. secretary general, is an example (J. Davis, *Island Time*, 123).

[119] H. Davis, *Henry Grady's New South*, 271–72.

of corn-shuckings, log-rollings or any social occasions or songs. "None of those tuneful melodies," Grady said, "with which he beguiles his work or gladdens his play-time acknowledge cotton as a subject or even an incident....I have never heard a negro song," he concluded, "in which the cotton field is made the incidental theme or the subject of allusion...."[120]

Almost certainly Grady gleaned these ideas from his pal Joel Chandler Harris, who as a folklorist was in a better position to know, but then Foner, the leading historian of Reconstruction, says former slaves abhorred cotton because of its association with slavery, even if constrained to produce it for the crop lien system.[121]

Grady went further: the farther up the chain from farm to factory, the greater the returns. When cotton left the fields, it was worth two-thirds less than when manufactured. "Will the South," he asked, "be content to see the whole of this added value realized by outsiders?" It was a stinging rebuke. Why should this profit go to the North, when the water that powered their mills ran freely in the South, year-round? Moreover, the cotton seed was not captured for its supreme value as fertilizer. At every turn, the value of the crop was handed off without being retained by its originators. What was right about this inversion? Moreover, Grady pointed to exceptions, such as New Orleans, where presses for cotton seed and use for fertilizer worked to huge advantage. "There is no question," he concluded, "that with one-tenth of the money invested in improved gins, cleaners, and pressers that would be required for factories, and with incomparably less risk, the South could make one-half the profit, pound for pound, that is made in the mills of New England." He went straight at Atkinson, saying that the impurities that move from Southern field to factory in New England could be eliminated if the factories were adjacent to the fields. Conceding that the farmer's dirty cotton was as profitable to the manufacturer as, say, dirty oil profits the refiners today, Grady's goal was simple. "Indeed," he concluded, "there is nothing so appeals to Southern pride as to urge the possibility that in time the manufacture of this crop as well as the

[120] Ibid.

[121] Foner, *Reconstruction*, 108–109.

crop itself shall be a monopoly of the cotton belt."[122]

Moreover, to Atkinson's thought that Southern heat in the summer would preclude manufacturing, Grady said that in the present summer, the hottest ever, not one mill was stopped. He then pointed to Northern winters as more prohibitive of continuous labor. He also noted manufacturing successes in Columbus , Augusta, and Atlanta. So it went. Finally, Grady pointed to mechanical changes that the Cotton Exposition would highlight, for example, an "attachment, or some machine of similar character for spinning the cotton into yarns near the field where it is grown, will be generally adopted throughout the South in the near future."[123]

The 1881 Exposition provided proof. October 27 was to be Governor's Day. All thirty-eight chief executives were invited, six attended, among them Governor Hobart B. Bigelow of Connecticut, who joined with Governor Colquitt for suit measurements. The sun was barely up on October 27 when cotton was picked from the international patches on the grounds. It was carded, spun, dyed and dried, cut and sewed into suits. That night, the governors appeared in swallow-tailed black suits at a reception in the executive mansion on Peachtree Street.[124] Attendees were astonished Grady was vindicated—from field at dawn to formal attire at dusk, mill to cotton indeed.

Grady's pleadings were as old as Alexander Hamilton's *Report on Manufactures*. Hamilton knew that if the Revolutionary nation were to compete on the trans-Atlantic level, it would have to grow cities made possible through manufacturing. Creating manufacturing would require technology stolen from England, who jealously guarded her manufacturing processes, especially in textiles. So, stealthily, Hamilton and associates brought managers and architects from the United Kingdom and started building a competitive manufacturing base. Its initial site would be across the Passaic into New Jersey where a hub developed that would become the city of Paterson. As Ron Chernow observed, "It was Hamilton's vision of America as a manufacturing behemoth, not Jefferson's of a society of yeoman farmers, that threatened the British."[125]

---

[122] Ibid., 273–77.

[123] Ibid., 282.

[124] H. Davis, *Henry Grady's New South*, passim.

[125] Chernow, *Alexander Hamilton*, 371.

Now Grady wanted to steal mills from the Northeast and bring them South, and Atkinson greeted that prospect with the same suspicion that London had held for Hamilton's scheme.

The 1881 Exposition would not be Grady's last. In his last three years there would be two expositions intersected by a Chautauqua, a triumphal march to the end. The Piedmont Exposition of 1887 was even more spectacular than the 1881 extravaganza, if for no other reason than that the president of the United States attended, the first Democratic president since Lincoln. Quickly emerging from the body politic (as Woodrow Wilson did later), Grover Cleveland was sheriff of Buffalo, New York, then governor of the state for two years, then president of the United States. He was a Liberal-Democratic reformer's delight—and a Liberal Republican's too.[126] Cleveland was anti-corruption, Tammany Hall especially, and pro-limited government to a fault. Grady stuck with Samuel Tilden, until that tired old hero of the party withdrew, then turned his support to Cleveland. By that time, Grady's rival at the *Charleston News and Courier*, Francis Warrington Dawson, was heading the Democratic Party's campaign in six of the Deep South states. Grady was cheerful enough in support.[127]

Now Grady was getting the prize. Working through Cleveland's personal secretary, Daniel Lamont, he got Cleveland to commit to the exposition, but then desperately tried to make it an exclusive visit—Atlanta as destination. A long letter to Lamont was plaintive, saying that stopping elsewhere would detract from Atlanta's luster. Alas, Cleveland started in St. Louis and made numerous stops along the way. Grady, always the publicist, declared the president stopping here and there, but on his way to Atlanta, the ultimate destination. He could turn the glint of mica into diamonds.

Cleveland arrived on October 17 in a day-long drizzle, but nothing dampened the enthusiasm. Grady introduced him to a throng of 50,000 in Piedmont Park. The exposition netted $58,000, which was dedi-

---

[126] In the nineteenth century, the terms Liberal Democratic and Liberal Republican were virtually interchangeable, although emerging out of two-party terminology. Liberal Republicans were critical to the election of the Democrat Grover Cleveland.

[127] E. C. Clark, *Francis Warrington Dawson*, 112–13.

cated to organizing another event two years later. By then, every Southern city of estimable enterprise was getting in on the shows, but Atlanta had pioneered and led the way. The Piedmont Chautauqua held in 1888 at Lithia Springs, twenty miles west of Atlanta, was not as successful. Still, some 30,000 participated in its events.[128] The resort already had a 500-room luxury hotel, The Sweetwater (named for the nearby creek), and as the name suggests, noted for its restorative waters. It was a little too far from Atlanta to serve its citizens' purposes as Chautauqua, but over its lifetime the resort and its therapeutic waters would attract the likes of Mark Twain, the Vanderbilt family, and presidents Cleveland, McKinley, Theodore Roosevelt, and Taft.

If cotton retained its tight grip on Southern agriculture, one would never know it from the pages of the *Constitution*. In one six-week span in 1882, "the newspaper printed the names of one thousand successful farmers."[129] The *Constitution* encouraged weeklies to do success stories, and when written up, Grady's newspaper ran with them. What farmer, what weekly, was going to deny success once proclaimed? Grady's instinct for publicity and its charms worked if actual numbers did not. In Colquitt's last campaign for governor, which Grady successfully managed, Grady developed a technique for mass producing letters that looked like originals. Although common today, it was novel then, and many a town or county official had a personal letter from the governor himself to prove it.

With the pea of farm publicity under one shell, Grady lifted the shell from another revealing industrialization as the farmers' ultimate salvation. With factories generating profits and wages locally, it would be spent on the produce of area farms. The symmetry of what Grady said was so perfect who could doubt that success was "at hand," if not yet "in hand."[130] Modern students of persuasion would call it "vision," a necessary component in leadership. Although modern historians have debunked the vision as mythic, in its time it spelled hope. If Grady had to cheat on conservatism's article of faith, free trade, what harm could come from moderate tariffs that supported factories that in turn yielded

[128] Nixon, *Henry W. Grady*, 278–80.
[129] H. Davis, *Henry Grady's New South*, 113.
[130] Ibid., 112–14.

farmers' markets?

Unrest among farmers was also abroad in 1887 with the formation of the Farmers Alliance in that year. It had always been present. Independent Democrats had scored notable victories, especially in the northern congressional districts of the state. They viewed the New South Creed with gimlet-eyed suspicion, especially as it seemed so Atlanta-centric. With Atlanta doubling its population in the eighties, with the capitol having moved there from Milledgeville in 1868, with all the railroads connecting there, and with the state's principal leadership choosing to live there even as Colquitt specifically and Gordon to some degree maintained their "planter" interests—Colquitt's wife's plantation in Baker County, Southwest Georgia, and Gordon's in Taylor, Middle Georgia—neither seemed to identify clearly with farmer interests and complaints.

Maestro of the House

The Atlanta Ring was never more than accusation. All who derided it lived outside its environs, a view that accounts today for the notion of "Atlanta" being separate from the "other Georgia." It was no "ring," as that imputes political control of all the levers in local politics. The Georgia Constitution of 1877, which eviscerated the Radical Republican constitution of 1868 in restoration of Democratic rule, was toothless. (The author's great grandfather, Oliver Perry Swearingen, was a member and chaplain of the convention.) It did embrace provisions that fought against state investment in railroads and industry, but even there could not escape the juggernaut of capitalism that would have its way. What the Constitution of 1877 did was make the state irrelevant, but—in the minds of capitalists and members of the Atlanta Ring—not impotent.

Thus did Grady become mastermind of a "Ring" that appeared impervious to the rest of the state and dominant, however weak it was. There had been an Atlanta Ring in the 1870s, but it was involved in local politics and existed little more than in appearance. Every city of estimable size had one. Certainly Milledgeville, the former state capital, was still ambitious to retain its status; nearby Macon had a greater population and dedicated space for a capitol building. Augusta and Savannah also had their claims, but it was hard to deny Atlanta. Still, it was Grady who made the difference. Without being asked, and to no one's later acknowledgment, he stepped in and engineered the Colquitt, Brown, and Gordon deal of 1880. The capital was temporarily moved from Milledgeville to Atlanta in 1867–1879 and made permanent in the 1877 state Constitution; talk of moving the capital away from Atlanta persisted into the 1990s. When Colquitt was vulnerable for re-election as governor in part because of the "deal" but also because of corruption in his administration for which he was not directly responsible, Grady became his campaign manager. He took a poll of county sheriffs and ordinaries around the state and predicted Colquitt's re-election totals as close as any pollster today.

All machinations of the Atlanta Ring were enshrouded in Confederate gray. When the state needed a governor to replace Colquitt, the hero of Olustee, that replacement turned out to be Alexander H. Stephens, the wizened vice president of the Confederacy, whom Independent Democrats courted and thought they had corralled, but who turned out to run as a regular Democrat, and thus a Grady choice. When Stephens died in office 120 days later, Grady engineered his most spectacular feat as Warwick of Georgia politics.

The odds-on candidate was Augustus Octavius Bacon, who seemed destined to be Georgia's next governor but for the Atlanta Ring and Grady's manipulations. A native of Bryan County near Savannah, he graduated from the University of Georgia in 1859 and took a law degree the following year. He mustered in Confederate service with the 9th Georgia and fought with it in the 1861 and 1862 campaigns of the Army of Northern Virginia, obtaining the rank of captain. He returned to Georgia and remained a supply officer for the war's duration. He opened his law practice in Macon and served in the Georgia House from 1871 to 1886, holding the speakership for two successive terms. He was highly respected but a cold man personally. Because Bacon's loyalties would be to Macon, Grady had to stop him. Bacon had desperately wanted to succeed Colquitt as governor, but when Stephens acceded to the regular Democratic nomination, Bacon was sullen but did not run for the office.

Stephens did little in the days remaining to him other than a slew of pardons that included Edward Cox, the murderer of Bob Alston, but in Stephens's death, Grady found opportunity. Atlanta would give him a spectacular send-off. Military companies marched down Forsyth Street, and bands from all over Georgia followed in solemn procession as the "Dead March" announced a hero's passing. "Little Aleck" was buried temporarily in Atlanta's Oakland Cemetery. Only Grady could orchestrate such a dramatic display for the thousands who packed trains into Atlanta and swelled the crowd. Atlanta lived up to its billing as the "Gate City" that none within Georgia could rival.

The question of who would succeed Stephens remained, and Bacon was chief pretender. The president of the Senate, James Boynton of Griffin, assumed the governor's position until a special election could be held, and Boynton himself developed pretensions. A nominating convention was to assemble in Atlanta on April 10 with the election set for April 24. As the convention opened, Grady had guessed wrongly that Boynton would be at or near the top in a field of five. Bacon was at the top although through the first day's balloting he did not get a majority. Ironically, Bacon's campaign manager was Grady's fraternity brother, Nathaniel E. Harris from Hancock County, for whom Grady had personally obtained a scholarship when Harris was struggling to get through the University of Georgia. The benefactor Grady arranged on that occasion was none other than Alexander Stephens. Fortunately for Grady's purposes but unfortunately for Harris and accordingly Bacon, Harris had to leave the convention to attend an ill son.

Grady moved into the Kimball House and did not leave until he had his way, even to abandoning house guests in his brand-new home on Peachtree Street. (He later wrote them an apology, saying that had he abandoned the delegates for his guests, all could have been lost.) Grady persuaded the delegates, who had already been through seventeen ballots, to appoint a special committee that would break the deadlock. As the convention considered the proposal, Grady worked tirelessly through the night to get the prospective committee members to throw their support behind Henry D. McDaniel from Monroe who was far behind in ballots and had given thought to withdrawing. Perhaps unsurprisingly, the convention appointed the committee and the committee in turn recommended McDaniel, who went on to win the election unopposed. Grady had reason to believe that he could get the unspectacular McDaniel, who had grown up in Atlanta, to do his bidding. He could and did. At his inauguration, made all the more painful because McDaniel was a stutterer, a young Atlanta attorney overheard a Tennessean to say, "Georgia was exchanging a governor who could not walk [Stephens] for one who could not talk [McDaniel]." The young attorney was Woodrow Wilson.[131]

From July 1882 to April 1883, Grady engineered the election of two governors, Stephens and McDaniel, and one U.S. senator, Colquitt. He was also behind the machinations of 1880 that resulted in Brown's appointment to the Senate and Colquitt's election to a second term as governor. Now all Grady needed to do was assure that McDaniel and Brown would have no opposition when running for full terms in 1884. Grady's ace this time was a presidential election in which the Democrats were almost certain to win. The party had not held the presidency in twenty-four years. Although he knew that Samuel Tilden, the sentimental favorite, was unlikely to run, Grady believed that booming his prospects would result in Brown and McDaniel both running unopposed in their races. Grady got the desired result: whether his strategy caused it, he at least steered the political conversation in Georgia away from contested state races.

There was a last shot for the Central and South Georgia crowd to get Bacon in—1886. Bacon's loss would give Grady his last hurrah, politically speaking. Bacon was clearly the man to succeed McDaniel, but further manipulation from Atlanta would be transparent and futile. What Grady needed was a last Confederate trick. It materialized. Even the *Macon Telegraph* and its pro-Bacon publisher, John Fletcher Hanson, sensed that John Brown Gordon would be the card, and so it was. Gordon, who had stepped down from the Senate in 1880 thereby enabling Joseph E. Brown's ascension, had failed in most of his many business ventures. Although not without means, he was no success. The governorship was the one office he had not held, and it would assuage disappointment that resulted from his civilian failures. So Grady seized on the hero of Appomattox and added Jefferson Davis to a gathering entourage, and in so doing he outdid his triumph with Alexander Stephens's funeral dirge.

Alabama was laying the cornerstone to its Confederate Monument in Montgomery. Jefferson Davis had been persuaded to attend from his

---

[131] Ibid.

Gulf Coast Mississippi home, as had Gordon. Grady saw his chance. Atlanta was preparing to unveil a monument of Benjamin Harvey Hill at the intersection of Peachtree and West Peachtree streets. Why not have the two most famous heroes of the Lost Cause make a journey through Georgia? It happened. From the Alabama-Georgia state line on to Atlanta, then to Savannah, and back through Macon, the most vivid symbols of the Confederacy bowed and doffed hats to reverential throngs. Gordon, most often with arm on Davis's slumped shoulders, spoke for Davis from the train's platform as it made stops along the way. Afterward there was no doubt: Gordon would be governor of Georgia through the end of the decade. Grady, the impresario, made it happen. Although the rise of the Farmers Alliance in the last three years of the decade portended change, Grady had secured his decade as the Warwick of Georgia politics.

Relations between Grady and Gordon soon soured, in part because the prickly Gordon heard reports that Grady was "the master hand" in his election as governor. Then in 1888 a boomlet started for Grady to succeed Alfred Colquitt in the U.S. Senate. Flattered, Grady took a nod, as more than seventy legislators had vowed their support, but not a word of support issued from Gordon. Quite the contrary, his office became headquarters for the opposition to Grady. Then in 1889, with Senator Brown seriously ill, Gordon sent the editor a blistering letter charging him with leaking to Brown's family that Gordon wanted the senator's seat. Although the letter has not survived, it was testified to by others—Grady's secretary saying that "Governor Gordon's conduct hurt him [Grady] more than the outside world ever knew." Grady did not respond or retaliate. Gordon's biographer said, "This collapse of the friendship of two of Georgia's most prominent public figures reveals a darker side of Gordon's character." He continued, "Resentful of the gifted newspaperman's immense abilities or perhaps fearful that Grady would eclipse him in the hearts of the Georgia people, Gordon turned on the man who had provided him with such invaluable advice and guidance. Gordon's treatment of his friend, wrote one Grady intimate, 'marks a tale of ingratitude which has not its parallel in the history of Georgia.'"[132]

Bacon would be elected to the United States Senate in 1894 and serve four successive terms, becoming the first popularly elected senator from Georgia by provision of the Seventeenth Amendment, ratified in 1913 and calling for the direct election of senators. Bacon died in 1914 not long after commencing his final term. He was the Senate's ranking Democrat and mourned by that chamber at his passing. Gordon won election to the Senate in 1891 and served until 1897. Gordon died in January 1904 while wintering with family at Florida's Biscayne Bay.

The New South

Grady's vision of the New South had its cornerstones: slavery was over and secession renounced; the future lay in industrialization; the end of one-crop agriculture (diversification); with White supremacy and one-party politics as the solution to race relations. His New South rhetoric romanticized relationships between Blacks and Whites in slavery and touted a balanced future for industrialization and agriculture. The New South of Grady's urgings could not and never would be reality, but it prevailed as vision in the late nineteenth century, perhaps more reluctantly among diehard Southerners. His views would be adopted in the era of Constitutional segregation for its own purposes, even as its affections and aspirations eventually would dismantle the era of Jim Crow segregation. As will be seen in part two, there was a hand-off. Grady as chrysalis represented a "butterfly effect" that would transform the South and the nation by mid-twentieth century.

Grady biographer Harold Davis correctly observed that Grady was too inconsistent in his views to be judged an intellectual.[133] He was right. Nowhere was this inconsistency more evident than in his efforts to address "the farmers and the cities." A transformation was underway that would make America an urban nation, which the census would verify by a national majority in 1920—although not in the South.

---

[132] Eckert, *John Brown Gordon*, 295–96; Hain, *Murder in the State Capitol*, 223–24; Nixon, *Henry W. Grady*, 328–29. Clark Howell was the "intimate" friend reference.

[133] H. Davis, *Henry Grady's New South*, introduction.

Grady's imagination was fertile although it was hard to separate the weeds from the garden. On the one hand, Grady lauded the independent yeoman of subsistence farming, corn over cotton, who survived on less money in exchange for greater independence. Happiness would result. Then Grady would advocate applying business principles to farming that would grow surpluses to feed urban markets, all of which were frustrated by freight rates, middlemen, and credit. Capitalism that had been built on slavery did not make the conversion to wage labor on farms or even family farms easy: its demands for profits created yet another kind of slavery.

Grady wanted to believe in crop diversity and applying business principles to farming and therefore advocated otherwise: that it was not another form of slavery. Farmers were not all impressed. The *Constitution* itself acknowledged as much in 1882. "Now the farmers," it opined, "have objected to the annual crusade of the *Constitution* in favor of diversified crops, because we are theorists. They have replied to our arguments with the boast that one practical farmer was worth a dozen editors, and that they knew more about their business than we could ever teach them."[134] Grady was a theorist. He believed in Jefferson's sturdy yeoman, even as his hero Jefferson was a slave master and perhaps a horticulturist but never a farmer. Grady believed the yeoman farmer could maintain his independence by crop diversification and the application of business principals to the farm. As theory, it was symmetrical if not applicable as the Southern farmers struggling to adjust in a new capitalist order and seeking ways to escape symbols that had "grouped in the powerful and persuasive myth of the southern plantation."[135]

Grady knew little better than most. He read many reports on trends, yet he was back and forth on cities versus farms. He could never resolve the tension, so he romanticized both to the satisfaction of neither. As Henry Nash Smith put it,

> The steam engine was not only to subordinate the yeoman farmer to the banker and the merchant of the new Western cities; eventually it transformed him into a producer of staple crops for distant

[134] *Atlanta Constitution*, March 1, 1882.

[135] H. Smith, *Virgin Land*, 172.

> markets and thus placed him at the mercy of freight rates and of fluctuations in international commodity prices. One of the most significant facts of American intellectual history is the slow and inadequate fashion in which the momentum of the forces was appreciated.[136]

Grady's urging of the business solution could only have frustrated an already aggravated situation. A year later Grady added fuel to his rhetorical fire when he said that the adoption of business principles would "attach the wings of progress to their plowshares and make themselves independent so far as plenty and comfort are concerned."[137]

The Farmers Alliance first made its appearance in Georgia at the Interstate Farmers' Convention that Grady addressed in 1887. He encouraged the Alliance's development, interviewed its principals, "explaining how they hoped to help themselves through organization and cooperation." In December 1888 and continuing through the early months of 1889, "he personally supervised a page in the Sunday *Constitution* in which farmers were invited to discuss their problems and advance solutions." He took only one trip outside the region to address the Southern Society of New York in April 1889 and otherwise used spring and summer months for speeches to farmers in Georgia.

At the same time, Grady "commissioned a compositor in the *Constitution* office to purchase a suburban farm," and he planned it with great care. Grady's friend Joel Chandler Harris defended the imaginary farm, writing, "The farm of course was a dream, but it was a very beautiful one while it lasted, and he dwelt on it with an earnestness that was quite engaging to those who enjoyed his companionship. The farm was a dream, but he no doubt got more enjoyment and profit out of it than a great many prosy people get out of the farms that are real."[138] Grady was going to have fun no matter the gravamen of subject or situation, and the Alliance was serious business as Grady prepared to go to Elberton and address their concerns.

Grady's speech in Elberton, northeast of Athens and just over the line from South Carolina, on June 9, 1889, formed the pattern for a

---

[136] Ibid., 182.

[137] *Atlanta Constitution*, May 25, 1883.

[138] Joel Chandler Harris, *Life of Henry W. Grady*, 18–20.

dozen other speeches he made, mostly in rural Georgia over the next two months. He opened with an idyllic flourish: "I stand here in this beautiful morning, so shot through and through with sunshine that the very air is as molten gold to the touch—under these trees in whose trunks the rains and suns of years are compacted, and on whose leaves God has laid his whispering music...." It was the nineteenth-century style of orating, and he spared no audience, not even farmers, its excesses. He could also wink, as when he described the smell of barbeque being prepared for dinner on the grounds, and said, "I shudder when I think that I, a single, unarmed, defenseless man, is all that stands between this crowd and that dinner. Here then, awed by God's majesty, and menaced by man's appetite, I am tempted to leave this platform and yield to boyish impulses...." He concluded, "and as for you, when the time comes—as it will come—when you prefer barbeque shoat to raw orator, and feel that you can be happier at the table than in this forum, just say the word and I will be with you heart and soul."[139]

He then launched into the meat of his subject and spoke for two hours. On any Saturday afternoon, in any part of Elbert County, Grady said you would find a farmer "saddling his plow-horse, or starting afoot and making his way to a neighboring church or schoolhouse." There he would find neighbors of similar determination—"the earnest, thoughtful faces, the serious debate and council, the closed doors and the secret session...." "It is a meeting," he said,

> of men who feel that in spite of themselves their affairs are going wrong—of free and equal citizens who feel that they carry unequal burdens.... This is a meeting of protest, of resistance. Here the farmer meets to demand, and organize that he may enforce his demand, that he shall stand equal with every other class of citizen....[140]

Grady was describing a gathering of Alliance men and anointed them with the balm of their own feelings. Grady was what would be today called a "total empath," and it showed in every speech he gave. Audience identification was his métier. His empathy also contributed to his inconsistencies, often saying the same things in different ways to

---

[139] Ibid., 159.
[140] Ibid., 160.

different audiences, certainly with differing emphases.

In Elberton he said everything he had said before, but it was to the Farmers Alliance that was on the cusp of seizing the Georgia legislature. The alliance had been around as the Granger Movement of the seventies and would morph into the Populist movement of the nineties. As Alliance, North and South, Black and White, segregated by region and race, but with common purpose speaking now against the day. Although the nation would tilt urban by the 1920s, the South would fall under rural control long into the mid-twentieth century—the county unit system (1917–1962) giving to the smallest Georgia counties two-thirds of the votes allotted to the largest, thereby wiping out 1500 votes with multiples in Fulton County at a swoop. Atlanta stood no chance against 150 rural counties of the state's total 159. In Elberton Grady acknowledged the movement of population from farm to city and provided facts to prove it. He waxed eloquently on farmers as the rock-solid element of American democracy. He lamented the demoralizing effects of urban life and said,

> I rejoice in Atlanta's growth, and yet I wonder whether it is worth what it costs when I know that her population has been drawn largely from rural Georgia, and that back of her grandeur are thousands of deserted farms and dismantled homes. As much as I love her—and she is all to me that home can be to any man—if I had the disposal of 100,000 immigrants at her gates to-morrow, 5000 should enter there, 75,000 should be located in the shops and factories in Georgia towns and villages, and 20,000 sent to her farms.[141]

Grady laid into mortgages held in New York and Europe on Southern farms as an egregious tax. As before, creditors, middlemen, and merchants soaked up profits from farmers as staples moved up the supply chain. Then Grady pivoted to Republicans who were attempting a Force Bill, so styled by Southerners, to oversee elections in the South that were transparently suppressing and intimidating Black voting, and from there he moved to pensions for Union soldiers which Southerners paid without recompense. Those pensions were "bought" votes for the Republican majority, so the enemy of the Southern farmer

[141] Ibid., 164.

was transferred from freight rates and middlemen to national politics; after all, Grady had employed the same approach in the 1884 national election for Cleveland to draw local attention away from local opposition to Gordon and Colquitt for governor and senator. It worked then. He was trying it now.

Then Grady made his final turn to "centralization," the evil of the century. Because of his audience, urbanization was a part of the evil, but not central to it. He had railed against atheism and anarchism as centralizing urban maladies, but these were not the issues concerning him now. For these farmers, and indeed as he had argued consistently, it was capital—the single individual capitalist who could lock up wheat from the market by buying and warehousing it until he exacted his millions, and other capitalists who could lock up other staples like cotton for same. All money had funneled to the top, impoverishing those who produced wealth. Government, Grady said, was the solution:

> It can top off these colossal fortunes and, by an income tax, retard their growth. It can set a limit to personal and corporate wealth. It can take trusts and syndicates by the throat. It can shatter monopoly; it can equalize the burden of taxation; it can distribute its privileges impartially; it can clothe with credit its land now discredited at its banks; it can lift the burden from the farmers' shoulders, give him equal strength to bear them—it can trust the people in whose name this Republic was founded; in whose courage it was defended; in whose wisdom it has been administered, and whose stricken love and confidence it cannot survive.[142]

The farmer ideology was never as consistent or probative as Grady wanted to believe that day. The forces of urbanization and civilization far outdistanced its grievances and prejudices. The farmer ideology would acquire political influence in the West and South but not the future. Especially in Georgia, its populist leaders would retrograde into racial politics and crippling economic policies, all in the name of Jeffersonian democracy, which never had or would succeed. From the Feltons to Tom Watson and on to Gene Talmadge and his machine, it would cripple the state and its farmers until the Grady imagination would re-emerge in the last half of the twentieth century.

---

[142] Ibid.

Coda

Grady idealized a New Southman as a person New England-educated who would move to the region and work wonders with northeastern capital. He got it in Sidney Root, only Root had already made the journey. Born in 1824 in Massachusetts, Root and his family moved to Craftsbury, Vermont, to farm. Root yearned for a career in art and therefore in New York, and his father did allow him to apprentice and later work for a jeweler in Burlington. From there a brother-in-law in Georgia enticed him to Lumpkin, Georgia, fifty miles south of Columbus. There he prospered as a merchant in the firm of Rawson and Root, a cash-only dry-goods store that, because of its cash-only business model, could sell for less. By 1855, it was Root's business alone. In 1849, he married Mary Harvey Clark, and they had two sons and a daughter. The first son was named John Wellborn Root. Both sons would become architects.

By 1857, he sold the business at a handsome profit and moved to Atlanta as the more opportune place for business. His wife's dowry brought with it three slaves, so he became a slave-owner also. Still, success in Atlanta was the ultimate striving and a partnership with John N. Beach created the ultimate opportunity as they became the most successful of Atlanta's antebellum merchants, which included international trade. The Beach and Root partners in dry-goods built the first three-story cast-iron building in Atlanta and inaugurated a new era of architecture. They eventually entered into cotton and banking as well and by the outbreak of war had become the most lucrative firm in Atlanta.

As the secession crisis loomed, Root came under suspicion for his New England background, but at age thirty-seven he enlisted in the Minute Men of Fulton County, thereby removing some of the doubt. More importantly, he accompanied Jefferson Davis from Ringgold, Georgia, to Montgomery for his inauguration. Davis tapped him to handle blockade-running operations from Charleston to England and Europe. He was as successful as could be, eventually collecting a flotilla of twenty ships out of Liverpool to run operations. In the meantime, his wife and mother-in-law moved to the safety of Cuthbert, Georgia, for the war's duration. (Andrew College, founded 1854, in Cuthbert, was the second college authorized to confer degrees on women. Wesleyan, founded in 1836, in Macon was the first.) Sidney Root smuggled his son John Wellborn through the blockade to Liverpool and accordingly an introduction to European culture. His father made sure John Wellborn was not drafted into Confederate service; it was a close call, given the Confederacy's desperate need for manpower. Grady himself, five and a half months younger, avoided the call, but others of that age did not. Root also joined those who advocated arming slaves and petitioned Jefferson Davis directly. Davis in turn sent him to Robert E. Lee's tent. Lee also thought slaves should be armed, but loud objections from diehards throughout the South and fast-closing events of the war rendered the issue moot.

At war's end, Root was in Europe at President Davis's request. He was trying to drum up support for the Confederacy's own version of emancipation. (Many in the South had concluded that armed Back Confederates should be given freedom. Jefferson Davis somewhat agreed, but it came to nothing.) Root then took a circuitous route back from Europe and rejoined his family. In Atlanta he found his commercial buildings destroyed, but not his house, a concrete structure that served as headquarters for Union Major Edward Beckwith during the occupation. He labored mightily to restore Atlanta's and his own fortunes. Among other things he established the Atlanta Board of Trade, which would become the Atlanta Chamber of Commerce, but by 1868, Root sold his house to Joseph E. Brown and moved to New York for his children's educations. He also became an even more devout member of the Baptist church, a denomination he adopted soon after moving South in the 1840s. Also interested in Negro education, he played an important role in convincing fellow Baptist John D. Rockefeller to endow what became Spelman College in Atlanta. As "resident trustee," Root also played a role in the transformation of the Atlanta Baptist Seminary into what became Morehouse College.

When African American Baptists in New York approached him in 1876 about ministering to a mission they had established, he at first refused. When they persisted, he relented but only on the understanding that his ministerial role would not entitle them to become his social equals. The congregants soon numbered a thousand and the mission became the Mount Olivet (Mount Olive) Baptist Church of New York

City in 1878, the year Root returned to Atlanta. Upon his return, he threw himself into the life of the city. He became a director of the Atlanta Cotton States Exposition of 1881 and fulfilled his interest in parks and greenspace by convincing his friend Lemuel Grant to build Grant Park in 1883.

His son, John Wellborn Root, moved to Chicago and soon established the architectural firm of Burnham and Root, which would do much to transform the Chicago skyline as it built back from the great fire of 1873. Like Grady, John Root would die early from pneumonia, but not before he had designed Chicago's World Columbian Exposition of 1892–1893, a spectacle to equal the spectacle in Paris that was crowned by the Eiffel Tower. John Root's death in 1891 also occasioned great mourning, if not on the scale of Grady's passing. His life and contributions would be immortalized in Erik Larson's *The Devil in the White City: Murder, Magic, and Madness at the Fair that Changed America*.

Another Georgian of Grady's age was born in 1852 in Columbus just fifty miles up the road from Lumpkin where John Root had grown up. George Foster Peabody also exhibited New South characteristics. When Sherman's raiders burned his father's mercantile store and ransacked their house and ate their supper as the horrified family looked on, the Peabody family decided to move in with relatives in Brooklyn, New York. By age twenty-eight, Foster Peabody formed a partnership in investment banking with his friend Spencer Trask. Over the next twenty-five years they amassed a fortune in railroads (out West and in Mexico and Latin America), utilities (one becoming General Electric), and sugar beets. He retired in 1906 to manage his philanthropies, among which were Negro education, various peace movements, and the University of Georgia. He served on the boards of several Negro colleges, including the Tuskegee Institute.

A staunch Democrat, George Foster Peabody was on its executive committee for over twenty years, becoming close with Woodrow Wilson and Franklin Roosevelt. Peabody encouraged FDR to purchase the property at Warm Springs, which became the Little White House, believing as did Roosevelt that the waters would be therapeutic.[143] Peabody became a friend to all UGA chancellors and became the university's leading benefactor of all time—his gifts totaling over thirteen million dollars in today's equivalent. He married once, Spencer Trask's widow Katrina (Kate). He was sixty-nine; she was sixty-eight. Already ill, she died eleven months later. Peabody soon thereafter adopted Marjorie Waite, a young widow who had come to Yaddo, the Trask Estate at Saratoga Springs, to run a school for working women. Yaddo would become the famous artists' and writers' colony.

Peabody died in 1938, outliving Grady and Root by almost fifty years. The University of Georgia named its famous awards for excellence in electronic media for him. The George Foster Peabody Awards are considered the most prestigious in the industry, the equivalent of Pulitzers in journalism. Grady, Root, and Peabody, another Georgia triumvirate, each embodied the values Grady had in mind for an urban and urbane New South.

---

[143] Peabody and Roosevelt made another friend through Warm Springs, Tom W. Loyless, a New South journalist, who, although a generation younger than Peabody, will figure prominently at the end of Part 3.

Part 2

The New South

> "Of all the talents bestowed upon men, none is so precious as the gift of oratory. He who enjoys it wields power more durable than that of a great king.... Whoever can command this power is formidable."
>
> —Andrew Roberts on Churchill

The Earthquakes

On the night of Tuesday, August 31, 1886, Grady was as usual in his living room chair, reading and jotting notes for the day coming, when at just before ten o'clock, he felt a rumble, quickly increasing to a roar, "like a street car running through the house." A 7.6 earthquake that started on the Atlantic coast at 9:53 p.m. rushed north and west at a speed of 7,200 miles per hour through the tectonic plates of the continent all the way up to Maine and over to Terre Haute, Indiana. Gas chandeliers swayed, crystal rattled and smashed to the floor. The Gradys rushed out of their Peachtree Street home to see a chimney that had crashed through a neighbor's house. All were safe but aftershocks continued.[1]

Grady headed immediately to his office, a mile away down a dusty Peachtree Street. After assessing incoming dispatches from the Associated Press and the *Constitution*'s own special correspondents, he noted that only Charleston was silent. Soon rumors abounded; one claimed Charleston had fallen into the ocean as it collapsed before the onrushing waves of a tsunami. When the disaster was confirmed by ten o'clock the next morning, Grady, Evan Howell, and three other Atlantans who wanted to help caught the first train to Augusta. On reaching

[1] Nixon, *Henry W. Grady*, 4–7; S. Williams and Hoffius, *Upheaval in Charleston*, 1–3; E. C. Clark, *Francis Warrington Dawson*, 138–41.

that half-way point, they discovered that the tracks had been washed out by a breaking dam on Langley Pond just east of the city. Grady promptly wired the superintendent of the South Carolina Railroad and arranged for a special engine to meet the Atlanta contingent on the other side of the pond.

Taking a small boat, they paddled the pond to meet the oncoming engine, fired and waiting. Because there were no turn-around tracks, the engine backed all the way to Charleston, or as near as they could get. Meanwhile, perched upon the wood-tender, Grady recorded copious notes on all he observed. On arriving in Charleston at ten o'clock Thursday night (September 2), exactly two days after the first shocks, he spent the next four hours interviewing victims and filed a 4,000-word story by two o'clock Friday morning. He telegraphed it to the *Constitution*, the *New York World*, and other papers, each over his full name. Without undressing, he slept a few hours, arose at sunrise, and soon sent out 10,000 words more.

Thus did Grady, a few weeks later, receive his invitation to address the New England Society of New York, the turning point of his all too brief career. He already had a national reputation, but as journalists know, there is nothing like covering a natural disaster to cement a reputation. Grady's herculean coverage of the Charleston earthquake confirmed his national standing, resulting in an address that in its day was the equivalent of Martin Luther King Jr.'s "Letter from Birmingham Jail" or "I Have a Dream" speech. It spoke of a national reconciliation that was a necessary precondition to all the good that eventually would come even from all the bad that occurred over the next seventy-five years, especially in terms of racial separation and degradation.

Grady's triumph, and the earthquake that led to it, sparked a controversy with fellow New Southerner and founding editor of the *Charleston News and Courier*, Francis Warrington Dawson, who was one of only two prophets of the New South who fought in the Civil War (the other was Henry Watterson). Dawson was born in England, May 17, 1840, and for his first twenty years carried the name Austin John Reeks (pronounced Ricks). As a Catholic, he experienced rank discrimination and identified with Irish Home Rule and Gladstonian Liberalism. It also caused him to identify with the South's strike for independence and under a *nom de guerre* set steam to run the blockade, entering the Confederacy at Morehead City, North Carolina. Beginning at Mechanicsville in June 1862, he fought in most of the engagements of the Army of Northern Virginia until taking his third wound at the Battle of Five Forks, just outside Petersburg and just before Appomattox.

Starting in artillery, Dawson ended the war at the rank of captain and chief of ordnance for Fitzhugh Lee's cavalry division. He was a hit with Richmond society, getting close to the Pegrams of Virginia's Southside and the Carys of Richmond. He even engaged to marry one of the beautiful Haxall sisters but married Virginia Fourgeaud in 1847.[2] To his mother he exclaimed, "It seems so strange that I should have had so few friends in England, when I have such hosts of them here."[3] It would be surprising if he did not make the acquaintance of Grady's good friend Robert Alston, although there is no direct evidence of it.

At war's end, Dawson entered journalism in Richmond and eventually made his way to Charleston, where he and a friend acquired first the *Charleston News* and soon the South's oldest newspaper, the *Courier*. Following his first wife's death, he met and married Sarah Fowler Morgan, whose family was from Louisiana. Her irrepressible and sometimes irresponsible younger brother, Jimmy, introduced them. Dawson had been introduced to James Morris Morgan while in Richmond, and Sarah had written the second most famous diary of the Civil War, *Diary of a Confederate Girl.* Together she and Dawson wrote a series of commentaries in the 1870s on the "Woman Question" that was as forward in its thinking as that of John Stuart and Harriett Taylor Mill's advocacy in England. Indeed, C. Vann Woodward said that Dawson, along with E. L. Godkin of *The Nation,* "spoke with the voice of Manchester to the New South."[4]

Thus, Dawson was an estimable figure when he and Grady crossed swords. Pique and envy set in when Dawson scored his own triumph with the earthquake. Dawson too was at home when the quake struck (Sarah and their two children were in Europe). He was in his third-

---

[2] Mary Haxall jilted him for Alexander Cameron of tobacco fortune and fame; Dawson had introduced the pair.)

[3] E. C. Clark, *Francis Warrington Dawson*, 19.

[4] Woodward, *Origins of the New South*, 146.

floor study, enjoying the quiet of a summer evening, when a soft rumbling noise soon became a roar. The great Bull Street house "seemed literally to turn on its axis." Dust and debris choked the room as the ceiling cracked and plaster scattered. A water tank in the attic burst, flooding the bedrooms and sending water cascading down the spiral staircase. The quake wrenched statues and lamps from their bases and hurled them to the floor. The large porch, or gallery, as Sarah called it, with its massive pillars and solid marble steps "was swept away as though it had been shaved off with a razor." The time was 9:51, two minutes before Grady felt it.

Like Grady, Dawson headed immediately to the newsroom and produced his own herculean feat. Because the September 1 edition of the *News and Courier* was always dedicated to an annual review of Charleston's economic and commercial activity, seven of its pages had already been composed. Dawson quickly added an eighth with headlines that blared "A TERRIBLE EARTHQUAKE—CHARLESTON SHAKEN FROM CENTRE TO CIRCUMFERENCE—THE WHOLE CITY INJURED—SAD LOSS OF LIFE—FIVE SUCCESSIVE SHOCKS—Scenes and incidents—The Most Disastrous Event in the City's History." He did not exaggerate. Thus did a stricken city come to read of its disaster within hours of being shaken to its foundations. The paper did not appear on September 2, and as Dawson explained in a letter to Sarah, "it was not because of any injury to the establishment, but because of the cowardice of the compositors." Conceding he may have been too harsh in that assessment, he nonetheless begrudged their thinking "more of running to their families than sticking to their posts."[5] He could be imperious, hectoring and ordering staff around. Still, even to staff he remained admired and respected.

The city of Charleston sang his praises as he worked tirelessly for the relief of its stricken citizenry. Another notable New South editor, Patrick Walsh of the *Augusta Chronicle*, wrote, "As a rule every great emergency develops its hero, and in this instance Capt. F. W. Dawson has become master of the situation."[6] So what happened between him and Grady? Certainly it was not Grady's reporting from the scene. He

[5] E. C. Clark, *Francis Warrington Dawson*, 138–39.

[6] *Augusta Chronicle*, September 15, 1886.

interviewed Dawson and numerous others and wrote vividly about the catastrophe in Charleston. He said it was greater than what Sherman's army had wrought. The division came later when Grady crowed that readers of the *Constitution* learned more about the quake and its aftermath than readers of the *News and Courier*. Grady also called Charleston "the last Citadel of the old regime." Dawson chafed at the insinuation that Charleston was mired in its past.

The *Constitution* stumbled on a key element of the controversy when it observed that while Mr. Grady was in New York striking a "note of harmony and fraternity" with his New South speech, Charleston alone gave the it no notice, even though "at the very moment the speech was made Charleston was enjoying the benefit of $800,000 contributed by the stingy and puritanical North." In a now-that-you've-mentioned-it editorial, Dawson charged that Grady had won acclaim for his coverage of the earthquake though he belittled the significance of the earthquake damage, thereby limiting the relief that otherwise would have flowed freely from the North. Dawson went on to suggest that the response of the American people to the Charleston earthquake, much more than Grady's speech, proved the harmony existing between the sections. Dawson accused Grady of being a latecomer to the field of sectional reconciliation and compared the Atlantan to "a leaf on the bosom of a broad river. As a leaf, he partakes of the flow of the mighty stream without directing or influencing it."[7]

For Dawson the earthquake's aftermath was both emotional and personal. On the morning of November 10, 1886, he found a new silver service on his breakfast table. Because Sarah and the children were still in Europe, it was a quiet moment. He opened the accompanying card. It read:

> It is today exactly twenty years ago you first came to Charleston and cast your lot with its citizens. In that period have happened, in quick succession, events which will always be counted as among the most momentous in the history of Charleston. In the narrative of all these

[7] *Charleston News & Courier*, December 30, 1886; E. C. Clark, *Francis Warrington Dawson*, 142.

> events, your name will appear as one of the chiefest actors, and always in the part of striving for the weal of our city and its citizens.[8]

What more could one want in "staid old Charleston" than an embrace seldom accorded an outsider. "Perhaps nothing more than the Charleston earthquake of August 31, 1886," wrote Jonathan Daniels, "could have made his acceptance final among his neighbors." After turning "to the English-born editor for leadership," the representatives of the oldest families were only then willing to give this "newcomer by Charleston standards the accolade of their appreciation and acceptance."[9] Thus, in Dawson's mind, the unappreciative Grady was the newcomer.

As a result of his full name being plastered all over the North as byline to the earthquake stories, Grady received an "urgent" invitation to address the New England Society of New York a few weeks later. As previously detailed, the speech was a smashing success. It was praised throughout the South, and the few objections raised came mostly from free trade journals opposed to Grady's protectionist views. Six days passed before the speech appeared in the *News and Courier*, and the editorial reply never mentioned his name or speech. To Grady's assertion that the nation had at last found in Abraham Lincoln the first "typical American," Dawson said "wrong" and denied "absolutely that among thoughtful Southerners there is any such thing as an intelligent recognition of Mr. Lincoln as a typical American." The South was willing to give him credit for "his shrewdness, his knowledge of men, his loyalty, his perseverance," but "he was never a typical American, unless such an American must necessarily be coarse while kindly, vulgar though good-hearted, ill-bred while acute, awkward while amiable, and weak in act while strong in word." Although unwilling to praise Lincoln as a model American, Dawson did perceive in him traits that made him a "typical western man," or "perhaps a type of new class who are rising to prominence in parts of the New South." Well, it was tangential to the whole of Grady's remarks, although it went straight at the most successful utterance of the night at Delmonico's.

---

[8] Friends to Dawson, November 10, 1886, and Dawson to Sarah, same date, Dawson Papers, Duke University Library.

[9] Jonathan Daniels, *They Will Be Heard*, 201.

Dawson and Grady were coming at the most fundamental tenet of the New South, apart from race: its history—arguably even the most important because accounting for White supremacy remained the central theme of Southern history. The most damning characteristic of this new class of Southerners was their willingness to adopt what one South Carolinian termed "policy and expediency as standards."[10] They appeared all too eager to admit President Garfield's dictum that the North was "eternally right" and the South "eternally wrong" in an effort to gain economic concessions from the North. Again with Grady in mind, Dawson agreed with the *Augusta Chronicle* that "conversions under excitement and enchantment" led to this kind of cowardly confession in the midst of "post-prandial pledges." Dawson condemned those who by the "witchery of pen or voice" would seek to extinguish "the principle of the 'Old South.'" He reminded those who would be expedient or politic that "it is not for the sons to apologize for their fathers, whose homes and honors they inherit."[11]

Dawson had seized on a wedge issue and would take it as far as it would travel. The issue had nothing to do with all that Grady had done to rewrite history in celebration of its "Lost Cause," which was central to his New South message. The process of rewriting history began with the war's last shot. A victorious Union that had trampled out "the grapes of wrath" and thereby restored union and freedom would write the history of the victor. The South would as assuredly compile a history of the vanquished, blurring any and all differences between old and new. As Henry Louis Gates recently put it, Grady was "the diabolically clever" editor whose New South speech was "an ingenious rebranding of the Old South in the guise of the New."[12] Yet, in the wake of Grady's declaration a moment came for venting and hashing out its meaning. Dawson accepted two invitations to address national audiences, even as he confessed to Sarah it would mean being burdened with "an awful o-

---

[10] J. J. Pringle to William Porcher Miles, June 29, 1877, Miles Papers], Southern Historical Collection, University of North Carolina.

[11] *Charleston News & Courier*, December 30, 1886.

[12] Gates, *Stony the Road*, 84. Gates also cites Grady's "Dallas Speech" for the editor's declaration "that the white race must dominate forever in the South because it is the white race that is superior to that race by which its supremacy is threatened" (86).

r-a-t-i-o-n to write; & I can't orate."[13]

The first at Cooper Union Hall in New York sounded like any other New South speech designed to assuage Northern fears with Southern pledges of union and reconciliation. It received more than polite applause; Dawson was too deprecatory about his own oratorical abilities. Still, he was no Grady. In the second speech in Baltimore, prepared for the eighth annual reunion of the Association of the Maryland Line, a Confederate survivors' association, Dawson did better because it was before a more empathetic audience. Concerning both speeches, Dawson wrote that "as Grady had been reaping the harvest of reconciliation & praise from the seed that I had been among the first to sow, I thought it advisable to keep to the front myself."[14] The Baltimore speech did have its moments. He told the survivors,

> It is well enough to cover our wounds and hide our scars. But never let it be denied—that the scars and wounds are there, not to rankle or irritate, but as signs and tokens of the days that are dead, the glories and disasters whose memories we could not blot out if we would, and would not if we could! Too much history has already been written for us. Too little has been written by ourselves, and for the justification of our people. It is, then, but meet and right that, on such an occasion as this, the truth shall be told, and the whole truth, even if hurts the feelings of our "friends, the enemy."[15]

The private reaction to Dawson's Baltimore address expressed more clearly the perceived differences between Dawson and Grady. Coming largely from "professional southerners," men whose chief ally seemed to be inertia, made Dawson appear more a patron of the old order than he was. One South Carolinian wrote that a recent trip North made him feel "even more keenly than before, the false position we were sought to be placed in by the utterances of Henry Grady, and it was therefore with additional pleasure that I read the antidote so promptly and efficaciously applied by you the other day." The correspondent also referred to Dawson's editorials while North "as evidence

---

[13] Dawson to Sarah, December 1886, and February 8 and 11, 1887, Dawson Papers, Duke University Library.

[14] Ibid.

[15] *News & Courier*, February 23, 1887.

that his [Grady's] ideas by no means meet with universal acceptance."[16] Another writer praising the speech as "one of the most valuable contributions to the history of the 'lost cause,'" commended Dawson's courage not to indulge in "weak and cowardly concessions to the dominant sentiment and the repudiation of principle for the sake of securing policy."[17] William Gordon McCabe, founder of the University School at Petersburg offered similar sentiments, and Charles Colcock Jones Jr., critic of the New South and staunch defender of the faith, found the address truly "admirable" and promised to circulate copies among his friends.[18]

To be sure, Grady would have disagreed with little other than inflection in Dawson's speeches and writings. Grady was not close to forgetting or apologizing for the past. Grady would have made no objections when Dawson opined that sectional pride preceded sectional reconciliation, that the "vindication of the South, at last, is the vindication of a part of the Union, and it will be to the honor and strength and glory of the whole Union that that vindication shall be full and complete as it surely will be."[19] A sure sign that the South had accepted defeat came in Grady's famous opening to the New South Address when he declaimed the South of slavery and secession was dead. Only after the second part of that proclamation, that "a New South of freedom and union was living, breathing, growing every hour," did he offer the exclamation, "Thank God."

Again Dawson's tone was a bit different, when he said it was enough to teach the children "that it was might that triumphed over right, in order that the ways of Eternal Providence should be made manifest—for our good in the end, for the good of the sinning and the sinned against."[20] As Dawson leaned one way and tilted the other, his quarrel with Grady was his belief that the Atlanta editor was saying

---

[16] Philip E. Chazal to Dawson, February 26, 1887, Dawson Papers, Duke University Library.

[17] W. L. T. Prince to Dawson, June 28, 1887, ibid.

[18] W. G. McCabe to Dawson, June 13, 1887; and C. C. Jones Jr. to Dawson, June 7, 1887, ibid.

[19] *News & Courier*, February 24, 1887.

[20] Ibid., November 30, 1882.

that the war was about slavery. Dawson preferred his reason for enlisting, that like the rebellious Irish, it was a strike for Home Rule. In the end, the quarrel was probably a result of their age difference more than anything else. As Broadus Mitchell put it, "Dawson was not an orator, and had none of the flourish of Grady." Dawson's attack was "direct and concentrated," too prosaic to fire the imagination. Yet on the more practical concern of bringing cotton mills South, "In this thinking...the *News and Courier* preceded the *Constitution* by ten years."[21] And yes, Grady was ten years and one week younger.

Rewriting History

History is the purest form of identity politics. From the totem pole to the Rosetta stone to Hammurabi's Code to the Bible and Quran to a modern textbook, history records the striving of peoples to establish their identity, their purpose, and the ways they have gone about finding that purpose. In a nation of tribes, sections, rebels, and loyalists, each develops a lore that explains who they are, and thus, why they are. It is ineluctable, inevitable. When the nation was preserved by arms, it was as assuredly to contest its historical grounds, secessionists protecting their right to have established a new nation, Unionists their hallowed ground. Thus when Grady yielded on slavery and secession and embraced union and freedom, he gave up a whole chunk of Southern identity, but his perspective was more rationalization of outcome than embrace of the victor's rationale. The settled determination to maintain White supremacy meant that Grady and the South would seek new ways and means to maintain old racial assumptions. The Confederate nation did not die. It lived on by other means that necessarily involved a reinvention of its history.

John Brown Gordon emerged from out of the North Georgia mountains as leader of the Racoon Roughs and wound up as the hero of Appomattox, leading the last cavalry charge against the victorious Union. Tall and ramrod erect, mustachioed, and with penetrating eyes, he fit the ideal image of a military general. Confederate generals like Gordon found it easy to trade on their celebrity and wind up with sinecures as titular heads of railroads and insurance companies. They

---

[21] Mitchell, *Rise of the Cotton Mills*, 114.

traded on their reputations to advance the penetration of Northern capital into Southern markets. Gordon wound up as head of two organizations. One was the Memphis-based Southern Life Insurance Company, a front for the Ku Klux Klan, for which he would become Grand Wizard. The other was the University Publishing Company, a New York-based publishing house dedicated to purging Yankee history from Southern schools (White only) and supplanting it with a curriculum and history written for and about White Southerners. Both made money for Gordon—but not enough to satisfy his avarice. He considered the companies as a contribution to the Lost Cause—in today's world he would have argued it as tax deductible.[22]

Under congressional investigation, Gordon testified that the Klan, if such existed, was a "peace organization," in effect, the only way to regulate irresponsible and dangerous Negroes incited by Radical Republicans. In his neo-Confederate way of thinking, this reasoning made sense. Mastered in slavery, Negroes could be tamed, dominated and docile, even affectionate—the happy darky. Free, they could be sullen, indolent, and, given their animalistic appetite for sex, a threat, especially to White women. White supremacy had to be protected by violence and vigilante justice—the Klan as peacemakers. The Negro was "child by tiger," at once savage and child-like: "Did He who made the lamb make thee?"[23] In any event the Negro, however docile and domestic, was the ultimate threat to purity and not to be trusted. The masters' own lack of purity, their sexual predation of Black women—proven by the existence of mulatto children—was ignored.

Truth is both history and destiny. The South would at last win. It was to be thus and not otherwise. C. Vann Woodward famously said that the three Civil War amendments, Thirteenth (end of slavery), Fourteenth (civil rights), and Fifteenth (voting rights), were the result of a "moral capital" built through war.[24] The same occurred with World War I and passage of the Prohibition (Eighteenth Amendment) and the women's right to vote (Nineteenth). Then with World War II came

---

[22] Eckert, *John Brown Gordon*, 133–40; Hain, *Murder in the State Capitol*, 116.

[23] "Child by Tiger" is a chapter title in Thomas Wolfe's *The Web and the Rock* and is drawn from William Blake's "The Tyger."

[24] Woodward, *Burden of Southern History*, 84.

the realization of the New Deal and *Brown v. Board of Education* with accompanying civil rights movement. War has yielded moral imperatives that have moved the nation forward from the American Revolution on, but all advances have been resisted, revised, and transmogrified by the politics of Whiteness. We were a nation of Whites and should be ever after, and if other colors, cultures, national origins, religious affiliations, or other human attributes impinged, Whites should sanitize them by co-optation or reject them. White flight to suburbs and ghettoization confirmed the visceral United States, a recasting of *e pluribus unum* into only one and White.

Vann Woodward, the sage of twentieth-century American history with special emphasis on the South, says that America has had to explain only two failures: first, the Southern strike for independence and second, the subsequent national attempt at Reconstruction, which in the mind of the South became the tragic era. Grady's image was more nuanced if no less definite, as revisiting Delmonico's will show. His Augusta friend, Marion J. Verdery, a pal from college days, accompanied Grady to New York. Verdery observed that on arrival for the momentous occasion Grady was "crowded with attentions." In the two preceding days he was given a reception by the Press Club and feted at the Union League Club. When asked what he was going to say, he replied, "The Lord only knows. I have thought of a thousand things to say, five hundred of which if I say they will murder me when I get back home, and the other five hundred of which will get me murdered at the banquet." Another reporter said he appeared "a trifle overcast with anxiety for the result."[25]

Indeed, he should have been. He had only scribbled notes on the back of his menu card. Grady seldom wrote speeches, and when on the few occasions he did, he went off-script—a "reading" and a "speech" are two different things. He wrote prolifically as a journalist, both commentary and news. From it, he had an immense vocabulary and wealth of knowledge for speaking, which he practiced in college and honed with experience. He had little doubt about the moment except its chance of failure, but that had always been his tightrope and it would sustain him now. In the days and weeks before, he had imagined what

[25] *Atlanta Constitution*, December 22, 1886.

he would say, turning a phrase this way and an anecdote another. No doubt by the time he arrived he was "loaded for bear" as the reporter who thought him a trifle anxious noted.

Now it was time for all his Phi Kappa and Washington Society days to come to his aid. Some 360 packed the banquet hall. Delmonico's at that time was located on the south side of Twenty-sixth Street between Broadway and Fifth Avenue. "Never have so many members tried to get seats for the annual feast," the *Tribune* reporter observed. The speaker's table was at the south end of the room; another six tables ran the full length of the hall. The unlucky junior members occupied the walls. At the center of the head table was Horace Russell, at one time New York's district attorney, and now president of the New England Society. On his right was DeWitt Talmadge, Brooklyn clergyman, and to the left was Grady. The other guests of honor included General William Tecumseh Sherman, "grizzled and serious," and business and professional leaders such as J. Pierpont Morgan, Lyman Abbott, Russell Sage, Seth Thomas, Elihu Root, H. M. Flagler, and Grady's friend and sponsor, John H. Inman. Inman represented those New Southers who at war's end had gone North to New York City and made fortunes.

The occasion celebrated the 266th anniversary of the landing of Pilgrims and Plymouth Rock. In Dr. Talmadge's response to "Forefathers' Day," he set Grady up for his most joyous line. "Let us remember," Talmadge said,

> that the coming American is to be an admixture of all foreign bloods. In about twenty-five or fifty years the model American will step forth. He will have the strong brain of the German, the polished manners of the French, the artistic taste of the Italian, the staunch heart of the English, the steadfast piety of the Scotch, the lightning wit of the Irish, and when he steps forth, bone, muscle, nerve, brain entwined with the fibres of all nationalities, the nations will break and cry: "Behold the American!"

(Grady had his cue—it would be his tribute to Lincoln as the first model American.) Not that any the audience would have disagreed, but Talmadge had described a European American, the ideal for both North and South, at least until the anti-immigrant, eugenics movement emerged at the end of the century, and even it might have swallowed the European mixture, excepting perhaps Italians.

Rising to the occasion, Grady was compact at five feet, eight inches, a little above average for the day, with a round, cherubic, but handsome face. "What a radiant, charming and accomplished man he was!" exclaimed Josephus Daniels. "His countenance radiated the charm that won all to him…." On an ordinary day Grady "wore a slouch hat, overcoat turned up at the collar, nothing that looked like being tailor-made, and yet he wore his clothes with distinction. You could not look at him without feeling that you were in the presence of a real person with an individuality and a flavor of rare quality."[26] Sculptor Orion Frazee, whom Grady had attracted to the artist colony he established in Atlanta, saw Grady almost daily and did a bust that captured the editor perfectly. Frazee would also do Grady's death mask.

This was no ordinary day, and Grady was in formal wear. His voice was in the tenor range but resonated with precise inflection and was mesmerizing for an age that found oratorical excess a form of entertainment and hours-long speeches both entertaining and informative. Douglas McArthur, whose father was a Civil War Medal of Honor recipient at Shiloh, carried the same oratorical gravitas into mid-twentieth century, but Grady also had humor, McArthur seldom did. The "New South" speech as taken by reportorial dictation was shorter than most but no less mesmerizing. In the opening he toyed with the theme of a culture clash between Virginia cavalier and New England puritan, suggesting that both were essential, then went on to proclaim Abraham Lincoln the first model American. They were now eating out of his post-prandial hands. "Let us, each cherishing the traditions and honoring his fathers," he said, "build with reverent hands to the type of simple but sublime life, in which all types are honored, and in our common glory as Americans there will be plenty and to spare for your forefathers and for mine."

He then turned to the theme of the returning foot-sore Confederate soldier, an army marching home "in defeat and not in victory—in pathos and not in splendor, but in glory that equaled yours, and to hearts as loving as ever welcomed heroes home! … Ragged, half-starved, heavy hearted, enfeebled by want and wounds…[he lifts his] tear-stained eyes for the last time to the graves that dot Old Virginia

[26] Josephus Daniels, *Tar Heel Editor*, 382.

hills, pulls his gray cap over his brow and begins the slow and painful journey."

> At last arriving home, he finds his house in ruins, his farm devastated, his slaves free, his stock killed, his barns empty, his trade destroyed, his money worthless, his social system, feudal in its magnificence, swept away.... Crushed by defeat, his very traditions are gone; without money, credit, employment, material or training; and beside all this, confronted with the gravest problem that ever met human intelligence—the establishing of a status for the vast body of his liberated slaves.

Grady extemporized the Confederate soldier because De Witt Talmadge had brilliantly portrayed the return of the victorious Northern armies. Thus, playing off Talmadge, Grady struck a blow for the North by proclaiming Lincoln as the model American, and lifted up the Confederate soldier, slouching South toward home and redemption.[27]

Then, after a list of such woes, Grady pivots, finds this same soldier rolling up his sleeves and going to work building a New South. With that nod to pluck and industry, he even threw in a little humor, borrowed from his friend Bill Arp. Arp, Grady said, "struck the keynote when he said: 'Well, I killed as many of them as they did of me, and now I am going to work.'" Arp even had a word about the returning veteran, who while roasting corn on the side of the road, said to his comrades, "'You may leave the South if you want to, but I am going to Sandersville [Washington County, Georgia], kiss my wife and raise a crop, and if the Yankees fool with me any more I will whip 'em again.'"

It was then that Grady turned to Sherman, and with a twinkle in his eye and a wink said, "I want to say to General Sherman, who is considered an able man in our parts, though some people think he is a kind of careless man about fire, that from the ashes he left us in 1864 we have raised a brave and beautiful city; that somehow or other we have caught the sunshine in the brick and mortar of our homes, and have builded therein not one ignoble prejudice or memory."

Grady next launched into a litany of accomplishments, "the sum

---

[27] See W. B. Yeats, "The Second Coming," poetryfoundation.org/poems/43290/the-second-coming.

of our work." We have learned that "the free negro counts more than he did as a slave. We have planted the schoolhouse on the hilltop and made it free to white and black." (That would not long be true; only years later, after integration, did it come to be true.) Towns and cities have replaced "theories" and "business above politics." We are challenging "your spinners in Massachusetts and your iron-makers in Pennsylvania." Cotton worth $400,000,000 annually "will make us rich when the supplies that make it are home-raised," interest on money has dropped from "24 to 6 percent," and bonds are floated at 4 percent. "We have learned that one northern immigrant is worth fifty foreigners." The list of New South accomplishments continued until it ended on a startling note: "Above all, we know that we have achieved in these 'piping times of peace' a fuller independence for the South than that which our fathers sought to win in the forum by their eloquence or compel in the field by their swords." A sentiment like that is what stuck in the craw of the "professional Southerners" who flocked to Grady's rival, Francis Dawson.

There was more. Now playing unabashedly to his audience, Grady said,

> We understand that when Lincoln signed the Emancipation Proclamation, your victory was assured, for he then committed you to the cause of human liberty, against which the arms of man cannot prevail—while those of our statesmen who trusted to make slavery the corner-stone of the Confederacy doomed us to defeat as far as they could, committing us to a cause that reason could not defend or the sword maintain in sight of advancing civilization.

Openly and unequivocally he asserted that slavery was the *bellum causa*. That kind of thinking had to be rebutted, and revisionist historians would soon see to it.

No sooner had Grady said it than he began his own revisionist account, the argument "let he who is without sin cast the first stone." In the next paragraph, Grady denied that Robert Toombs, one of Georgia's most vivid fire-eaters, had ever said "that he would call the roll of his slaves at the foot of Bunker Hill." Grady reasoned that he had not said it because it would have been foolish. (Toombs's reputation for the outrageous was one good reason for calling him "Fighting Bob.") Grady carried it further: Toombs would not have said it "for he might have known that whenever slavery became entangled in war it must perish." Now Grady was dancing on the head of a pin over the word "might" instead of "would." In truth Toombs's legacy renders moot Grady's even suggesting that he did not say it. Yet Grady was headed in another direction and no doubt needed the smokescreen. Still, the war itself had ended slavery in the border states, beginning with Virginia, and by 1864 slaves spilled over into Union lines and joined Sherman's exodus from Atlanta. Slavery was essentially over, and not even a negotiated peace could have resurrected it.[28]

The New South editor's objective point was New England's complicity. He observed that "the chattel in human flesh ended forever in New England when your fathers—not to be blamed for parting with what didn't pay [slavery]—sold their slaves to our fathers—not to be praised for knowing a paying thing when they saw it." It was at best a simplistic and elliptical reading of slavery as it ended in New England and spread throughout the South. Moreover, it was the old Southern *tu quoque*, that you are just as bad as we are.

Even Lincoln broached the thought when he met with Alexander Stephens and other Southern mediators on February 3, 1865, at Fort Fisher in Hampton Roads for a possible end to the war. Although tough and nonnegotiable, Lincoln did say to Stephens and company that he was willing to compensate Southerners for their slaves. When Secretary of State Seward objected, Lincoln said, "If it was wrong in the South to hold slaves, it was wrong in the North to carry on the slave trade and sell them to the South." Despite this concession on the part of the Great Emancipator, the talks at Hampton Roads were at an end, and no quarter was given to the Southern supplicants.[29] Still Grady was not far off where Lincoln stood on compensation and complicity, North and South, on slavery.

Grady's feint at Delmonico's was done so quickly perhaps his listeners could not grasp the prestidigitation—because the orator performed another quick sleight of hand to talk about the close and cordial the relationship between Southern Blacks and Whites. He noted that

---

[28] Glatthaar, *General Lee's Army*, 314.

[29] Chernow, *Grant*, 468.

both Southern and Northern Whites had used and abused these faithful people, as Grady referred to them, even as both protest the "injustice to this simple and sincere people. To liberty and enfranchisement is as far as law can carry the negro. The rest must be left to conscience and common sense." Most important, "it must be left to those among whom his lot is cast, with whom he is indissolubly connected, and whose prosperity depends upon his intelligent sympathy and confidence"—in brief, the White folks at home.

Having "snatched victory from the toad's head of defeat," the New South "presents a perfect democracy, the oligarchs leading in the popular movement—a social system compact and closely knitted, less splendid on the surface, but stronger at the core—a hundred farms for every plantation, fifty homes for every palace—and a diversified industry that meets the complex need of this complex age." The New South, he said, "understands that her emancipation came because through the inscrutable wisdom of God her honest purpose was crossed, and her brave armies beaten." What more could he have said? The ovation was thunderous, New England consubstantial with the New South. It was Grady's dream and, in time, would transmogrify into the radical racism of the next three decades and on to the present day of racial politics.

The transmogrification was a reality that went back to the beginning. Jefferson's notion of a free man being debt free; Jackson's antipathy for Native Americans; the Know Nothing party, aka American Party, and its nativist, anti-Catholic predilections; Liberal Republicans and Southern Democrats holding similar negative reactions to immigrants and Blacks; the America First advocates of the late 1930s and 40s; the John Birchers and White Citizens Councils of the fifties and sixties; the Goldwater movement and George Wallace's resurgence of the American Independent Party label; the Republican "Southern strategy" of Richard Nixon's and Ronald Reagan's fashioning; on to the Koch brothers and Donald Trump's alt-White nativism. The concept is visceral within American politics: Whites founded this country and should still govern it. (All this will be examined in Part 3, Grady's Legacy.)

The assurances Grady gave the conservative business leaders in his audience was all they could have asked, and their ovation gratified Grady. James Buchanan Duke, the tobacco magnate who in 1924 gave the endowment that changed the name of little Trinity College to Duke University, was one appreciative Southerner. For years after, the wealthy North Carolinian carried with him a newspaper clipping of Grady's tribute to the footsore "hero in gray with heart of gold." "It reminded me a lot," he said, "of my own father," who "hustled and harvested like the man in gray."[30] When Grady in his peroration asked whether New England "would permit the prejudice of war to remain in the hearts of the conquerors, when it had died in the hearts of the conquered," the audience shouted: "No! No!" then cheered the hero of the moment "in a manner seldom witnessed in New York."[31]

Though it was midnight when the banquet ended, Charles R. Miller, editor of the *Times*, rushed back to his office and editorialized for his morning readers that it was "the speech of the evening.... It was eloquent. It swept the whole range of emotion, of sentiment, and of patriotism.... In all its four score years the society of Plymouth Rock worshippers never heard a speech that was better worth its while to hear and think about."[32] The Democratic *New York World* opined that the speech was "truly eloquent, in the highest meaning of that much misused word," citing specifically Grady's passage, "I am glad that the omniscient God held the balance of battle in his Almighty hand, and that the American Union was saved from the wreck of war." Although the Republican *Tribune* had reservations about the South's continuing "prejudice and fraud" in suppressing the Negro vote, it felt that the speaker had "reached a high plane in contemporary oratory."

Because Grady seldom came to New York for only one reason, he was also there to fundraise for the upcoming Piedmont Exposition and more generally to promote investment in the South. As a result, he was much pleased with the reaction of the New York *Commercial and Financial Chronicle* that in its December 25 issue carried a flattering review of the speech. Grady arrived back from New York on Christmas Eve, just in time for his favorite holiday. Although on a few occasions, strapped for money, he could not on this holiday get the presents he wished for Julia and the children. (As Joel Chandler Harris observed,

---

[30] Nixon, *Henry W, Grady*, 246; Winkler, *Tobacco Tycoon*, 183.

[31] Nixon, *Henry W. Grady*, 247.

[32] Ibid., drawn from Bauer, "Henry W. Grady."

he could have written himself rich had he placed "his pen at the disposal of men interested in speculative schemes," also by speaking for fees, but he showed little interest in personal wealth.) Still, it was the holiday that appealed to him most, and there was the memorable Christmas Eve he hosted a gathering at the *Constitution* for the city's poor and destitute. Exhausted but pleased with his success, he was happy to be with his adored family that Christmas.

"The speech" changed him, the watchful and observant Harris wrote. "He put away something of his boyishness, and became, as it seemed, a trifle more thoughtful. His purpose developed into a mission, and grew in his mind, and shone in his eyes, and remained with him day and night." Grady was fulfilling his "ardent desire to aid in the reconciliation of the North and South," a "desire that rapidly grew into a fixed and solemn purpose."[33]

The New South

What was the New South? First it was a return to American nationalism, no more talk of secession and Southern nationalism. Grady and compatriots advocated acceptance of the verdict of war and a new nation born of it, tantamount to the British accepting the outcome of the Revolution. Yet altered its terms; saying that acting under the first Constitution, the South had marched to defend states' rights and sundered the nation accordingly and within their so-called rights. So then, who was to blame for the war? Well, the winner takes all—except in this case history. And there the South would make its last stand—and win. Just as Southerners then wanted to write their own history, so did African Americans make the same claim at mid-twentieth century with less success but not without consequences. Or as Herbert Butterfield put it, "History is a clash of wills out of which emerges something that probably no man ever willed."[34]

The White South would have its way first. What follows is a historiography of the pivotal period in American history from 1863–1877, when the Republic stretched the Constitution to accommodate its Af-

[33] Joel Chandler Harris, *Life of Henry W. Grady*, 66.

[34] Butterfield, *Whig Interpretation of History*, 46.

rican American population as citizens. The debate over what Reconstruction meant has now reached 155 years and is much alive today, and the calls ranged from Black Lives Matter to reparations, which seem to be a variant of the unfulfilled promise of "40 acres and a mule." This essay began because I was born in 1943, which resulted in my doing a senior thesis at Emory University in 1965 and not some other time. Bell Wiley, the eminent Civil War historian, assigned me a project dealing with the latest historiographical controversy over the Civil War and Reconstruction. John Hope Franklin had just set the stage with his volume in the Chicago History of American Civilization series, *Reconstruction: After the Civil War* (1961). Franklin summarized and expanded a mounting revisionist response to William A. Dunning's American Nation Series volume *Reconstruction, Political and Economic* (1907). Earlier voices had been silenced, especially Black voices such as John R. Lynch's *The Facts of Reconstruction* (1913) and W. E. B. Du Bois's *Black Reconstruction* (1935). Now Franklin, building upon a substantial body of revisionist scholarship that reflected the civil rights movement of the fifties, also known as America's Second Reconstruction, threw down the gauntlet.

My callow assignment, based more on proximity than knowledge of the topic, was to drive to Athens, Georgia, and interview the venerable, if discredited, E. Merton Coulter. He was a beloved mentor and teacher of generations that had preceded mine. His volume in the History of the American South Series, *The South During Reconstruction, 1865–1867* (1947), amounted to an embrace of the Dunning School, the regnant canon on Reconstruction well into the twentieth century.[35] Sitting in Coulter's office in Phi Kappa Hall (Henry Grady's literary society of choice, still housed in the same building on the Old North Campus), I watched and listened as Coulter proved impervious to the winds of revision and seemed only too happy to serve as counterpoint to its proponents, especially Franklin. The exchange with Franklin

[35] Franklin had sparked the controversy much earlier, when shortly after Coulter's publication, Franklin wrote a stinging rebuke in "Whither Reconstruction Historiography?" (*Journal of Negro Education* 17/4 [Autumn 1948]: 446–61). My notion that the controversy was fresh owed as much to the novelty of youthful discovery as to Franklin's recent book.

would forever condemn Coulter, master teacher of his time, to historiographical calumny.

This controversy is a perfect example of how history is built. History is a way of knowing, a method. As method, it is interpretive. It satisfies what Jurgen Habermas called the historical-hermeneutical "interest" in knowledge, as distinct from the empirical or critical. By extension, one may properly understand "history" as a *faculty* and, in that respect, not unlike mathematical reasoning. Some are more adept at it, or do it better, or with more awareness than others. As a problem-solving discipline, it resembles in argumentative form the parallel case. In this respect the past is, in the language of aesthetics, like a single line on a canvas. It is neither here nor there, more or less, until a second line, "the present," is drawn, establishing a tension and creating motion, expectation, energy—in sum, a dialectic.[36] So the past lies dormant until parallels are established with the present (the second line if you will), which in turn creates history's dialectic, its dynamic. Also like argument from parallel case, history is perhaps the most persuasive form of argument (people believe it is the great lesson-giver) even though it is the easiest to undermine by counter example. Emerging from out of this mix is "historiography," an unfolding, ever-changing, often contradictory, and certainly evolutionary understanding of the past.[37]

As I walked out of Phi Kappa Hall, little did I understand the significance of my assignment, much less the entrails of historiography. I got some of the picture. Coulter defended the explanations of my youth

---

[36] Indebted to John Updike for the canvas metaphor (*Seek My Face* [New York: Knopf, 2001]).

[37] Walter Isaacson's biographical *tour de force* on Leonardo da Vinci emphasizes that the "master" built his artistic and scientific career on that precise methodology. Untutored and thought unlettered because his father would not legitimize his birth, da Vinci still made his way. "He turned out to be good in geometry," Isaacson writes, "but he never mastered the use of equations or the rudimentary algebra that existed at his time." Still, "one skill that was emphasized was how to draw analogies [parallel cases by another name], a method that Leonardo would use repeatedly in his later science. Analogies and spotting patterns became for him a rudimentary method of theorizing" (Isaacson, *Leonardo da Vinci*, 31–32). It made his genius. So perhaps the past is redeemable when not put to political ends, and historians have a method after all, but then no one entering that sphere is without political interests.

in South Georgia; after all he had written the Georgia history I read in the ninth grade. By these lights, Reconstruction was truly a tragic era in which ignorant and rapacious Negroes, with their carpetbagging and scalawagging allies, plundered the South. It was an image that with all its scholarly appurtenances did as much to fire the popular imagination as it did to influence the academic. It would be picked up from Thomas Dixon's *The Clansman* (1905), which became D. W. Griffith's pioneering movie *Birth of a Nation* (1915), which would then be etched permanently in the national lore with Margaret Mitchell's and Richard Selznick's *Gone with the Wind* (1936 and 1939 respectively). Coulter picked up on all this.

Before Dixon's and Mitchell's novels (and the resulting films), there was "Miss Millie." Mildred Lewis Rutherford, the daughter of Williams Rutherford, Grady's mathematics professor at Georgia and his most admired teacher, was a prolific writer. In all show wrote some twenty-nine books and pamphlets, all of which memorialized the Old South and its Lost Cause. Just a year younger than Grady, her maternal uncles were Howell Cobb and Thomas R. R. Cobb, eminent figures in secession and Civil War legend.[38] Millie attended the Lucy Cobb Institute in Athens, graduating in 1868, the year before Grady graduated from the university. After teaching history and literature in Atlanta, she returned in 1880 to the Cobb Institute as its principal.[39] Like John Brown Gordon with his University Publishing venture, she wanted not only Georgia children but also Southerners in general taught from textbooks written by and for them. Also like Gordon, who formed the Society of Confederate Veterans in 1891, Rutherford served as president of the Georgia Division of the United Daughters of the Confederacy from 1899 to 1902. She also served as the historian-general of the national UDC from 1911 to 1916.

"Miss Millie" advocated traditional roles for women and opposed

---

[38] Southerners mourned Tom Cobb, who died commanding Georgians behind the stone wall at Fredericksburg, as a "Christian hero," his Calvinist zeal so apparent in his personal character. Tom's older brother, Howell, continued as a leading figure in Georgia thereafter.

[39] A. E. Marshall, "Mildred Lewis Rutherford, 1851–1928," *New Georgia Encyclopedia*, www.georgiaencyclopedia.org/articles/history-archaeology/mildred-lewis-rutherford-1851-1928.

women's suffrage. She did so although she herself took to the stump and made countless speeches urging her view of the Lost Cause and women's roles in it. Entrusted with so many girls' education, she would become their arbiter. By force of personality and copious written works, she had a dramatic effect on textbooks, but it would be a mistake to think this control of the Southern narrative in schools was some countercultural move. When the nation abandoned Reconstruction, it relinquished not only its putative war aim of freedom for African Americans but also its justification for doing so. The New South narrative started at war's end, and men like Grady and Dawson did so much to promote it. It became the nation's history by acquiescence—the central tenet of which was the Negroes' incapacity for citizenship, the Fourteenth and Fifteenth amendments notwithstanding. As Drew Gilpin Faust put it succinctly, those that tied the narrative to the UCV and UDC in the last decade of the nineteenth century, attached the Confederate narrative "to the virulent politics of Jim Crow, disfranchisement, and states' rights. Confederate memory became in the 1890s a force that effectively undermined the emancipationist, nationalist, and egalitarian meaning of the war."[40]

Returning to the scene in Dallas, Texas, where Grady almost twenty years before delivered his speech on the "South and Her Problem," Rutherford quoted Grady as saying "the civilization of the Old South has never been surpassed, and perhaps never will be equaled by any people or nation upon the Globe." The artist Lucy May Stanton joined Miss Millie in Athens. She also never married, and her paintings, while more nuanced than Rutherford's pleadings, also contributed to Rutherford's theme, not of a New South but "the Old South remade." Stanton's portraits of Blacks were especially respectful. Stanton grew up in Atlanta across the street from Joel Chandler Harris and began her career as an artist in 1896 (among her mentors were J. Emile Blanche, Augustus Koopman, James Abbott McNeil Whistler, and Virginia Richmond Reynolds). After studying in Paris and living in New York for a year, she moved to Athens and lived there until 1926. Miss Millie was a good friend; although Stanton was a suffragette and pacifist, they shared a similar reverence for the Old South. Among

[40] Faust, *This Republic of Suffering*, 247.

Stanton's more famous portraits were those of Joel Chandler Harris, Howell Cobb, and Atlanta mayor Charles Collier. Historian Grace Elizabeth Hale captured both women perfectly in "Some Women Have Never Been Reconstructed: Mildred Lewis Rutherford, Lucy M. Stanton, and the Racial Politics of White Southern Womanhood, 1900–1930."[41]

Whither Reconstruction

Reconstruction was the most critical period in American history because it represented the nation's first comprehensive attempt, at least for male inhabitants, to make manifest its founding declaration of equality. Although a failure, Reconstruction would shape, as no other set of principles, the discourse of the twentieth century. Its historiography unfolds over four periods of roughly thirty-five years each. In its first, a national consensus built as to what Reconstruction meant, and the meaning was anything but ennobling. The next thirty-five years, running to 1930, elaborated and reinforced the "tragic era" conclusion. Beginning in the thirties, a re-visioning of Reconstruction set in, aided by a collapse of the nation's vaunted capitalism, which in turn provided justification for New Deal liberalism and the interventionist state. Liberalism's salad days reached maturity on the race question in Gunnar Myrdal's *American Dilemma* (1944), which in 1954 became the evidentiary cornerstone of *Brown v. Board of Education*, thereby ending *de jure* segregation if not *de facto* segregation.

By 1965 the social and intellectual fervor of the civil rights movement was spent, as was the first wave of revisionist historiography. The final thirty-five-year run up to 2000 began in a rage of Black power, New Left, and anti-war rhetoric. Racism was viewed as systemic, obdurate, persistent, and toxic. Postrevisionism in historiography was called neo-abolitionism, reflecting as it did an infectious revolutionary impulse to remake America, even as it talked of darker, institutional forces that made it impossible to do so—the result being that Radicals,

[41] Inscoe, *Georgia in Black and White*, 173–94. See also B. A. Fowler, "Lucy May Stanton (1875–1931)," *New Georgia Encyclopedia*, www.georgiaencyclopedia.org/articles/arts-culture/lucy-may-stanton-1875-1931.

scalawags, carpetbaggers, and African Americans got a much better reception in historiography, especially as contrasted with the opposition. Eventually this later period edged toward neo-conservatism, as historians took a more benign view of those caught in the middle, historical actors who pulled back from Reconstruction's more far-reaching aims for Black citizenship. The principal architects of this historiography, stretched toward sixty years, were William Archibald Dunning, Gunnar Myrdal, C. Vann Woodward, John Hope Franklin, and Eric Foner.

The Dunning school, although widely credited with establishing the darker view of Reconstruction, was less a school than a ratifying convention of recent experience and historical explanation, much as *Plessy* codified late nineteenth-century social, statutory, and juridical thought on segregation. Today Dunning is mentioned only four times in the massive *Encyclopedia of Southern Culture* (1989) and receives no biographical profile. However, what William Archibald Dunning brought to the subject was the legitimacy of the new historical scientism, which was developed first in the seminars at Johns Hopkins where Herbert Baxter Adams was developing his own Southern view (Woodrow Wilson being one of his charges). Columbia and the University of Chicago were quick to follow. Adams introduced the "Teutonic germ theory" of American history, that Germanic origins by way of England explained American exceptionalism; thus Blacks were per se inherently inferior, lacking the Germanic germ.

Dunning himself was a student of John William Burgess who brought graduate study in history to Columbia. Burgess was the son of a pro-Union slaveholder from Tennessee and produced his own study of *Reconstruction and the Constitution* (1905), which itself was an extended condemnation of Radical Reconstruction along White supremacist lines. The following year, James Ford Rhodes published his seven-volume *History of the U.S.*, which took matters up to 1877 and disparaged Reconstruction, employing now familiar racist assumptions of Black inferiority. Dunning first published on Reconstruction in 1885, but the work for which he is most cited came with his assignment to do a volume in the American Nation series, which he titled *Reconstruction: Political and Economic, 1865–1877* (1907).[42]

The Dunning school had the following story elements. First, Abraham Lincoln promised a speedy and magnanimous restoration of the South. He decreed that, when 10 percent of the 1860 electorate in any state that had seceded swore an oath of allegiance and a pledge to abide by the 13th Amendment, the state could be reintegrated. But Radicals were bent on vengeance and used the president's martyrdom to further their own vendetta against the South rather than Lincoln's aims. Second, Andrew Johnson offered a continuation of Lincoln's leniency, and in summer and fall 1865 extended an olive branch to Southerners, who already had accepted the verdict of war and promised to deal justly with their former slaves. But Congress refused to recognize the governments Johnson created and refused to seat their representatives, thereby setting the stage for the prolonged agony of Radical Reconstruction.

Dunning's story continued: radicals, resorting to demagoguery, won electoral majorities in 1866 and set about to reconstruct the South thoroughly. By 1867 they had placed the South under military occupation, disfranchised its leadership class, made inferior Negroes the political equal of Whites, and ushered in an era of corruption and excess unprecedented in American history. Radicals impeached the president and came within one vote of removing him from office, thereby paving the way for the presidency of U. S. Grant and national political corruption every bit as base as that worked on a prostrate South—the only difference being that the North was not saddled with Negro rule. To cement their vindictive ends, radicals forced Southern states and, through them the nation, to accept the Fourteenth and Fifteenth amendments to the Constitution. This "tragic era" set the stage for White redemption, which, though attended by violence, was justified by the abuses of radicals, carpetbaggers, scalawags, and Blacks.

Dunning did bring for the first time a national, as opposed to a strictly regional, look at Reconstruction and its implications for federalism although the contours of his narrative in *Reconstruction: Economic*

---

[42] Woodward, *Origins of the New South*, 441–42; Ayers, *Promise of the New South*, 423.

and Political (1907) did little to alter the narrative already worked out among Southerners like "Miss Millie," Gordon, Toombs, Stephens, and Grady. Dunning also brought new discipline to the marshalling of evidence, pioneered in the "seminars" of German universities. His views against "presentism," meaning seeing everything in light of the present, bear repeating. "The realities of the past," he wrote, "will never be scientifically apprehended so long as the student of history stands contemplating in stupor of admiration the reversals of ancient beliefs effect in our own age. Contempt for those who lacked our (present) light is the worst of equipments for understanding their deeds."[43] His students at Columbia would spread his gospel and his metaphor. Among them were the great pioneers in Southern history: Ulrich Bonnell Phillips, previously noted, whose "Central Theme of Southern History" remains to this day the interpretive key for understanding the dominance of race in regional and national history; Charles W. Ramsdell and J. G. de Roulhac Hamilton, who helped pave the way for Chapel Hill's lordly dominance in fashioning Southern history; and William K. Boyd, Holland Thompson, and Walter L. Fleming, who all worked in the shadow of the "Old Chief" as Dunning was affectionately known. Most of these did state histories of Reconstruction to flesh out the details of its various implementations.

Frank Lawrence Owsley, a second generation Dunningite, studied under William Edward Dodd at the University of Chicago. Dodd would later serve as Ambassador to Nazi Germany and become the subject of Eric Larson's best-selling *In the Garden of Beasts: Love, Terror, and an American Family in Hitler's Berlin* (2011). Owsley would join the history department at Vanderbilt and fit comfortably among the Agrarians, who wrote wistfully of an older South, more virtuous than prosperous, that was still under siege by Northern and New South industrialism. In his essay for the agrarian manifesto *I'll Take My Stand* (1930), Owsley said that Southerners "must ultimately come to scorn the condemnation and the philosophy" of their conquerors, "or their soul should and will perish." He called for a stout resistance. "The most outstanding instance of this toughmindedness," he wrote, "is found in

---

[43] Kraus, *Writing of History*, 374.

the Northerner, William Archibald Dunning, and the group of Southern students whom he gathered about him to study the history of the Civil War and Reconstruction. It was among this group that the Southern renascence began and the holiness of the Northern legend was challenged."[44]

Thus, by 1930 the White South would have the most favorable reading of its history imaginable. The great hermeneutic traditions of law (*Plessy*) and history (Dunning) had settled accounts. Francis Dawson and Henry Grady need not have feared. Moreover, the failed diplomacy that led to World War I encouraged historians to believe that the Civil War was itself needless. Even if Southerners had not written "the" history, at least not exclusively, it certainly had been written for them. North and South had combined to blame those who would bring on war, no matter how just the cause, and especially those who advocated Negro equality. Thus George Fort Milton, Chattanooga publisher and Democratic political activist, led the way with his biography, *The Eve of Conflict: Stephen A. Douglas and the Needless War* (1934). Eminent scholars like James G. Randall, *The Civil War and Reconstruction* (1937), and Avery Craven, *The Coming of Civil War* (1942), lent professional weight to Milton's more popular effort.

Part of this view owed to reading history backwards. The horrendous death and dying of the Great War in Europe disposed intellectuals to peace at almost any price, the armament conferences of the twenties, and the Kellogg-Briand Pact (1928), which offered hope that diplomacy vigorously pursued could have avoided yet another bloodbath. Thus if World War I was avoidable, reasoned Bowers and Milton, one should not read the horrors of an earlier war in America as irrepressible (reasonable men could negotiate differences), and radicals of the 1850s who eschewed compromise even unto the last should receive no vindication at the bar of history. The compromising Stephen Douglas was their hero. The other part of the historical indictment of radicalism owed to the nation's congenital loathing of the African American. If nothing else, World War II would prove these revisionists wrong.

---

[44] Ransom, et al., *I'll Take My Stand*, 66.

Pivot

The collapse of the nation's economic system in the thirties brought new possibilities for seeing history. Even Southerners of the thinking sort began to divide amongst themselves (not yet on the Negro question, but soon there also). Agrarians at Vanderbilt and regionalists at Chapel Hill looked to the past and found differing inspirations for the future. Although the period produced a historiography of Reconstruction only marginally revised from the Dunningites, it did sow the intellectual seeds for profound historiographical change in the latter half of the twentieth century. At the heart of this debate was liberalism, its nexus with equality having been firmly if only rhetorically established in Civil War and Reconstruction.

Equality is a frail creature. Nurtured only by rhetoric, it strains against nature. It is pure ideology. Unlike its siblings, life and property, liberty as fraternal twin of equality exists only as an idea, subject to public opinion and lawmakers. In twentieth-century America, the land of abundance, equality of citizenship and opportunity gave the appearance of ascendancy. Historians who assessed our moral worth as a people used it as a standard of judgment. However, equality survives best when clustered with other values into an ideograph, a habit of thought rather than a set of propositions. For example, "progress" is a key ideograph in measuring the materialization of equality. How many more enjoy abundance today than yesterday, and if not enjoying prosperity, how many more have access to good-paying jobs? (At this writing, stagnant wages drove the last presidential campaign, and income inequality continues the debate.) For all its interpretive power, equality, as it has come to be associated with liberalism in the twentieth-century state, remains our most fragile national treasure. It is the "L" word in politics. Polls demonstrate that, given the opportunity, few Americans would vote for the Bill of Rights, especially as they might advantage the disadvantaged. Only its instantiation in the Constitution, and then only by compromise, allows it to survive. All other "ologies" threaten equality—sociology, ethnology, psychology, even biology. Rooted as they are in the empiricism of nature, the other "ologies" make equality appear unnatural and, by political reduction, absurd.

The tendency is to treat the authors of *I'll Take My Stand* (1930), Ransom, Tate, Davidson, Lytle, Warren, Owsley, and friends as latter-day Jeremiahs who lost contact with the drift of America, perhaps even with Southern history. They are seen as curiosities performing an intellectual sideshow. Some of their ideas resonate with recent critics of consumerism and mass society, but the Nashville Agrarians seem too parochial to be cited as intellectual forebears. At best they are used to illuminate tensions that once existed between the Old and New South or perhaps, ruminating as they did in the roaring twenties, a spirit of alienation from Fords, flappers, and fanatics. Indeed, they did reflect contemporary intellectual disgust with modernity and materialism—Joseph Wood Krutch's *The Modern Temper* being one conspicuous parallel.

The Agrarians wanted to convince Southerners not to abandon their folkways. As traditionalists, they sought to convert *is* into *ought*, to represent the concrete sociology of experience against the dangerous abstractions of liberalism. Although couching their arguments in the essays of *I'll Take My Stand*, literary narrative was their métier. One Agrarian, Donald Davidson, complained about "The Briar Patch," an essay of another Agrarian, Robert Penn Warren. Davidson wrote, "behind the essay are implications which I am sure we (traditionalists) don't accept.... It doesn't *sound* like Red [Warren] at all—at least not the Red I know. The language, the catchwords, somehow don't fit. I am almost inclined to doubt whether RED ACTUALLY WROTE THIS ESSAY."[45]

Part of the reason was that Warren was arguing for Negro education, if awkwardly from a present perspective. (It was essentially Grady's position before his death in 1889. Make of the Negro an artisan not an artist, but even at that, Grady's brand of New South rhetoric was anathema to most. The Agrarians rejected liberalism for its centrifugal tendencies, pulling individuals away from their tribal identities toward a recognition of essential equality. (Ideology as serial argument explodes outward.) For traditionalists nature was centripetal, drawing people into close tribal arrangements—birds of a feather, like-to-like, etc. (Mythology implodes inwards.) To be sure, mythology can stand in service of liberalism and ideology for traditionalism, but the natural

[45] Donald Davidson to Allen Tate, July 21, 1930, quoted in Carpenter, *History as Rhetoric*, 187.

element of each is the reverse. The agrarians rejected the homogenizing thrust of modern liberalism along with its twin industrialism.

They attacked industrialism specifically because its organizational requirements forced contacts between the races on more or less equal terms, thereby violating the "sacred differential," a differential that applied to sex as well as race.[46] Theirs was a Volksgeistian Conservatism, a term Joel Williamson used to describe a small, turn-of-the-century group of Southerners who were influenced by, among other things, this Hegelian idealism.[47]

Sociology, sans numbers and statistics, the articulate sociology of pre-Civil War George Fitzhugh, confirmed the Agrarians' sense of nature. They were convinced that as much as Chapel Hillians might study poverty and tenancy or the deleterious effects of racial subordination, their social scientific numbers could not overcome the natural determination of White people to stay on top. At their ameliorative best, the Nashville traditionalists sided with Warren's argument in "The Briar Patch." It called for paternalism and a recognized place for Black Americans—menial but respected, which was essentially Grady's argument. As of 1930 when *I'll Take My Stand* made its appearance, no one at Chapel Hill came to a radically different conclusion for African Americans. At best, they argued for a gradual adjustment in relations between the races, but it was an uncertain change that would come in generations not years.

The agrarians were not long for the stage. Hashing out their thoughts in the roaring twenties, theirs was an affordable if indulgent complaint. The Great Depression with its forced out-migration of peoples from the South made their social views look fanciful, mere idylls of an isolated, Old South elite. The best of them, Warren for example, soon put it behind, but the traditionalists did contribute one student well-regarded in rhetoric circles, Richard Weaver. His *Southern Traditions at Bay* (1960) was his dissertation at Vanderbilt, completed in 1940. What Weaver clung to was a kind of Platonist, essentialist view of the world. Stripped of its institutional value in social change, it provided only critique. As Eric Foner observed, "writers like Russell Kirk

[46] Graves, *Fighting South*, passim.

[47] Williamson, *Crucible of Race*, 414–15.

and Richard Weaver rejected the 'relativism' that had supposedly corroded Western self-confidence (white-over-black) and called for the reassertion of absolute (traditional) values grounded in religion and time."[48] Race also played a role in Weaver's hierarchy of virtue. His view was one to which many White Southerners, and truly many others, subscribed, for Weaver never completely divested himself of the belief that Negroes were lesser figures of the Southern landscape, not part of the "ideal" unless in their place. His spiritual conservatism still resonates among the religious right, especially in the South.

All of these arguments came to a nonacademic head in 1941. Two Southerners wrote powerful impressions of life and mind in the South. Will Alexander Percy, scion of a distinguished planter tradition in Mississippi, wrote an elegiac book of a South that inhabited Grady's mind's eye but was long gone, *noblesse oblige* writ large. The title, *Lanterns on the Levee: Recollections of a Planter's Son*, foreshadowed its theme. Set in Greenville and nearby Leland, Mississippi, and the family's Pantherburn plantation, it remains a classic of Southern literature. Reviewers were without exception in noting its "kindness." As the title also suggests, it was set against the Mississippi River flood of 1927, subject of John Barry's tour de force *Rising Tide* (1997). Percy was a poet and an only child, groomed by his mother and father, grandparents, and exceptional tutors. His father, LeRoy, was a U.S. senator, the last elected by the legislature. The coarse James K. Vardaman, an extreme racist in the Tom Watson mode, defeated LeRoy Percy in 1911. Will Percy attended Sewanee, The University of the South in Tennessee (Arcadia as he styled it), and after a European tour headed to Harvard Law School. Following service with Herbert Hoover's Belgian Relief Commission, he became a commissioned officer training Black troops in Europe in World War I.

Percy never married, but upon the suicides of his cousin LeRoy Pratt Percy in 1929 and LeRoy's wife Bolling Phinizy Percy two years later, he adopted their three sons, one of whom was Walker Percy, who also entered the Southern literary hall of fame. Another cousin of the boys was Shelby Foote, who spent considerable time in Will Percy's home and became "the voice" of Ken Burns award-winning PBS series

---

[48] Foner, *Story of American Freedom*, 309.

on the Civil War. Cousin Will was thereafter known as Uncle Will.

What Percy achieved in *Lanterns* is a most charitable view of the Negroes' contributions to Southern culture and a romantic view of the Delta and its hard demands. Indeed, he viewed Negroes as creative, inventive, loving, and essential to his own education as a young man. He never disparaged, except in the case of "White trash." His view was made of the same materials of Grady's New South that glowed with descriptions of Black faithfulness and White reciprocity, but he humanized it. He has been compared with Henry Adams and rightly so. What was transformative in *Lanterns* was a boundless embrace of the classical tradition and the luminous language of poetry. It stands alone. Not even *The Education of Henry Adams* exceeds it or even Adams *Mont St. Michelle and Chartres. Lanterns* appeared in 1941 under the Knopf imprimatur and sold out many times over. Percy had only months to live, dying in January 1942.

Also weighing in from the non-academic quarter was journalist Wilbur J. Cash, born in Gaffney, South Carolina, educated at Wake Forest University, who spent most of his time as a writer/journalist in and around Charlotte, North Carolina. His pen, too, was eloquent, and he wrote *The Mind of the South,* also published by Knopf in 1941. His view of life and labor in the Old and New South squared with the Howard Odum School at the University of North Carolina at Chapel Hill. Thus, Percy with the Agrarians at Vanderbilt and Cash with the North Carolinians squared off in the literature of the South, not willfully but by accident of time and circumstance. Cash's *Mind* gathered all the forces of progressivism in a sweeping narrative not of the Old South, but where terrace and labor found itself on the cusp of change. Historians have since found flaws, but Cash gave his immediate audience reason for pause about current conditions and reasons for change. He received a Guggenheim fellowship to Mexico City, where communists and left-leaning thought-leaders were assembling. There he committed suicide on July 1, 1941, in the city where the exiled Leon Trotsky had been assassinated in August 1940.

The Percy family was beset with suicides. Will Alexander's death was not suspicious, but Cash's death by his own hand was foreshadowed. In 1935, Clarence Cason, who founded the journalism program at the University of Alabama in 1928, published a memorable book on the South, *90 Degrees in the Shade*. It also pulled back the covers on Southern manners and morals, including lynchings (four in Tuscaloosa alone in 1933, one occurring at the fourth hole of the city golf course across from where Cason lived). Anxious about the book's reception, he closed the door to his office in the Old Union Building (now Reese Phifer Hall) and took his life with a handgun. He was thirty-nine.

Although the philosophical distance between Vanderbilt and Chapel Hill was not all that great (especially on the central theme of Southern history, White supremacy), the Agrarians considered Chapel Hillians their intellectual enemies. So intense was the animosity that a young historian at Chapel Hill had to sneak into a gathering of Agrarians under disguise.[49] C. Vann Woodward's later dominance of Reconstruction historiography would be fashioned of materials gathered in this debate. For all its sound and fury, little happened, at least not immediately. Liberalism at Chapel Hill, rooted as it was in the new regionalism, proved skin deep. As noted above, traditionalists at Vanderbilt and social critics at Chapel Hill slept in the Procrustean bed of race. That was soon to change. A pipeline from Emory University in Atlanta to Chapel Hill, C. Vann Woodward being its progenitor, raised up a new generation. Grady's reputation would rise with them, as the Agrarians receded into the past.

Sowing Cities

Tacitus, the first non-Christian to write about Christianity, said that Romans persecuted Christians not for the burning of Rome but for their "hatred of mankind." Although he did believe Nero was scapegoating them, Tacitus also believed Rome was a magnet for all sorts of cults and extreme religiosity, "*superstitio*" he called it. Specifically, Christians did not pay taxes that even Jews paid, they refused military service, they held property communally, and they gathered in secrecy to break bread and drink wine—the body and blood that smacked of cannibalism, even if only consubstantially. In brief, they were not good Roman citizens. In its early form, Christianity was an urban religion. The term pagan itself is of Roman origin (*paganus*) meaning dwellers

[49] Woodward, *Thinking Back*, 18.

on the country-side, farmers and shepherds if you will. Christianity depended upon the relative anonymity and liberality afforded by a city like Rome. In the same way, African Americans experienced slavery differently in cities than on the countryside, finding the urban environment more fluid and flexible, providing some element of freedom.[50]

Grady's own thinking was a little too rhapsodic about an agrarian paradise to embrace fully his view of cities as other than markets for farmers. Still urbanization was synergy, and Grady argued that the more towns and cities were sown, the better for rural Georgia, the South, indeed America. Therefore, his pursuit of industrialization was not at the expense of farms but for their profit, as he consoled himself. What Grady did not fully comprehend was "urbanization," although he pursued it with full intensity. Grady's decade was moving toward it, but it was fully thirty years before America would tip from rural to urban, and long after that in the South. Thus, it may well be said that what Grady envisioned, urbanization, was ahead of his own time and would be realized long after his death.

What may have obscured Grady's vision was his own competitive instinct about Atlanta. He was continually in conflict with the ambitions of Macon, Milledgeville, Augusta, Columbus, and Savannah, or perhaps it was them against Atlanta. Perhaps too much can be made of the conflict, for on occasions each city congratulated the other. However, it was then as it is today, Atlanta against the rest of Georgia. No one doubted that Atlanta was the behemoth, the capitol escheated to Atlanta, the rail hubs all centered there, it exploded with growth. In the end Atlanta would change everything from race relations to national politics, not by Grady's design but by his energy. Grady's last three years were all about his urban vision, however inchoate.

His vision was to be sure commercial and industrial, but it was also art and design, plans for these forces to cohabit on a happy scale. It did not begin with Samuel Noble's plans for Anniston, Alabama, a planned community a full year before George Pullman developed his own in Chicago. Grady not only touted the Anniston plan but invested in the joint stock operation. Noble consulted architects in England who had

[50] R. Wade, *Slavery in the Cities*; author's notes from a 1964 Oxford class with Wade.

already thought of industrial socialism, manufacturing married to labor in an industrial paradise. It worked well enough, Pullman in Illinois, Noble in Alabama, and still later Tennessee Coal and Iron (U.S. Steel) in Birmingham, Alabama in the twenties and thirties. Although not perfect, such planning was an effort to temper the relationship between capital and labor, especially after the horrors of convict-leasing in all those industries—and at least a stab at incentivizing labor.

At the beginning of the eighties and Grady's tenure in a leadership role with the *Constitution*, Atlanta was growing (population 37,000), but it was still a rather crude gathering place. One reporter assigned to streets said the dust in drought and mud in wet made streets impassable except with stilts.[51] Grady weighed in. Feeling that Atlanta's streets misrepresented her, Grady later called for a separate department of streets since "the division of labor and responsibility works well." "Whatever else it does," Grady wrote, "we hope that the municipal government will bear in mind that a city is something more than an aggregation of people deposited in a mud-hole."[52] It got better with paving stones and macadamized streets as the decade wore on, but maintaining the roads remained a challenge.

One thing Grady never addressed was Negro residential segregation (not that anyone else did except at least one *Constitution* reporter who took it on as a onetime assignment). Noting that great material improvement had been made in Atlanta as of 1881, "the city also had its seamy side." The enterprising reporter "set forth to investigate the haunts of the lowly and vicious—Pig Alley, Happy Hollow, the Ant Hole, the Beaver Slide, Campbell's Row, Hell's Half Acre, and other romantic and classic abodes." He began honestly enough, "Few people in Atlanta ever stop to consider how the colored people of the city live." Then, despite professed affections, "by far the largest portion of the negroes [*sic*] are really never known to us," he wrote. "They are not employed in private homes, nor in the business houses, but drift off to themselves, and are almost as far from white people, so far as all practical benefits of association are concerned, as if the two races never

[51] Garrett, *Atlanta and Environs*, 2:15–17.

[52] *Atlanta Constitution*, July 30, 1880, and December 29, 1882.

met."[53] So much for Grady's vaunted affection between the races.

The smell of fried fish, mullet especially, spelled Decatur Street and the beginning of Negro Row, and so it went from Pig Alley to Ant Hole, fit places "to bear a harvest of criminals and doubtless many daring crimes had their conception there." And so the report continued with the editor inserting, "The reporter could have gone on all night picking out these localities, but this dose will do the reader today."[54] These scarred streets and neighborhoods would mar Atlanta for years into the future. Grady ignored them for the most part, offered no solutions, as did Atlanta until today, when it at least makes for "talking points."

So as Atlanta grew, indeed doubling its population by the end of the decade, Grady ignored the divide and certainly offered no solutions. It was Blacks living as Blacks and Whites as Whites with never the twain meeting, except when the presence of a Black domestic servant confirmed a White family's social standing. The shacks that shambled throughout Negro quarters well into mid-twentieth century were an abomination. The urban housing that replaced them or the old homes left behind by White flight were not much better by the end of the century. The twenty-first century has witnessed a transformation as multi-unit dwellings, a new Beltline, and parks have drawn millennials and Whites back into the 4th Ward as a better accommodation to work-realities than suburban isolation.

The original shacks, crowded side by side, gave rise on May 21, 1917, to Atlanta's worst fire. Beginning south of town, it spread through the 4th Ward, all the way across Ponce de Leon to near Highland Avenue, fueled by wood shingles and clapboards from a nearby sawmill that gave Slabtown its name. Ironically, the city had passed an ordinance to replace wood shingles with more fire-resistant asphalt or tar but had not yet enforced it. Moreover, fire engines, many horse-drawn, and hoses were outdated and inadequate. The result was a con-

[53] Garrett, *Atlanta and Environs*, 2:25; *Atlanta Constitution*, July 20, 1881.
[54] Garrett, *Atlanta and Environs*, 2:25–26.

flagration that burned through 2,000 buildings and left 10,000 homeless, mostly Blacks.[55] The claim some made that it was worse than Sherman's fire is exaggerated, certainly given Atlanta's population when the city burned in 1864, but the 1917 fire invited comparison.

Grady had a keen interest in parks and green space. "As well might a man try to live without lungs, as a city to get along in health and comfort without these breathing spots." The aesthetic function of parks was often conjoined with the argument for sanitation and health. "It should not be forgotten that trees have a known sanitary value," reminded one editorial. "They soften the heat and dryness of the hot season. They absorb carbonic acid. They keep both earth and air moist." Today, Atlanta remains rightly advertised as the "City of Trees." Moreover, Grady said that to remove land from the profit motive of speculative capital required more than sentiment. "We repeat," he wrote, "that city is wise that secures its parks when land is cheap, for all cities must secure them at last."[56] One historian saw the movement toward parks and its effect on planning as paving the way "for acceptance of modification of the prevailing laissez-faire outlook toward the growth of American cities."[57]

The 1881 Cotton States Exposition was held in Oglethorpe Park, two miles to the west and north of downtown, with one of its leave-behinds being a cotton manufacturing building that Edward Atkinson had encouraged as the centerpiece. The structure measured 720 feet long by 400 feet wide constructed on modern factory lines and in the shape of a Greek Cross—so more than two and a half times the size of a modern football field.[58] It became home to the Exposition Cotton Mills that continued in operation from 1882 to 1969. Piedmont Park, north of the city, started as a driving club (horses and carriages) for Atlanta's elite, who shortly thereafter entered into an agreement with the Piedmont Exposition Company to use a portion of the land it had acquired for the Piedmont Exposition of 1887. Many members of the Piedmont Driving Club also were directors of the Piedmont Exposition Company, so it was an easy alliance. The landscaping and build-

[55] Burns, "Second Burning of Atlanta," 86–89.

[56] *Atlanta Constitution*, September 23, 1888, and April 23, 1884.

[57] Glaab, *American City*, 245.

[58] Garrett, *Atlanta and Environs*, 2:29–33.

out for the 1887 Exposition enhanced the park and its utility for recreation and relaxation.[59] The idea for the exposition and the naming of it was hatched in Grady's office. Grady was vice president of the Exposition Company and a director of the Driving Club.[60]

Grady and Atlanta were fortunate with the return of Sidney Root in 1878. Atlanta's "merchant prince," it will be recalled, had left the city for New York in 1868 for the education of his children—both sons becoming architects with John Wellborn Root designing the Chicago World's Columbian Exposition of 1893. John died in 1891, like Grady at age 39 and also from pneumonia, but not before handing off designs for Atlanta's Equitable Building, one of the city's architectural gems. It later became the Trust Company of Georgia, but the building was demolished in 1971 though its massive columns and name panel can still be seen at Sun Trust Bank, across from Woodruff Park.

On Sidney Root's return in 1878, he threw himself back into the life of the city with special attention to its parks and greenspaces, especially Grant Park. "Indeed," remarked Franklin Garrett, "his love of trees and nature inspired him to suggest to Colonel [Lemuel P.] Grant that the land be donated to the city." By 1883, Mayor John B. Goodwin appointed Root chairman of the park commission board. Already Root had toured Europe in order to advise Atlanta on its 1881 exposition build-out. Root had the sensitivity of Frederick Law Olmsted for how park space should conform to nature, and he supervised the construction of Grant Park until his death in 1897. Garrett concludes, "The city should erect in the park some fitting memorial to the man who induced the owner to give it and whose genius developed it."[61] (A small shopping center with an eatery near Grant Park does bear his name but it is not in the park.)

Parks were but a first step in the larger consideration of health. With the general acceptance of the germ theory, there came a greater and more urgent demand for "Hygeia, or the City of Health." "The new industrial environment," wrote Lewis Mumford, "was so glaringly lacking in the attributes of health, that it is hardly any wonder that the

---

[59] Mayo, "Stumbling into History," 10–13.

[60] Nixon, *Henry W. Grady*, 264–66.

[61] Garrett, *Atlanta and Environs*, 2:41.

counter-movement of hygiene provided the most positive contributions to town planning during the nineteenth century."[62] Epidemics were the scourge of the last half of the nineteenth century, and 1888 was a particularly bad year. Southern coastal states were especially vulnerable, but disease seldom came inland though it was always a threat. "When the epidemic strikes us," Grady warned, "people will lose their heads, and in their panic necessary precautions will be forgotten. Now is the time to make our preparations."[63]

After Cleveland's failed reelection, Grady immediately turned: "From politics to sewers is not such a distance that it can't be covered quickly. To have the way cleared so that mistakes will be impossible, let us call to our aid the best sanitary engineer that can be had in America. Such a man," it was announced, "will make in one hour a suggestion that will pay the whole expenses of his engagement."[64] Grady got what he wanted, a founder of modern environmental technology. "Prior to 1880 Atlanta had no sewer system worthy of the name," writes Garrett. "By 1890 it had what for that time was a most-modern system, designed by Rudolph Hering, the eminent sanitary engineer."[65]

Urban socialism was real, from parks to health, and Grady weighed in for community over private enterprise. He particularly favored strengthening the national role in public health.

> Instead of abolishing the national board of health, its powers should be greatly enlarged. At present it cannot do much more than collect statistics and promulgate theories; it should have supervision of all sources of disease whether of men or cattle, and its recommendations should be final. When the health or even lives of people are at stake, there is no sense in talking about small expenditures, or in declaiming against federal interference. The whole world knows that the states acting separately will take no effectual steps to keep out epidemics or to crush them after they have obtained a foothold.[66]

One can find no clearer case for governmental intervention—Grady

[62] Mumford, *City in History*, passim.

[63] *Atlanta Constitution*, February 20, 1888.

[64] Ibid., November 18, 1884.

[65] Garrett, *Atlanta and Environs*, 2:209.

[66] *Atlanta Constitution*, February 20, 1880.

pre-figuring Atlanta's Centers for Disease Control and Prevention. Prevailing theory had to yield to the new facts of urban life.

These thoughts were lent urgency by a yellow fever epidemic that entered through Jacksonville and perhaps other coastal towns and threatened to spread inland. One town after another accused others of harboring the spread. Atlanta was almost antic in sloughing it off to Alabama towns and denying its own vulnerability. In the end, it was not so serious in any inland places, but the finger-pointing was not pretty, and the panic was real. The city's year-end report noted, "The Board of Health had its hands full during August, 1888, when the city became host to a large influx of refugees from Jacksonville, Florida, where a yellow fever epidemic held sway. Happily, however, no actual case of yellow fever was brought here, nor did a single case develop among the thousands of refugees who passed through, or who remained in Atlanta."[67]

In the end, the real escape from urban reality and blight was suburban. First Edgewood, then Kirkwood and East Lake, eastward it moved along the Georgia Railroad Line. Then north to Piedmont Park and northwest to Oglethorpe, Whites found their escape. Grady offered no resistance. Initially, he saw suburbs as detached centers for "handsome country places" or "purely pleasure resorts" with "good drives and fine suburban villas, farms and parks." As indeed they were, as evidenced by Bob Alston's estate in East Lake, John B. Gordon's estate, "Sutherland" in Kirkwood, and Joseph E. Brown's house in Edgewood, which, in 1868, was owned by Sidney Root. All these fine accommodations were away from the Black and middling classes. "An extended suburban area would be practically a part of our city," Grady wrote, "and from many points of view the distribution of our population in this way instead of packing it in within narrow limits would have obvious advantages.... Her [Atlanta's] suburbs are her children and her allies."[68] But for Whites only. "Few but white Americans of means could afford them, and in cities like Atlanta [where Frederick Law Olmsted and his sons planned the suburb of Druid Hills] passed

---

[67] Garrett, *Atlanta and Environs*, 2:149–53. A similar outbreak in 1876 brought Joel Chandler Harris and his family to Atlanta from Savannah.

[68] *Atlanta Constitution*, July 4, 1886.

ordinances to codify residential segregation."[69]

As always, transit was the essential driver of suburban development. By 1889 Atlanta had completed a Nine-Mile Circle, or beltline, for electric trolleys. It began at Marietta and Broad streets and ran out Broad to Peachtree to Houston, and out Houston and Highland Avenue to Virginia Avenue; thence from Virginia Avenue to Boulevard and up Boulevard back to Highland and from there onto Houston and back to its starting point. One rider exclaimed, "You just can't appreciate the electric cars until you have ridden on them. They are so different from any other kind of conveyance that you hardly know what you are riding on. The best way I can describe it is by saying it makes you feel like a boy and riding to town in the carriage instead of the big wagon." One could make the circle for five cents, and it immediately became popular for picnic and sightseeing excursions. Grady liked that it knit the suburbs to the city in a unified way.[70]

Grady was no "New South Funder," a group that got its name by opposing all expenditures until bonded indebtedness was paid off, a steeper task as interest rates multiplied in the eighties. Funders were primarily bondholders and their lawyers who styled themselves as Conservative Democrats. In Virginia it took the form of Funders versus Readjusters, a group following William Mahone, former Civil War general and businessman who argued for adjusting the debt downward, thus cramming bondholders. In Georgia it was a little different, with Independent Democrats threatening to link up with Republicans to oust the Atlanta Ring, the fruit of Grady's political labors. The controversy was most vigorous from 1880 to 1884. C. Vann Woodward said of the Funders that laissez-faire economics "became almost a test of Southern patriotism," but Grady ran counter to this orthodoxy, for he had already "yielded...to the pressing needs for government services, regulation, and action."[71] Grady wrote,

> Just at present the difficulty does not so much consist of meeting the interest account and all customary expenditures, as in finding

[69] Horwitz, *Spying on the South*, 407–408.
[70] Garrett, *Atlanta and Environs*, 2:190–91.
[71] Woodward, *Origins of the New South*, 65.

> means to meet the public wants of an enterprising and rapidly increasing population. More and better public schools are needed; the police force is not large enough; new pumps and mains are a necessity before another summer comes around; a paid fire department and fire-alarm system are required to give adequate protection to property; the city has no building of its own; and a great deal of work must be done before streets and bridges and sewers and sidewalks of the city are rendered useful. Convenient and health giving....[72]

The picture is a little less clear on public schools where the New South record revealed declining support, especially for Negro schools. Atlanta had eight schools for White children, including Boys' High and Girls' High, while Black children attended three schools. The White schools each listed the eighth as their final grade, but the Black schools showed no particular level of grade required and did not show instructors by grades or incomes, as shown for the White schools. With two exceptions, Girls' High and Calhoun Street School, a male was listed as principal and the salaries ranged from $1410 to $1600. The two female principals had salaries of $1200, Girls' High, and $525 for Calhoun Street. The three Negro schools had two male principals and one female. The males earned $600 each and the female $500.[73] What is known is that throughout the South school terms for African American students were considerably less than for Whites. Considerably less was expected of them, and therefore less given. It would only worsen in the 1890s and well into the twentieth century. Not only did "separate" never approximate equal education, in Richmond County (Augusta, Georgia) the Supreme Court said it need not fund a Black school at all even if one was provided for Whites.[74] The issue remains as Republican governors and legislators try to find paths to destroy public education and evolve a "choice" system for Whites, primarily through charter schools and whatever out-of-district schools those White students and families prefer.

Grady favored practical and industrial education, especially for Blacks with an eye toward manufacturing, but even here Blacks were

[72] *Atlanta Constitution*, January 3, 1882.

[73] Garrett, *Atlanta and Environs*, 2:72–73.

[74] *Cumming v. Richmond County Board of Education*, 1899.

frozen out of meaningful employment, especially in textiles, which were dominated by White women and child labor. Skilled labor was more prevalent among African Americans in slavery because planters attached value attached to developing construction and craft skills among their own plantation labor force.[75] However, in the emerging industrial order of Jim Crow segregation, Black labor became increasingly marginalized, especially in skilled occupations where most were barred.

In the spirit of the age Grady was a leading proponent of advanced technical education and rallied the city to establish a seat of technical learning in Atlanta. It was a bitter fight, in that Macon had led the way for the establishment of such a school. In a conversation between Major John Fletcher Hanson, owner of a textile manufacturing operation in Macon and later president of the Central of Georgia Railroad, and Nathaniel Edwin Harris, soon to represent Bibb County (Macon) in the legislature and later as governor, the idea was birthed in May 1882. Hanson also owned the *Macon Telegraph*. Hanson told Harris that as much as the state needed such an institute, he doubted it would succeed "as it would take a million dollars to establish it." Harris took the challenge, saying he would rather be author of such a law than governor, and accordingly ran for the legislature on such a plank and got his wish. Harris introduced a resolution on November 24, 1882, authorizing the creation of a committee to visit other institutions to learn what would be required. The legislature approved the resolution in December, and a committee of ten undertook the task, reporting at the summer session of the legislature in 1883. Although Hanson and Harris deserve credit, Henry Grady had editorialized for such a school countless times from 1882 until its adoption.[76]

A bitter fight ensued as "funders" in the legislature were loath to allocate any money for public higher education, its miserly allocations to the university in Athens being indicative. Accordingly, the 1883 bill failed. Harris did not give up and made it a major issue in the election

---

[75] In Tuscaloosa, the major span of the Warrior River was engineered by a Black man, Horace King, the most demanded bridge-builder in the South. King died in Lagrange, Georgia in 1885. As will be seen, the building for the Negro exhibition hall at the famed 1895 Exposition in Atlanta was also designed and built by a Black man from that city.

[76] Garrett, *Atlanta and Environs*, 2:169.

of a new legislature. With Governor McDaniel's support, the Legislature approved the measure on October 15, 1885, and allocated $65,000 for public higher education. The fight was now on to see which city would get it. The principal rivals were Athens, Macon, and Atlanta. A five- member committee chaired by Nat Harris was to decide. Athens argued to use the money to add a department in the university, but the bitter fight as usual would be between Macon and Atlanta.[77]

As usual, Grady took the lead by calling together twenty-five to thirty of Atlanta's leading businessmen. He opened the meeting personally pledging $1000 and all in attendance pledged the same amount each. In all, Atlanta subscribed $50,000, plus land, and an annual maintenance fee of $2,500 from city hall.[78] The *Macon Telegraph*, Hanson's paper, called Atlanta unfit by reason of being poorly drained and unhealthy. The *Constitution* struck back accusing the *Telegraph* of an "amazing pitch of stupid hatred." Still, the five-member commission for site selection went twenty-four ballots before Atlanta got three of the five ballots, and the Georgia School of Technology opened on its Atlanta campus in 1888. At the inaugural ceremonies, Nat Harris confessed that "his heart was almost broken," but then knowing Grady was to speak after him, he launched into an encomium of praise for Grady and his city:

> Atlanta did not get on well at one time with the middle and southern portion of the state. Her people were not like our people, the push and energy of her citizens, the rapid strides which they made in wealth and progress, gave her more the appearance of one of our western or northern cities than of a southern metropolis. She had such a wonderful press to blow her own horn, and did it with such unceasing and inevitable persistence, that often when smarting under the sting of defeat we forgot she belonged to the state. "Get there somehow" was the motto on which she acted, and it went into everything she took a hand in, from a baseball game to a governor's election. Yet she grew and distanced all her rivals and made her influence felt in every hamlet and every neighborhood and in every gathering in this great state of Georgia. She purified her politics, she gathered the influence of the great around her, till by sheer force

---

[77] Ibid., 172.

[78] Ibid.; Nixon, *Henry W. Grady*, 222.

> of will and energy she made the people recognize her as part of the commonwealth equally with Rome, with Macon and Savannah.[79]

Speaking of baseball, Grady led in that too. He was always an athlete, from childhood in Athens where he was followed around town and environs sparring and playing games, and as an adult he stayed active in sports. He loved baseball especially. Soon after Grady became managing editor of the *Constitution*, Evan Howell noticed a sharp jump in telegraphic services. Grady bragged that the Constitution spent more on telegraphic news than any other paper in the South. Upon further inspection Howell found that a lot of those charges were for stories about sporting events and told Grady if he did not stop it, "I'm going to have to charge it up to you." Whereupon Grady replied, "That's alright. Charge it. I don't care. But I'm going to have the baseball news just the same." That was in 1881. By 1884 Grady was leading a movement to organize a Southern baseball league among cities of over 25,000 in population. The meeting was finally held in Montgomery, Alabama, on November 24. The organizers who wanted a leader with "character and prestige" turned to Grady and asked if he would accept its presidency. He did. In its first season, summer 1885, with a new stadium at the newly developed Peters Park between North Avenue and West Peachtree Street, Atlanta won the first league title. During that season, several teams threatened to withdraw, because "Grady was so strict about keeping down rowdyism and, more especially, because he insisted the players keep away from questionable characters off the field."[80]

A Twice New City

Writing of the Urban Frontier and the rise of western cities, Richard C. Wade observed, "A city is many things: it is a cultural focus, a social resort, a political center, but before all though not above all—it is a place where people earn a living." He noted that "this priority is especially striking in young cities where a vigorous social and cultural life must await the establishment of a stable economic structure."[81] Atlanta

---

[79] Ibid., 283.

[80] Garrett, *Atlanta and Environs*, 2:76–77.

[81] R. Wade, *Urban Frontier*, 39.

got two chances; first in the late 1830s as Terminus became Marthasville, which in turn became Atlanta. That period ended with the de-population of the city as Sherman entered it in 1864 and left it in ruins exacted by both Confederate and Union forces. The second period began with Sherman's exit and ended twenty-five years later with Henry Grady's death and the beginning of the "Brave and Beautiful City" he imagined and championed.

Grady described it this way, "Atlanta, the 'Gate City'...is essentially a new place—modern, cosmopolitan, democratic—a fresh production, wholly practical, without antiquities or prejudices, with no history save the dramatic ups and downs of a brief self-made career, achieving phenomenal fortune by native genius and enterprise." In his favorite imagery of the phoenix, Grady concluded, "From the black baptism of ashes has arisen the present magnificent ideal of a city."[82] The Phoenix became the official seal of the city in 1887. In 1889 on the inaugural centennial of George Washington, Grady waxed eloquent again, "Here is a new centennial opening up; the richest spot on earth about to give its treasures and resources into the hands of commerce, and a comparatively undeveloped section preparing to give the world a taste of the riches and treasures that lie hidden in hills and in its valleys."[83] Nor did he leave it to the prying forces of Northern capital alone. He wanted Atlanta to establish a Chamber of Commerce Investment Company, alongside the manufacturing association it had already created. Activity was the order of the day. Atlanta had to be "the busiest city in the union." C. Vann Woodward called this attitude "a public zeal that, in the Carolinas, Georgia, and Alabama, converted an economic development into a civic crusade inspired with a vision of social salvation" and cited Atlanta, Charlotte, and Charleston as exemplars of this kind of boosterism.

Grady did not set aside cultural plans for commercial exploitation. In 1882 he envisioned Atlanta as one of the best "summer resorts" with an art exposition "second only to the cotton states exposition held last year." Earlier he had argued for a "musical union. There is no reason why Atlanta should not stand at the head of musical affairs in the

---

[82] *Atlanta Constitution*, July 24, 1887.

[83] Ibid., May 5, 1889.

South, as Cincinnati leads the west." He had championed the creation of a Young Men's Library Association, and as Joel Chandler Harris put it, the library was never more successful than "when Mr. Grady was booming the town in its behalf."[84]

Grady was a good friend of artist Horace Bradley, born into Atlanta's tightly knit Irish Catholic community in 1860. Another entrant two years earlier, 1858, was James Joseph Haverty, also Irish Catholic. They would become fast friends. Bradley, an artist/illustrator for *Frank Leslie's Illustrated* and for *Harper's*, was a highly respected artist with studios in Atlanta and New York. Haverty would become a self-educated art collector of extraordinary gifts. Grady recruited Bradley to do an art column for the *Constitution*, and in the last months of his life signed Bradley to be "chief of fine arts" for what would become the 1895 Cotton States and International Exposition.[85] Grady wanted to nurture an artists' colony in Atlanta, and in the year of the Chautauqua, 1888, took major steps in that direction.

Another important player in Grady's plans was Canadian-born James Henry Moser—"Jimmy" as known to Grady. He arrived in Atlanta in 1879. He illustrated pamphlets, magazines, and books, and he specialized in depicting urban Black community life. Striking was *The Bookworm,* showing a Black girl intently poring over a book.[86] He also illustrated Joel Chandler Harris's *Uncle Remus Tales*. When the Gradys moved into their spectacular new home on Peachtree, Moser decorated the guest room with a mural of *Uncle Remus* characters.[87]

Moser and Bradley did most to energize studio art in the city and both would move on to New York City by the end of the decade, but they left an indelible imprint on Atlanta. Art was being studied intently at the Female Institute under the watchful eye of Mrs. J. J. Ballard. To the list of celebrated artists, the *Constitution* noted Minnie McAfee, "one of the youngest," but "her work shows a delicacy of touch and fine finish rarely seen outside the academies." The paper bemoaned the fact that Mrs. Charles A. Loring had not yet set up a studio but described her touch as "masterly." Fortunately, Mary Gregory had set up a studio

[84] Ibid., June 25, 1882; Harris, *Grady*, 59.

[85] Pollack, *Visual Art*, 15.

[86] Ibid.

[87] Nixon, *Henry W. Grady*, 189.

fifteen years before and "since then has worked side by side with those who have wrought our growth and progress." Moreover, she won a reputation for her portraits and especially a most interesting one of former Confederate vice president and Georgia governor Alexander Stephens.[88]

Haverty was the future of art collection in Atlanta. He perfected the family furniture business and expanded the brand throughout the South. His wealth was extraordinary. He named his family estate Villa Clare, for his beloved wife Clara and after County Clare in Ireland from which the family had departed for New Orleans during the potato famine. Clara died in 1918, and in the 1920s and 30s, Haverty would open Villa Clare on Sunday afternoons to any and all who wanted to view his collection. In 1926 he convinced Mrs. Joseph Madison "Hattie" High to donate her mansion as a museum for art; thus Atlanta's High Museum.[89] Grady integrated visual arts from production to collection into his vision of where Atlanta was going.

The most interesting figure in the story of art was Henry Ossawa Tanner. Born in Pittsburgh in 1859, between Haverty (1858) and Bradley (1860), he was the first African American artist to gain international acclaim. His father was a bishop of the African Methodist Episcopal Church, and his mother had escaped slavery by the Underground Railroad. The family moved to Philadelphia in his youth where he attended the Robert Vaux School, one of the few African American schools to offer a liberal arts curriculum. As a young man, he enrolled in the Pennsylvania Academy of the Fine Arts. Although Philadelphia's racism chapped him, he became a student of the influential Thomas Eakins, who had considerable influence. Tanner was a favored student of Eakins. Eakins's portrait of Tanner is memorable and rare for a student to be so honored. Tanner experienced racism in Philadelphia because of its close ties to the planter class in the South, many of whom had sent their daughters to Philadelphia academies for the well-to-do. Indeed, Grady's wife Julia was educated there. Tanner's autobiography *The Story of an Artist's Life* describes the racism he experienced.

---

[88] Garrett, *Atlanta and Environs*, 2:215; *Atlanta Constitution*, November 30, 1890.

[89] W. Smith, *Villa Clare*, 66–67.

"I was extremely timid," he wrote, "and to be made to feel that I was not wanted, although in a place where I had every right to be, even months afterwards caused me sometimes real pain."[90]

When Tanner moved to Atlanta in 1887, in part to escape the hypocritical racial atmosphere of Philadelphia, Horace Bradley soon hired him to run his studio. However, his lasting association was with Clark Atlanta University, the city's primary African American institution, where he taught art. (Spelman and Morehouse were just emerging at the time. Clark, established in 1869, was one of the few African American schools offering a liberal arts education.) Tanner had his own gallery as well. Within another three years he would exile himself to Paris where he spent the rest of his artistic career. For Tanner, as for Ta-Nehisi Coates more than a hundred years later, Paris defined cosmopolitanism. For Atlanta his presence was a brief shining moment. Unfortunately, organizers of the 1895 Exposition tarnished it by consigning Tanner's invited art to the Negro Building, a sign of what Grady's New South could never overcome, the segregation its own racism preferred. Tanner handled it well enough, and former president Grover Cleveland and other dignitaries made sure to attend the exhibits in that building as well as the Woman's Building.

J. J. Haverty would continue collecting Tanner's work into the twenties and thirties.[91] Tanner's paintings are still displayed in the High Museum, a gift of J. J. Haverty's descendants. Tanner died in May 1937, Haverty in October 1939. They had been born within a year of each other. What journeys they had made in the name of aesthetics.

Grady would have been pleased to know that his vision of an aesthetically beautiful city would have resonated with art historian and collector Deborah C. Pollack, whose *Visual Art and the Urban Evolution of the New South* (2015) impressively describes Grady's contributions in inspiring and organizing an artistic challenge to the New South. He also worked with the formation of Atlanta's Music Association, transforming DeGive's Opera House into a hall of joyful noises. He encouraged libraries and literature, championing not only "Jake" (as he called Joel Chandler Harris) and many others but especially William Tappan

[90] Bruce, *Henry Ossawa Tanner*. See also Mathews, *Henry Ossawa Tanner*.
[91] W. Smith, *Villa Clare*, 79–80.

Thompson, editor of the *Savannah Morning News* for his hilarious *Major Jones's Courtship*, and Mary Edwards Bryan, editor of *Sunny South*, a literary weekly started in 1875. Grady described Bryan as "the most brilliant, fecund and versatile authoress." She was exuberant, writing, "There is a growing demand for art-work, and the artist's work becomes more steadily remunerative."[92] Art in Atlanta was not monochromatic.

In the last half of the nineteenth century, the Ruskin movement emphasized the aesthetic as a liberating force; Grady's knowledge of the movement is unknown, but he certainly got some insight into how fragile the movement was. Fine art could be erotic, and the female form was considered the root of all evil. So it was that in 1884 officials arraigned Daniel Pitchford, who owned a shop on Whitehall Street, for displaying female nudes in his window. They were replicas of famous paintings, ergo fine art. A trial followed with prosecutors claiming Pitchford's lewd intent. Grady and the *Constitution*, along with the new art community, rose up. The *Constitution* made it clear that the outside world would ridicule Atlanta and "called upon the court to refrain from putting the city in an embarrassing situation before the rest of the country by enforcing Pitchford's obscenity charge." They urged the court to put it in context of what other "fine art" cities were doing. The judge finally ruled that the paintings were "nude without being vulgar."[93] Even as by the nineties, Grady and Atlanta had almost grasped the ring, it was no sure thing.

Haverty's great-grandson said it got worse in the first decades of the twentieth century as virulent racism and evangelical Christianity came to see all art as subversive or worse still, lewd and lascivious. It led H. L. Mencken to charge Georgia as the worst state in the "Sahara of the Bozart" (his playful substitute for the French Beaux Arts), his way of saying that the South in general and Georgia in particular had resisted the fine arts of the late nineteenth century and become a cultural desert.[94] As will be seen in Part 3, there was a rapid devolution from the vision Grady articulated in the eighties, especially in the three decades following his death. Yet, as biographer Harold Davis put it,

---

[92] Pollack, *Visual Art*, 26.
[93] Ibid., 26–27.
[94] W. Smith, *Villa Clare*, 65.

Grady's death spared him "sights he would have disliked."[95]

Grady's image lives on in the art he inspired. In 1885, the year the Cyclorama artists showed up to sketch scenes of the Battle of Atlanta that would appear on that remarkable canvas, Orion Frazee also showed up. Born in New York in 1843, he was an Italian-trained American sculptor of immense achievement. He soon fell in with Grady and saw him almost daily. At Grady's suggestion, Frazee traveled to Mississippi to do a likeness of Jefferson Davis that would serve as his death mask. Grady thought that if Frazee molded the mask into a sculpted bust or statue, the artist's fame would grow. Ironically Frazee would all too soon do Grady's death mask, using a clay bust he had done of Davis and remolding it into Grady's likeness. That bust, completed in 1892 and done in a more modern style, is thought to be the best likeness of Grady as he was known to family and friends.

In the same year Frazee completed the bust, the city of Atlanta unveiled a heroic statue of Grady in oratorical pose, sculpted by Alexander Doyle, whose likenesses of Civil War generals and soldiers as well as statesmen populate battle fields, cemeteries, boulevards, and the nation's capital itself. Below Grady's towering pose are the figures of memory and history and the inscription from his last speech: "Give us the broad and perfect loyalty that loves and trusts Georgia alike with Massachusetts—that knows no south, no north, no east, no west, but endears with equal and patriotic love every foot of our soil, every State in our Union."

---

[95] H. Davis, *Henry Grady's New South*, 163.

Taylor-Grady House.

Courtesy Hargrett Rare Book & Manuscript Library, University of Georgia

Lucille Selig and Leo Frank, ca. 1909.

Mary Phagan, ca. 1913.

Monument erected in 1889 to honor the memory of the Confederate dead of Alexandria, Virginia.

Courtesy E. Culpepper Clark

William Tecumseh Sherman in ceremonial uniform, ca. 1880. This would have been the time period Henry Grady got to know Sherman personally.

Courtesy Atlanta History Center

Lillian Smith with her friend and partner.

Courtesy Rose Library, Emory University

Sketches depicting David Barrow (upper left) and Henry Barrow (seated). Members of the Barrow family owned four plantations in Georgia and founded the state's Agricultural Society.

Courtesy Rose Library, Emory University

Drawing of David Crenshaw Barrow, ca. 1900.

Courtesy Rose Library, Emory University

Alfred H. Colquitt, the first of three New South Governors of Georgia in the 1880's, installed and influenced by Grady.

Courtesy Hargrett Rare Book & Manuscript Library, University of Georgia

John Brown Gordon, Robert E. Lee's "Old War Horse" and later installed by Grady as a New South Governor of Georgia. Grady and Gordon would later have a falling out.

Courtesy Rose Library, Emory University

The image of Grady that Joel Chandler Harris thought looked most like Grady as *Constitution* staff knew him. Harris used it in his memorial volume on Grady's life and labors.

Mildred Lewis Rutherford, a founder of the United Daughters of the Confederacy and its State Historian. "Miss Millie" as she was affectionately known, did much to shape the "Lost Cause" mythology of the Confederacy.

Courtesy Hargrett Rare Book & Manuscript Library, University of Georgia

Grady's home, which he had built at 353 Peachtree Street, was later destroyed by fire.

Courtesy Atlanta History Center

The Grady's at home. From left to right: Henry's wife, Julia King, Henry King Grady (who later changed the King to Woodfin), Augusta "Gussie," and Henry.

Courtesy Rose Library, Emory University

Henry Grady's Chi Phi brothers at the University of Georgia. Grady is standing second from left.

Courtesy Hargrett Rare Book & Manuscript Library, University of Georgia

Part 3

Legacy

Sherman and Grady both had incredible intellectual energy and were kinetic in pursuing goals. Sherman was a chatterbox, issuing a stream of consciousness that would have been scattered had his aides not taken notes. He wrote copiously about his maneuvers and battles, so no historian could mistake where he was going or his strategy, even with the welter of commentary that followed. Grady was equally loquacious, if not quite as scattered, in pursuing campaigns for events like expositions and candidates for political office. Even his touted penchant for entertaining could be set aside for a cause. But Sherman was the warlord, and Grady the pacificator, so while totally different they were equally committed to their causes in their times.

Born thirty years before Grady, "Cump," as the family called him, graduated from the United States Military Academy in 1840 and immediately joined the Second Seminole war in Florida, where even with desultory fighting he learned the particulars of soldiering. After three years in Florida, he eventually wound up at Fort Moultrie on Sullivan's Island at the entrance to Charleston Harbor. A call to serve on a military tribunal brought him to Marietta, Georgia, in 1844 "to investigate some claims by former volunteer troops." A compulsive observer of terrain, during his six week stay he mapped the area, including the future Atlanta (although it was then known as Marthasville), which served him well in the campaign that ended in its capture and destruction twenty years later.[1] From Marietta, he proceeded to Bellefonte, Alabama, in the Northeastern corner of the state where he furthered his knowledge of the ground his army would later cover. Surprisingly, in his memoirs he claims to have visited Kennesaw Mountain frequently during his stay in Marietta.[2] As one who has walked that mountain, it is inconceivable to this author that Sherman would have ordered the

[1] O'Connell, *Fierce Patriot*, 26.

[2] Sherman, *Memoirs*, 1:149.

frontal assault on June 27, 1864, that ended disastrously. It was the only major blunder of his Atlanta campaign.

In this time, Atlanta began as only a spike in the ground driven in 1837 to mark the terminus of the state-owned Western and Atlantic Railroad designed to run from Chattanooga to an area south and east of the Chattahoochee River that held promise for converging railroads. It was to be the critical link between the Mississippi basin and the Atlantic, which it became. Yet in 1837, it was only a spike that gave Atlanta its first name, Terminus. In 1843 it would be named for governor Wilson Lumpkin's daughter Martha, thus Marthasville, and two years later Atlanta, some thinking it feminine for Atlantic, and for a time it was called informally Atalanta, the mythical Greek huntress, which would have been more correct and was Martha's middle name. When Sherman came through, it was but a small hamlet of its future. Lying between Decatur to its east and Marietta to the northwest, it was barely anything, its substantial Cherokee population having been deported in 1838 by requirement of Andrew Jackson's Indian Removal Act of 1830—ever after known as the "Trail of Tears." Twenty years later, Sherman himself would order a forced removal of the city's population by conquest—a defining moment in the war against the rebellion.

It was also in this time that John Tyler, Virginian and accidental president, who succeeded President William Henry Harrison on his early death in 1841, presented a treaty to annex the independent Republic of Texas. Because Texas had legalized slavery, the treaty spurred impassioned debate between North and South, thus setting the stage for all that would make Sherman, the soldier, and Grady, the reconciler, famous.[3]

Sherman's father died when he was nine. His mother, coping with eleven children, fostered him to the Thomas Ewing Sr. family in his hometown of Lancaster, Ohio. His foster father was a United States senator and a powerful figure in Ohio. Eventually at age thirty, Cump fell in love with his foster-sister Ellen, married, and had eight children with her. She was devoutly Catholic, he agnostic, but they were devoted despite later affairs he had in New York as general of the Army. She was his anchor. Sherman's younger brother John would become the

[3] Chernow, *Grant*, 38.

most influential figure in the Unites States Senate in the last half of the nineteenth century, authoring among other significant legislation, the Sherman Antitrust Act of 1890. John also became both secretary of the treasury and secretary of state. He retired in 1898 and died in 1900.

Sherman always thought the confluence of the Missouri with the Mississippi was the most powerful place in America and moved to St. Louis with Ellen and family in the 1850s. With uncertain prospects, he traveled to San Francisco and went into banking but eventually failed. That journey gave him a sense of America's vastness. In the days after the Civil War, he would comprehend it more fully, not only with the Indian Removal he led late into the century as chief of the army but also with the transcontinental railroads he also oversaw. The realization of America's vast designs should have entitled him to a place on Mount Rushmore. Before all that and having failed at banking in San Francisco, he made a detour to Louisiana.

The army posted Sherman to Louisiana during the Mexican War, and among the state's West Pointers, Braxton Bragg and P. G. T. Beauregard among the more famous, he had an outstanding reputation. In 1859 they and others wished to establish a Louisiana Seminary of Learning and Military Academy. The academy was an afterthought and motivated not by thoughts of impending Civil War but by the need of discipline for rowdy students.[4] War was pending, but Sherman persuaded Ellen that he should accept what appeared to be a stable position as superintendent, even if in Alexandria, Louisiana, the most central city in the state—and away from what could be a claustrophobic Ewing family.

He threw himself into the role of superintendent with his usual attention to detail and development. The school's board included the state's leading planters, businessmen, and former West Pointers. The board soon realized they had the right man. In short order, he developed a curriculum and manual of arms that would have been the envy of West Point and VMI. The faculty was superb, including David

[4] The University of Alabama did the same thing in 1859 when it adopted the Virginia Military Academy's manual to curb unruly student behavior. Their behavior issues involved Southern frontier craziness, guns and knives among hotheaded students. However, these issues were not uncommon throughout American higher education, Harvard included.

French Boyd in linguistics, who became the best friend Sherman ever had outside the military. (Today the name Boyd still marks the campus, which was named Louisiana State University in 1860.) Sherman secured arms from the War Department and a solid base of funding from the founders. They liked him and he them. It was going well until his brother John appeared to side with abolitionists in the impending crisis, which created a stir among the LSU board. On Sherman's appeal, his brother sent a back-tracking missive intended to defuse any thought that he was an abolitionist. What follows from Sherman's remarkable memoirs bears repeating in full. At a gathering of the board, Governor Thomas Overton Moore asked politely that Sherman explain his brother's comments. Sherman replied,

> I answered: Governor Moors [*sic*], you mistake in calling my brother John Sherman an abolitionist. We have been separated since childhood—I in the army, and he pursuing law in Northern Ohio, and it is possible that we may differ in general sentiment, but I deny that he is considered at home an abolitionist; and, although he prefers the free institutions under which he lives to those of slavery which prevail here, he would not of himself take from you by law or force any property whatever, even slaves. Then said Moore: "Give us your own views of slavery as you see it here and throughout the South."

I answered in effect that "the people of Louisiana were hardly responsible for slavery, as they had inherited it; that I found two distinct conditions of slavery, domestic and field hands. The domestic slaves employed by the families, were probably better treated than any slaves on earth; but the condition of the field-hands was different, depending more on the temper and disposition of their masters and overseers than were those employed about the house"; and I went on to say that, "were I a citizen of Louisiana, and a member of the Legislature, I would deem it wise to bring the legal condition of the slaves more near the status of human beings under all Christian and civilized governments. In the first place, I argued that, in sales of slaves made by the State, I would forbid the separation of families, letting the father, mother, and children, be sold together to one person, instead of each to the highest bidder. And again, I would advise the repeal of the statute which enacted a severe penalty for even the owner to teach his slave to read and write, because that qualified property and took away a part of its value; illustrating the case of Henry Sampson, who had been the slave of Colonel Chambers, of Rapides Parish, who had gone to California as the servant of an officer of the army, and who was afterward employed by me in the bank at San Francisco. At first he could not write or read, and I could only offer to pay him one hundred dollars a month; but he was taught to write and read by Reilley, our bank teller, when his services became worth two hundred and fifty dollars, which enabled him to buy his own freedom...."[5]

Sherman says that when he was finished someone struck the table and said, "By God he is right!" Sherman also said that afterward the debate went on for about an hour "on both sides and with fairness." He was glad to be relieved because "at that time all men in Louisiana were dreadfully excited on questions affecting their slaves, who constituted the bulk of their wealth, and without whom they honestly believed that sugar, cotton, and rice could not possibly be cultivated."[6] Then Sherman resolved it. "The more I think of it, the more I think I should be away, the sooner the better...." It was time to go. "I therefore bad adieu to all my friends, and about the 25th of February (1861), took my departure by railroad, for Lancaster, via Cairo [pronounced Kay-row in Illinois] and Cincinnati."[7]

Whether it happened that way is subject to the vagaries of memory. That said, it says a lot about Sherman's mind at the time of its writing in his memoirs. Moreover, the breaking point was yet to come. When Louisiana seceded, Sherman was done. He settled with the board and departed saying, "These are small matters in comparison with those in the present state of the country, which will cause sacrifices by millions, instead of by hundreds."[8] At war's end, his friend David French Boyd would take over the seminary which had become the Louisiana State University. Boyd always considered Sherman the founder. Not long after the institution reopened in Alexandria, it burned, cause unknown, and was moved to Baton Rouge, "where the same institution now is, under the title of the Louisiana University (now Louisiana State

---

[5] Sherman, *Memoirs*, 1:136–37.

[6] Ibid.

[7] Ibid., 143.

[8] Ibid.

University)." "I have been able to do them many acts of kindness," Sherman said, "and am still in correspondence, with Colonel Boyd, its president."[9]

Sherman's racialist thinking and Southern sympathies are well known, if argued variously and differently among historians. As a recent historian put it, "his vision of a blessed society also embraced racial bias as part of the natural order of things as well as pragmatic limits to some freedoms." When pressed by Lincoln and Grant on the question of recruiting Black soldiers within his command area, Sherman responded, "I have had the question put to me often: 'Is not a negro as good as a white man to stop a bullet?' Yes; and a sand-bag is better; but can a negro...improvise roads, bridges, sorties, flank movements, etc., like the white man? I say no." "Summing it up, he told a southerner and former acquaintance, 'I care not a straw for niggers.'"[10] Sherman used what today is known as the N-word commonly until the end of his days.

Sherman was equally passionate about the Union. Secession was a willful destruction of the Republic's sacred sovereignty. When the arsenal he had assembled for the Louisiana Seminary of Learning and Military Academy was seized by secessionists, he seethed. He harbored a "special hatred for the Southern intelligentsia," whose actions rent the Union asunder. To Ellen he wrote, "We must Kill those three hundred thousand I have told you of so often...."[11] The psychological profiles of Sherman are prolific largely because his mannerisms and actions lend themselves to such profiling. My readings of them would say at minimum he had a borderline narcissistic personality disorder, often found in charismatic leaders, his rapid and repetitive and often confusing speech being but one manifestation. Others have suggested manic-depressive disorder, now called bipolar, yet the ups and downs of how he experienced a remarkable career is in the end not important except as an attempted explanation of peculiar personality traits, certainly not his accomplishments. He was unique, complex, and beloved by his soldiers, and most of his commanders, however confused they may have been by

---

[9] Ibid., 149.

[10] Trudeau, *Southern Storm*, 24, 31.

[11] Ibid., 29.

his outbursts. Most importantly, as a soldier he pushed on to victory. Because he allowed nothing to stand in his way, he became the ultimate soldier himself, permanently mounted in the nation's bronzed statuary.

His burning of Atlanta and "March to the Sea" etched him forever in the South's eschatology of evil as he burned his way through Atlanta and on to Savannah with rape, pillage, plunder, and buried silver in his wake. Plenty of pillage and plunder occurred as his forces lived off the land with outliers, known as bummers, suddenly appearing on farms and plantations and taking whatever the army needed or the plunderers wanted. Houses and barns were often torched so as to leave a smoking trail, but it was far from total war, more like the "hard war" he and Grant justified based upon the rebellion and its purpose to rend the nation asunder.

What most astounds is the relative absence of rape. Most authorities now believe only one credible claim existed, with two others more dubious. Still more recent accountings go to the overall reports of gonorrhea and syphilis among White Union soldiers that indicate much higher rates of intercourse throughout the war. Those reports were not specific to the "March to the Sea" campaign but by reduction seem credible. The compelling evidence indicates far less rape than one would expect from an avenging army, yet with one important alternative report of White Union soldiers having sex with slaves with putative intent on the part of slaves to acquire food or other favors. For obvious reasons of family and home, any self-reporting would have been completely taboo for White women.

Sherman's March to the Sea became, in Southern memory, the most dastardly in the history of war—with a major motion picture in 1939, *Gone with the Wind*, to prove it. Georgia was prostrate, as were South and North Carolina to follow. Columbia, South Carolina, suffered arguably greater destruction from its burning. In a review of the book *Sherman's Ghosts*, James M. McPherson wrote, "The Bummers of the Civil War destroyed much property but few civilian lives...."[12] In *Saving Savannah* Bancroft Prize-winning historian Jacqueline Jones

[12] James M. McPherson, "'Sherman's Ghosts' by Matthew Carr," *New York Times Review of Books*, March 25, 2015. Available online: www.nytimes.com/2015/03/29/books/review/shermans-ghosts-by-matthew-carr.html.

notes, "The Yankees inflicted considerable damage on property, but unlike other conquering armies they did not massacre civilian men, women, or children." Herbert G. Gutman makes a more compelling case for rape of slaves by Union soldiers generally and some other instances of rape of White women and slaves on the March to the Sea. By combing the reports of Freedmen Bureaus throughout the South, the anecdotal evidence from self-reports of African American women certainly indicate that White Union soldiers were as callous as any. One reason for fewer reports of rape during the March to the Sea may have been the speed with which the march took place (three hundred miles in five weeks), thereby perhaps providing fewer opportunities for soldiers to target and attack.[13]

At least one atrocity from Sherman's march lives in infamy. It bears the name of Ebenezer Creek, a stream that runs south from the Savannah River (which generally marks the South Carolina-Georgia border) through Effingham County about twenty miles from the city of Savannah. It was not fordable when Union Brevet Major General Jefferson C. Davis (no relation to the South's president, although both were from Kentucky) approached with his division of Oliver O. Howard's corps on December 8. Desperate to keep up with Sherman's other columns, in part to get the brevet rank made permanent, he ordered his pioneers to throw out a pontoon bridge. Although no Blacks served under Sherman's converging columns, he did find able-bodied slaves serviceable as pioneers in clearing roads, building bridges, and removing obstructions. They were also his best source of intelligence about what Whites were up to. General Davis had other considerations. He was a hard-cussing fighter who had already killed one fellow officer who got in his way. Moreover, as a Kentuckian and Democrat, he had no use for Blacks, except as pioneers. Unfortunately, as with most of Sherman's columns, large numbers of slaves followed Davis's division as it moved toward Savannah, and their hoped-for freedom. (Estimates

[13] Gutman, *Black Family*, 386–400. Faust supports the notion that Sherman's March "targeted property rather than persons," but she also notes that there were collateral human deaths with sufficient anecdotal evidence. Still, clearly the march, for whatever reason, did not target civilians (*This Republic of Suffering*, 138).

indicate as many as 19,000 Negroes followed Sherman's march.) Sherman had advised his commanders not to allow slaves to impede their march, but it inevitably occurred in varying degrees.

What happened next was cruel. With Wheeler's Confederate cavalry nipping at his rear on December 9, Davis marched his soldiers over the bridge and immediately ordered the pontoons pulled from the frigid creek, which was in excess of 120 feet wide and ten feet deep at the crossing. When the slaves who were following saw what was happening, fearful cries wailed up. With Confederate cavalry advancing, many slaves believed they had no choice and started fording, only to drown by the hundreds. Although Wheeler's cavalry made no record of it, Union observers saw numerous slaves being slashed and shot. The lucky escaped into the woods, where many were rounded up and sent back to their plantations or farms. Exact casualty figures are unknown although historians use numbers ranging from four hundred to over a thousand. Several Union officers were so appalled that one wrote his congressman, who broke the story; whereupon Lincoln sent Secretary of War Stanton to investigate. Sherman defended General Davis on grounds of "military necessity," and Davis, under investigation, defended himself. The result was no charges brought and no consequences attended other than perhaps Davis's failure to obtain the permanent rank of major general. On December 25, Sherman handed Savannah over to Lincoln as a Christmas present.

Sherman spent considerable time in his memoirs on the subject of Stanton's visit with its implications that whether Ebenezer Creek was as described by the officer who reported it, Sherman's attitude toward Negroes, and especially whether to bring them within Union lines for their protection, was being questioned.[14] Stanton made it clear that harboring them within lines was a war imperative, as the Confederacy was actively considering their enlistment to support its cause. Then there was the oft-reported meeting of Stanton with a delegation of African American leaders, mostly ministers. To a series of questions running from their understanding of the Emancipation Proclamation and its implications for them as citizens to their opinion of Sherman himself, they were forthcoming. When Stanton got to the last question about

[14] Sherman, *Memoirs*, 2:118–31.

Sherman, he asked the general to leave the room. Sherman bristled but stepped away as requested. He need not have feared, for the ministers were fulsome in their praise of him.

Several years ago, then Georgia labor commissioner Michael L. Thurmond arranged a gathering at Ebenezer Creek, where the Reverend Thurmond Tillman of Savannah's famed First African Baptist Church consecrated the ground that so many slaves had hallowed with their lives in a desperate effort to gain freedom. A State Historical Marker was unveiled on that same occasion. Thurmond was the first and remains the only Black elected to statewide office in Georgia and in 2016 was elected to a four-year term as the chief executive officer of DeKalb County, Georgia. His book *Freedom: Georgia's Antislavery Heritage, 1733–1865*, vividly recounts the tragedy at Ebenezer Creek and much more.

Sherman included in his memoirs a missive from General Halleck that furthered Sherman's belief that radicals in Congress and other high places had serious reservations about his attitudes on race. He used it to dismiss Stanton's visit as political. One good thing came of it: Sherman's Special Order Number 15, which inched toward appropriation of land along the Southeastern coast for resettlement of slaves and making some provision for them. The order went as far as military necessity would allow, Stanton and Sherman correctly believing that a permanent solution would require governmental action. Still, it was an important step. Sherman never accepted the full prospect and implications of African American citizenship. He put it this way:

> The Negro question was beginning to loom up among the political eventualities of the day, and many foresaw that not only would the slaves secure their freedom, but that they would also have votes. I did not dream of such a result then, but knew that slavery, as such, was dead forever, and did not suppose that the former slaves would be suddenly, without preparation, manufactured into voters, equal to all others, politically and socially.[15]

---

[15] Sherman, *Memoirs*, 2:127. Land distribution was effectively halted by 1866 under orders of President Johnson and reverted to original White owners. The "forty acres and a mule" order had been issued by Freedmen Bureau Chief General O. O. Howard on July 28, 1866. Freedmen were to take the land and

Grady could have written that.

Ron Chernow's monumental biography of Grant stresses the friendship between the future president and Sherman. They were the two most remarkable generals of the Civil War, Southern generals included. When Grant in 1864 was made the nation's third lieutenant general (Washington the first and Winfield Scott the second), Grant more than lived up to Lincoln's confidence in his becoming general of all the armies of the Republic. Again the marvels of telegraphy made it work; the Union side had strung 15,389 miles of wire during the war, employing 1,500 linemen and operators. Thus was Grant able to coordinate a strategy among all the armies for the destruction, in detail and simultaneously, of the Confederacy's two principal armies, Lee's in Virginia and Joseph E. Johnston's in Georgia, along with other Union armies scattered across the South. When done, the principal figures would be Grant, Sherman, and Sheridan. But for Sherman's departure from Atlanta to Savannah, Grant was in constant telegraphic contact with his friend and fellow warrior. That coordination and the South's dwindling resources spelled victory for the mightiest armies ever assembled.

Grant had one other advantage over Sherman: "an ideological commitment to the war as profound as his military contribution." Commitment became conviction when Grant did two things: first, he resisted Peace Democrats such as General George McClellan and others who would attempt to come to "terms" with the South, for it would inevitably return slavery as a necessary condition of the South and therefore a compromised nation; and second, Grant was "all-in" for the recruitment and deployment of Colored troops for reasons both of necessity and of conviction of their worth. Sherman, no less the soldier, was wanting on both counts and thus lost a vital connection to the purpose of it all.[16]

Grant's commitment to citizenship for Blacks continued through

---

have three years to purchase the acreage (apparently from proceeds of farming it), but it all reverted to the original owners less than a year later under orders from Johnson. See R. White, *Republic*, 45.

[16] The parenthetical thought is a synthesis from among many but owes most importantly to Chernow, *Grant*, 440–41.

his presidency, even if fellow Republicans abandoned that commitment. Sherman himself grew estranged from Grant, saying his presidency had caved to Reconstruction requirements of emancipation and citizens' rights for African Americans, "that he had been surrounded by a weak cabinet, and had failed to restore harmony and fraternity among the different sections of the country—that a mistake had been made in putting all the power of the Southern states in the hands of the ignorant (Blacks and carpetbaggers), and substantially disfranchising the intelligent classes (Whites), and the South was in worse condition today than at the close of the war."[17] As a Grant biographer put it, "To understand Grant's position it is worth stressing that it was Liberal Republicans—self-righteous, good government folks—not conservative businessmen and Stalwart Party bosses who decided that Black citizens were suddenly expendable."[18]

Grady's nods to Sherman and the general's trips back to Atlanta were all essential to the national tableau of reconciliation. Each played his role, a role enacted by Robert E. Lee himself at Appomattox and later as president of Washington University (later, Washington and Lee). Indeed, had no united nation ensued, the evolution of the American South would have played out differently by guerilla warfare, continual disruption, and military force. Instead Grady's New South, evolving from Lee's defeated South, accepted as did Lee, the verdict of war and a new nationalism based on the nation's own recognition that the South had a problem—Negroes. No other section had come to terms with this issue, not to mention the North's own xenophobic and racialist thinking about immigrants, including Negroes. Thus did Sherman's natural sympathies coincide with Grady's vision of the future—the old soldier and the New South spokesman finding the middle ground of compromise through reconciliation, however costly to African Americans.

The Century

Before Vietnam, C. Vann Woodward observed that Americans had experienced only two defeats: the Southern strike for independence and

[17] Chernow, *Grant*, 809.

[18] Ibid., 740.

the Northern attempt at Reconstruction. The first came by force of arms, the second by force and other means. As a reporter for the *Constitution*, Grady chronicled the undoing of Reconstruction and, on assignment for a number of other papers, including the *New York World* and *New York Herald*, spread the word. He reported from Tallahassee on the electoral commission's resolution in favor of Hayes over Tilden. That resolution would lead to the permanent end of Reconstruction as federal troops departed South Carolina and Louisiana in April 1877. By the time Grady became managing editor of the *Constitution* in 1880, he had the opportunity through the power and wizardry of his pen to shape what people would think of those two failures all the way through to the mid-twentieth century. Powerful social, economic, and cultural forces were determinative. Yet Grady and other scribes of the era established the meaning of it all, gave it a language for engagement, and rhetorical touchstones for future historians to ponder.

Although a failure, Reconstruction did deposit three amendments to the Constitution that formed the scaffolding for freedom's struggle. Indeed, the relationship between American wars and reform is a close one, as in Woodward's notion that the Civil War created sufficient "moral capital" to get the Thirteenth, Fourteenth, and Fifteenth amendments into law. The American Revolution was born of a commitment to equality and eventually yielded a more perfect Union. World War I enabled woman's suffrage and the Prohibition amendment to pass, which, despite the latter's poor performance, was born of reformist instincts, among them avoiding wife abuse, which so often accompanied alcohol, alongside the right to vote. Then World War II provided impetus toward fulfilling freedom's promise through the Supreme Court's rulings on civil rights and a labor movement that helped address income inequality.

No sooner had the Thirteenth, Fourteenth, and Fifteenth amendments become law than the nation started walking them back. The South found ways to establish slavery by other means: denying equal protection of the laws, separating by both race and benefits, and suppressing African American voters before disfranchising them altogether. Through it all, the White South found a complicit nation and Supreme Court.

Chief Justice Morrison "Mott" Remick Waite presided over the court from 1874–1888 and best illustrates the temper of the times. Historian Richard White said Grant "mostly appointed mediocrities to the bench," but that Waite, who was born and raised in Toledo, Ohio, was "competent" if little known "outside Republican Party circles."[19] Mary Frances Waite, unmarried daughter of the chief justice, was a young woman of even disposition who liked to immerse herself in church work. For this reason, she astonished her father when he found her in a considerable state of agitation on a cheerful Sunday morning in May 1877. On further inquiry, he learned that she had returned from a church service in which she witnessed "the people of Charleston give thanks for their 'great deliverance'" from Reconstruction. Nany, as she was affectionately known, was accompanying her father on his tour of duty on the Fourth Circuit, a regional responsibility that members of the Supreme Court had to endure until 1891. The chief justice shared his daughter's concern. "The truth is," he observed "...the people here are really, at this moment, in heart further from reconstruction than they have been since the war. They have received the first fruits of success [removal of federal troops from the South]...and have gone back to their original idols." Despairing of his party's future in the South, he believed that his friend President Hayes's only option was to appoint men of genuine ability from the "enemy camp," then hope for the best. "The truth is," he conceded, "I am thoroughly disgusted."[20]

Waite was a strong supporter of the administration's Southern strategy. Ironically, he was in South Carolina to try election cases of voter suppression by fraud, intimidation, and murder. What he heard from the bench that spring sickened him. He sat through accounts of the brutal slaying of a boy who could neither hear nor speak and the murder of a Black father in front of his wife and children--even as he begged for his life and promised to vote Democratic.[21] Waite's education at Yale had given him a proper appreciation for the rights of property and of states. Of greater significance for the cases he was trying in Charleston, he did not believe that the acts of private persons, even in denying voting rights, fell under the purview of federal authority. Yet

[19] Ibid., 255.

[20] Waite to wife, May 24, 1877, Morrison Remick Waite Papers, Library of Congress.

[21] Magrath, *Morrison R. Waite*, 158–59.

in another letter to Mrs. Waite he complained, "You can hardly imagine the horrid details of our trial. There have already been developed about twenty murders in cold blood. I have never before conceived of such a state of society. The testimony this morning was…sickening." Moreover, he was stunned at the manner in which the Charleston press abused and misrepresented Negro witnesses even though deponents seemed "unusually intelligent for their condition."[22] Anxious to hear what possible excuse the defense could give for such atrocities, in the end he was forced to concede that the defense made a strong case against their liability under the particular indictment (violation of election laws) "but nothing to excuse the inhuman barbarity of the conduct of some of the persons implicated. More unprovoked murder was ever proven than has been shown in some of these cases, but unfortunately the guilty parties are not on trial for that."[23]

The South Carolina cases resulted in a mistrial and provided grounds for a new appeal for general amnesty from the state to President Hayes. When Attorney General Charles Devens sought Waite's opinion, he said simply. "The cases were thoroughly prepared, and, so far as I could discover, the government lost nothing through any fault of those to whom its interests were committed."[24] The president had his answer. Although Hayes waited another year, in April 1879, he gave up and decided to come to terms. The attenuation of the court's reach in civil rights cases even under the three amendments to the Constitution would be affirmed and confirmed in the three civil rights cases that came before the court in 1883. Effectively, the Supreme Court said that the Reconstruction amendments precluded states, but not individuals, from infringing rights. (It is the same argument now advanced by proponents of religious liberty legislation—if an individual by dint of religious conviction refuses service or aid to another individual, even to those in a protected class, that individual cannot be prosecuted for having violated rights.) Waite's court said states could pursue criminal charges against those who committed acts of violence as in the South

[22] Waite to wife, May 20 and 22, 1877, Morrison Remick Waite Papers, Library of Congress.

[23] Ibid., May 27, 1877.

[24] Devens to Waite, March 11, 1878, and Waite to Devens, March 25, 1878, ibid.

Carolina cases and in so many others across the South, but what Southern state was likely to do that?

For Waite, who fit all the qualifications of a liberal Republican and had all affinities with the South's upper-crust of New South partisans, the bottom line was that government belonged in the hands of the "best men." It did not belong to immigrants, to the Tammany Hall ilk who fed upon them, to no spoils system. It had to be about laisse faire economics, the gold standard, and certainly suspicion of, if not outright opposition to, Black participation for all the foregoing reasons. Thus, on departing Charleston, he concluded that the grandee of all South Carolina, Wade Hampton, who before the war was the largest landowner in the South with plantations in Mississippi as well as South Carolina, who formed Hampton's Legion at the beginning of the war and who was Lee's last commander of cavalry, was a "gentleman." Refinement had its courtesies.

Nevertheless, equally and beneath it all was the same violence that created slavery and war capitalism, and after a horrendous Civil War, the rogue military campaigns that followed to restore White rule throughout the South. Waite was sickened by it, but Henry Grady's counterpart in South Carolina, Francis Warrington Dawson, put it best. On receiving amnesty, his editorial caption warned: "Not Guilty, but Don't do it Again." Dawson hied the violent men away, saying that their own political preferment depended upon it. "We tell them in all frankness that South Carolina will not tolerate lawlessness at elections. This revolution must move backwards."[25] Yet still, and as Flannery O'Connor knew, "the violent bear it away."[26] The surrender of Reconstruction was complete. The New South would take up the story.

Century Magazine

Although the battle for a New South was over, a refrain would follow, full of sound and fury, and signifying a lot. *Century Magazine* succeeded *Scribner's Monthly Magazine* in 1881 and became a phenomenal success in the 1880s, reaching a circulation of 250,000 in that decade (another source says 130,000). Following a contretemps in the Scribner family,

---

[25] *Charleston News & Courier*, December 16, 1878.

[26] *The Violent Bear It Away* is the title of her last novel (1960).

Richard Watson Gilder would become its editor in 1881 until his death in 1909. Like Chief Justice Waite, he was a Liberal Republican, by among other things becoming a member of the Anti-Spoils League, but his liberalism was made of sterner stuff. He became a Progressive in the early twentieth century and took on the social ills of tenements in New York City, much like Jane Addams at Hull House in Chicago. Many Liberal Republicans made that journey. Indeed, Morrison Waite himself, despite his timidity on civil rights, endorsed federal regulations for the emerging giants of rail, coal, steel, and finance. As we have seen, so did Grady.

Gilder increased circulation phenomenally by publishing numerous human-interest accounts of Civil War veterans, including leaders from both North and South. *Century* was also touted for its illustrations and until its demise in 1930 did not move to photography. Gilder also encouraged robust debate on the topics of the day and thus entered George Washington Cable and Henry W. Grady in 1885. Cable, a prolific writer on Creole, quadroon, and octoroon culture in New Orleans was considered a master, if not *the* master of local color journalism. His novels outpaced even that. His *Old Creole Days* and *The Grandisimmes* led the way. He was also an original thinker, so original that Old and New Southers branded him as "not Southern," although he was born in New Orleans in 1844, fought with the Confederate cavalry in Mississippi, and until late in life claimed to be Southern. His father was of German ancestry, having settled in northern Virginia (not Southern enough), and his mother was of New England ancestry and from Indiana. It was enough to disqualify him as a Southerner if Southerners did not like what he had to say, and they did not.

As a literary figure, Cable was almost as prominent as Mark Twain, and indeed the two traveled together on the lecture circuit. And then came the invitation from Gilder to publish a lecture he had recently given to the Association of Social Scientists in Boston. He agreed, and in February 1885 it appeared in *Century* under the title "The Freedman's Case in Equity." Whereas Cable was a reluctant arguer, he was a superb debater. Grady loved an argument but remained more a persuader than a debater. In any event, they would clash in the pages of *Century* as Grady was invited to provide a rebuttal in April.

Gilder, the ringmaster, had set another show. Commencement addresses in 1883 and 1884 at Louisiana University in Baton Rouge, Ole Miss in Oxford, and finally the University of Alabama in Tuscaloosa presaged that Cable was going to talk about the "Negro Problem." He generally avoided doing so because he avoided conflict. Besides, fiction created opportunities to address it through characterization, a more congenial approach for him.

Cable began: "The greatest problem before the American people to-day is, as it has been for a hundred years, the presence among us of the Negro." He said that "no comparable entanglement" has beset a modern nation "with so serene a disregard of its ultimate issue, or with a more distinct national responsibility." The Negro had been brought to these shores "with cruel force," and the few who protested were "mobbed" with "public consent." Thus Cable attached a "moral responsibility" to the whole nation. Noting that recent amendments to the Constitution did as much as any constitution could to advance Black citizenship, he also noted that the Supreme Court overturned attempts of Congress to strengthen those guarantees. Moreover, "the popular mind in the old free States, weary of strife at arm's length, bewildered by its complications, vexed by many a blunder, eager to turn to the cure of other evils, and even tinctured by that race feeling whose grosser excesses it would so gladly see suppressed, has retreated from its uncomfortable dictational [*sic*] attitude and thrown the whole matter over to the States of the South." No modern historian has improved upon that assignment of responsibility or description of how the abandonment of Reconstruction came to pass.

Cable noted that the war to end slavery grafted into "one of the most intelligent nations in the world six millions [more like four at the beginning of the war] of people from one of the most debased races on the globe." Now the nation proposed to abandon them, to make it "a dead and buried issue" and "to recommit it to the silence and concealment of the covered furrow." With a nod to efforts being made in the South, Cable makes clear it is not enough and says that both the region and the nation must discover the "equities" owed the freedman and "the errors that are being committed against them." Failure to address these issues would lead to a "system of vicious evasions eventually ruinous to public and private morals and liberty."

Then Cable entered into the meat, or more like it, the gristle that would choke the Solid South. The original sin is that Whites treated the Negro as an "alien," and no amount of contact with the "superior race" could alter that consideration. Black Americans adopted the dress, the language, and the religion of Whites. Some bought their freedom and taught their children, some even shared White blood, but even that did not elevate the Negro from "zero" whether mulatto, quadroon, or octoroon: one drop of Negro blood equaled "zero." Thus did the Southern argument in amelioration that slavery civilized the Negro become the null hypothesis it had always been. Slavery had not become the schoolhouse of civilization. Those who attempted to rise were thrown "into loathsome jails as a common felon." "So the perpetual alien was made also into a perpetual menial, and the belief became fixed that this, too, was nature's decree, not ours." There was one exception; as Cable explained, "Thousands of pious masters and mistresses flatly broke the shameful laws that stood between their slaves and the Bible. Slavery was right; but religion, they held, was for the alien and menial as well as for the citizen and master."

At war's end, slavery ended but not its sentiment and thus the enduring problem and conflict. Here Cable pauses to say that the Negro in freedom renounced the old relationship and refused to go back into menial bondage. Thus, the Negro struck the discordant note that jarred continuing efforts through Reconstruction to retain the old sentiment. By his refusal to go back, "he has proved to us who once ruled over him that, be his relative standing among the races of men what it may, he is worthy to be free." Cable refers to the first Reconstruction as mandated by victory in war. What followed in Redemption of the Southern states was a pledge of "voluntary reconstruction." However, he scathingly notes it will never happen if the result is necessarily second-class citizenship. That was precisely where it headed. Cable then provides in detail the degradations that pend in a future of segregation. "See its every-day working," he wrote. "Any colored man gains unquestioned admission into innumerable places the moment he appears as the menial attendant of some White person, where he could not cross the threshold in his own right as a well-dressed and well-behaved master of himself." Nor did re-enslavement through the penal system and convict-leasing escape his attention. South Carolina alone, for the year

1881, committed 406 Blacks to prison and only 25 Whites, for a ratio of one in every 1,488 Blacks to one in every 15,644 Whites.

Cable also took on "the bugbear" of "social equality" in a plea against separation of the races in education. He labeled the argument that it was justified on differences in "race instinct" as "mere twaddle" completely lacking in proof. Cable closes his litany with the rhetorical question, "What need to say more? The question is answered. Is the freedman a free man? No." Throughout Cable notes that right-thinking people of the South have expressed approval of this sentiment but remain silent. In closing he expresses the hope that a sufficient change of sentiment will change the answer from "no" to "yes." But it is only a rhetorical hope against hope.

HWG's Rebuttal "In Plain Black and White"

Grady's opening was disingenuous at best. "It is strange that during the discussion of the negro question, which has been wide and pertinent, no one has stood up to speak the mind of the South." He was but joining the chorus of Old and New Southers who denied that Cable was a Southerner. He noted with some irony that the South no longer needs be silent because "the people of the United States have, by their suffrages, remitted to the Southern people, temporarily at least, control of the race question. The decision of the Supreme Court on the Civil Rights Bill leaves practically to their adjustment important issues that were, until that decision was rendered, covered by straight and severe enactment;" thus affirming Cable's distinction between compulsory and voluntary reconstruction. "In this article," Grady continued, "as in his works, Mr. Cable is sentimental rather than practical," but he does not speak for the South. Indeed, he is no Southerner. "Born in the South, of Northern parents, he appears to have had little sympathy with his Southern environment, as in 1882 he wrote, 'To be in New England would be enough for me. I was there once—a year ago—and it seemed I'd never been home till then.'" (Cable had been there for an event honoring Harriet Beecher Stowe.) "Among thoughtful men of the South…men who control and will continue to control, I do know, there is general protest against Mr. Cable's statement of the case, and universal protest against his suggestions for the future."

Grady proceeded to speak for the South, saying that it had accepted the arbitrament of war: the end of slavery ("for this all men are thankful"), enfranchisement ("done more in a sense of reparation than in judgment"), and by fixed enactment, the restoration of the Negro's social and civil rights ("and here for the first time the revolution faltered"). This, the third step, "wrong in purpose, has failed in execution. It stands denounced as null by the highest court, as inoperative by general confession, and as unwise by popular verdict." "The South will never adopt Mr. Cable's suggestion of the social intermingling of the races." Then Grady proclaimed what would become mantra for opponents of "indiscriminate mixing of the races": "Neither race wants it." This mantra would reverberate for the next seventy-five years even as the civil rights movement of the twentieth century revealed it to be a lie. "The South replies [to Mr. Cable] that the assortment of races is wise and proper, and stands on the platform of equal accommodation for each race, but separate." Ten years hence the Supreme Court, having remanded the issue to the Southern states, would ratify their separate-but-equal claims in *Plessy*, paving the way for the Jim Crow South.

As he often did, Grady said that if there were an equal division of the races in Wisconsin or Vermont, the result would be no different; thus his variant of the Southern *tu quoque*. He elaborated that efforts to join Black and White congregations, "earnestly, and honestly, we may believe," but universally failed in that purpose, neither race wanting it. He then denounced intermingling as a step toward "amalgamation." It would result in disorganization of society and worse in "an internecine war," as "whites, at any cost and at any hazard, would maintain the clear integrity and dominance of the Anglo-Saxon blood." Grady's article continues in the vein of how happily things are being resolved: "In the common sense and the sincerity of the negro, no less than in the intelligence and earnestness of the Whites, we find the problem simplifying."

Following this litany of happy outcomes from public accommodations to the courts and education, Grady turns back to the false light in which people like Cable have cast the South. Then he warns that, if the victorious Northern armies should be "rallied again from their homes" based upon this false testimony, under no circumstances could they enforce "the policy indicated in the Civil Rights bill." For this reason, "she [the South] has reserved to herself the right to settle the still unsettled element of the race problem, and this right she can never yield." "The domination of the White race in the South," is but the "assertion of the right of character, intelligence and property to rule." Grady closes his case for the South in equity, saying "she desires to silence no criticism, evade no issue, and lessen no responsibility. She recognizes that the negro is here to stay. She knows that her honor, her dear name, and her fame, no less than her prosperity, will be measured by the fullness of the justice she gives and guarantees to this kindly and dependent race."

Grady's propensity for mythmaking and romanticizing was relatively harmless when discussing farmers and cities, or industrialization and urbanization, but as applied to race it was absolutely harmful. Over and again he was dishonest about the actual condition of Blacks in a White-dominated world. Unlike Morrison Waite, who at least was sickened by the reign of terror that accompanied the restoration of White rule, Grady looked past grim realities and clung to myths as harmful and humiliating as the "happy darky," which is but a variant of his calling them a "kindly and dependent race." Grady could make useful applications of the "dream farm" that he invented to think about new agricultural applications and practices, even as real farmers rejected most he offered out of hand. However, nothing in his romanticized view of African Americans led to other than their debasement in segregation. Little comfort exists in the argument that it was going to happen in any event. That being so, his rhetoric did not mitigate but facilitated the slide into the radical racism of the three decades following his death.

No doubt the readers of *Century* found little to fault with Grady's response to Cable. Five years later, six days before his death, he presented all the same arguments found "In Plain Black and White." He felt a little greater urgency on that occasion as Henry Cabot Lodge of the Bay State threatened a "Force Bill" that would have brought back federal supervision of Southern elections. Richard White makes clear the Lodge bill "made no difference." The South was already in control with "grandfather clauses" and "literacy tests" that "made voter fraud less necessary in disenfranchising black voters."[27] For Grady it was the

---

[27] R. White, *Republic*, 635.

same—a plea for "benign neglect," as it would be styled by Daniel Patrick Moynihan in the Nixon years. In Boston the ovation was thunderous from the rich and powerful. Grady's assurances assuaged a city that was once the seat of abolitionism. Alt-right/White rule in Southern states today is not even a veiled echo of the past but an absolute silencing of any opposition to White nationalism. Republicans have gerrymandered African American voters into a few districts in order to maximize White Republican rule. They have been remarkably successful in their purpose, or based on history, perhaps it was to be expected.

Cable returned to the pages of *Century* in September in part to answer his Southern critics and Grady. In "The Silent South," he was as moderate and conciliatory as before and again claimed to be of the South, even to waxing eloquent about the statue of Robert E. Lee in New Orleans and how much it meant to him.[28] He thought that Lee represented "our whole South's better self," but alas, like Lee's statue, the better self was silent. Then in direct response to Grady's charge of encouraging social intermingling, Cable declared "social equality is a fool's dream." Again Cable held out the hope that the South would turn to fairness and take his lead. Alas, it remained silent. In 1888 Cable even tried an "Open Letter Club" to encourage discussion. The response also was largely silence, so few responded. Had Cable's critics been wrong? Although he denied embracing "social equality," it is difficult to read the policy implications of his plea for fairness and not find in it a necessary outcome. Having read in full his case for the "Freedman in Equity," one cannot mistake this author's view that Cable saw "the day of equality" coming.

One historian of that era drew parallel lines to explain racial thought: one-line Black, one White. "Radicals" (White) believed the lines were horizontal with Blacks being permanently on the bottom, never to meet. "Conservatives" (Grady by my estimate) believed the lines to be vertical, separate to be sure, but with Blacks free to raise their station as far as intellect and achievement allowed, but pessimistic that the two would meet on equal terms. Liberals, and only a few of them, like Cable, believing that the vertical lines could one day merge (similar

[28] The statue was removed from its towering pedestal in 2017.

to Einstein's railroad tracks at a perceptual convergence in a distant future, bending in the mind's eye toward convergence).[29] Almost no one in the late nineteenth century believed that social integration, should, would, or could occur overnight. At best it was a future and indefinite prospect. (No one used the term "integration" in that day. "Intermingling," with its explicit sexual connotation, was the currency.)

Of interest is how much fire Grady drew from Old Southers who complained that his rebuttal in *Century* had given away the company store. Grady's assertions could never mollify Southern poet Paul Hamilton Hayne. He complained that Grady "*concedes* so much to the North as this, that they were perfectly justified in abolishing Slavery, and that we ought rather to be grateful for the same." Moreover, Grady failed miserably in arguing the miscegenation point. He was "wretchedly superficial" in dismissing it in "a somewhat airy and insouciate [*sic*] fashion." Grady, in Hayne's estimation tried to have it both ways and got neither. On the one hand he denied the Negro sought "social communion and *amalgamation*," and at another point he raised the danger of intermixture. Hayne was corresponding with Cable nemesis in New Orleans, Charles Gayarre, who agreed with all Hayne was saying about Cable and Grady.[30] Indeed Grady was a master of equivocation, walking fine lines between audiences North and South, urban and rural, radical and rational, playing out lines and pulling them back. Still, Grady's oratorical pose and personality persuaded.

Ironically, in the spring following Grady's death, Cable made his way to Cartersville, Georgia, as a location for his last novel that attempted to explain the South. He studied the city in detail. He needed a place other than New Orleans, one that represented the quintessential South. Whether he met the local colorist Bill Arp, who was then living in Cartersville, is not known, but surely he did. Also in Cartersville was Samuel Porter Jones (1847–1906), or plain "Sam" as he preferred it. Jones was the most famous preacher in late nineteenth-century America, excepting only perhaps Dwight Moody. Jones was a hard-drinking man who gave up both liquor and his law practice following a religious

[29] Williamson, *Crucible of Race*, 5–7.
[30] Ibid., 103–104.

conversion, and started preaching far and wide. One convert in Nashville, Tom Ryman, owned a line of steamboats that in addition to cargo featured bars and dancing girls as well. Jones convinced him not only to give up that part of his trade but to build Ryman's Union Gospel Tabernacle.[31] In time it would become the Grand Ole Opry House. Also in Cartersville were the Feltons, Dr. William H. and Rebecca Latimore, wildly popular among Independent Democrats and foes of Grady. Indeed, Cable had corresponded with Rebecca Felton in 1886 about her opposition to the convict-lease system.[32] So Cable had every reason to settle on Cartersville as the most Southern place on earth.

Moreover, given that the novel was set in Reconstruction and post-Reconstruction times, he must surely have learned that Grady had edited two papers in nearby Rome. The novel titled *John March, Southerner* appeared in 1895. Cartersville became the city of Suez in "the State of Dixie." One historian called it "his most self-consciously Southern work of fiction."[33] Ironically, one character, Cornelius Leggett, a former slave who becomes a Reconstruction politico is a veritable caricature of Blackface comedy, and Cable's view of that era resembles prevailing Southern thought. Still, it did not change the *idée fixe* that Grady and many others cultivated of Grady's not being truly Southern. Indeed, Gilder, who published Cable's controversial views in *Century*, refused to publish *John March* and frowned upon his views about social equality.[34] Thereafter, Cable stayed away from Southern affairs and turned to romance and glory although his work was not completely devoid of Southern issues. He died in January 1925 in St. Petersburg, Florida—to the Gulf one more time.

Cable had an excellent relationship with Grady's pal Joel Chandler Harris. In 1882 Mark Twain and Cable told Joe Harris to meet them in New Orleans. Their purpose was an attempt to get the painfully shy Harris to join them on the lecture circuit. Harris did make the trip. Twain and Cable did all they could to entice Harris by explaining the rich rewards he would receive from sales of his books and lecture fees.

---

31 D. B. Parker, "Sam Jones (1847–1906)," *New Georgia Encyclopedia*, www.georgiaencyclopedia.org/articles/arts-culture/sam-jones-1847-1906.

32 Turner, *George W. Cable.*

33 Hobson, *Tell about the South*, 120.

34 Turner, *George W. Cable*, 293–96.

Yet Harris, almost pathologically shy and a stammerer, would not assent. He spent a second day with Twain in Cable's study with the two of them reading to Cable's and his sister Nettie's children. When asked to follow their lead, Harris refused, to the keen disappointment of the children. Much later, Cable described that evening in a letter to Harris's daughter-in-law Julia. "Your father could not overcome his shyness to read in our parlor to the family circle and Mark read for him. The children were inconsolable to find Uncle Remus nothing but a White man!" (Cable and Twain often referred to Harris as "Uncle Remus.") To Julia he kindly added, "I could tell you more about your father's diffidence, which often made his friends the fonder of him."[35]

Harris did join Twain in Hartford the following year, where Twain introduced Harris to James R. Osgood. Osgood would become Harris's publisher and with it came improved marketing and sales of his books.[36] Osgood was associated with both *The Century* and *The Atlantic Monthly*. He would later be a founder of Houghton Mifflin. He was a major force in publishing. Harris and Grady, who joined the *Constitution* together as associate editors in 1876, became equally famous, if Grady was more assertive of his influence on politics and policy, state and nation.

In 1887, Gilder was showing renewed interest in Harris and asked Grady about Harris's position with the *Constitution*. Grady responded, "We have no titles at Constitution, and little degrees of rank. Joe Harris is entitled to all the honor that can be gotten out of the *Constitution*, and I am glad to see him get it even if it is through misapprehension. By the way, he is a staunch friend of the *Century*, and of you, as we all are."[37] Clearly Gilder was inquiring about Harris's status with the paper. That an eminent friend of Twain and Cable would need vetting seems strange, and Grady was always aware of his friend's estimable fame.

---

[35] Ibid., 121; Cable to Julia Harris, July 22, 1917, Joel Chandler Harris Papers, Rose Library, Emory.

[36] Bickley, *Joel Chandler Harris*, 42–43.

[37] Grady to Gilder, January 18, 1887, H. W. Grady Papers, Rose Library, Emory.

The Pages

Grady was caught between the Pages, Thomas Nelson (Richmond) and Walter Hines (Raleigh), distant cousins who helped define the era as it moved forward. Thomas Nelson Page styled himself as an advocate of the Old South; Walter Hines Page, the New. The difference was almost a quibble, but of such are squabbles made. Thomas Page had used his commencement address at William and Mary in 1887, "The Old South," to take shots at Grady's New South Address in New York the preceding December. That same year he published *In Ole Virginia*, the collection of short stories for which he is best known. In it he idealizes antebellum life. In truth Thomas Page shared similar views with Grady about "New" and "Old," Grady romanticizing the old, Page accepting with qualifications the new. Walter Hines Page, five years younger than Grady, was unequivocally aligned with the New South. Both Pages would accept ambassadorial appointments under New South president Woodrow Wilson—Walter to Great Britain, Thomas to Italy.[38] Walter had an exceptionally fine career as a writer and publisher. He was chief of *The Atlantic Monthly* for a five-year stretch at the end of the century and entered into a partnership that created Doubleday, Page, & Co. Walter's son Arthur would become a leading figure in the emerging field of public relations, the Arthur Page Society being the elite club for PR professionals today. But then that was also Grady's métier, publicity as essential to progress.

So what was the difference between old and new? Thomas Nelson Page and Henry Grady "did look in different directions—," historian Fred Hobson writes, "the one backward, the other forward—and since the mid-1880s had been clearly placed in different schools of Southern thought." Where Page saw the South as "crucified and resurrected," Grady saw it as saddled with a slavery it did not choose and liberated from it by means it fought to the last. In Grady's view, the Civil War having freed the South from slavery, all else depended on pluck, energy, and modernism.[39] The future would see it that way also.

---

[38] Hobson, *Tell about the South*, 138–39.

[39] Ibid.

The Legacy

Grady's influence on the eighties was palpable. Atlanta's historian, Franklin Garrett, called him "man-of-the-decade." The outpouring of sympathy from all over the nation that followed his death underscored his importance. Some particulars should be noted in a final assessment. He never used "nigger" in columns or speeches although he is said to have used it in casual conversation. (The author has seen its usage in one instance of Grady's correspondence, but only once and as a marginal notation without reference to anyone or explanation, the word dangled in the left-side column.) He never subscribed to White nationalism that embraced what W. J. Cash called the "Savage Ideal," a belief that assumed White superiority and the idea that lesser races, Blacks particularly, would revert to an inherent barbarism and accordingly to extinction—in brief, radical racism. Historians have labeled this kind of thinking as "regressionist thought." Grady's notions of blood inheritance came close to embracing the Social Darwinist perspective on superior and inferior races, but he never said so explicitly. He even entertained the thought that an intermingling of blood might improve the Negro race but at what cost to the "superior race," yet he would not say so with any definition. At best, he thought separation was the ideal, with the Negro free to rise to whatever level capable. At worst, he did not believe in social equality, but even there he was more prone to mince than dance.

In the fall before his death he got a glimpse of the ugly future. Lynchings in the eighties were few in the early years but began to rise later, and most lynchings were in the Southern part of the state, so they remained relatively out of sight and out of mind. Grady and the *Constitution* dismissed them casually with callous headlines like "Jerked to Jesus," "The Rope Necklace," "Dacey's Drop," "By the Neck." Even Grady's mentor in Athens, Professor Williams Rutherford, father of Miss Millie, rebuked him for such barbarisms. When Grady was twenty-seven, Rutherford wrote, "No man ever gained a reputation for a writer and established a character for greatness who wrote in the style which I am now criticizing.... My young friend you are making a grievous mistake."[40] Nor did the *Constitution* bear down on the convict-lease

[40] H. Davis, *Henry Grady's New South*, 148.

system that was truly "slavery by another name." The Reconstruction legislature adopted it as an economy measure, but that was no excuse. The convict-lease system was awful, and Grady's triumvirate profited from it. His friend Bob Alston may well have lost his life by opposing it in 1879. It bore more scrutiny than the *Constitution* gave it; moreover, incendiary headlines actively encouraged it.

Then in 1889, the issue of race relations got Grady's attention. Negroes gathered in Atlanta and Macon to say they were not content, despite Grady's insistence otherwise in speeches to Northern audiences.[41] Moreover, Republicans at the national level were showing greater interest in weighing in on issues of equality—Thomas B. Reed, John Sherman, and Henry Cabot Lodge were but the most conspicuous. For example, it was they who threatened a "Force Bill" to supervise Southern elections. Grady's message of contentment and charity between the races was ringing hollow and his trip north in December 1889 was to shout down any evidence of discontentment. That trip became more urgent by the appointment of a Republican postmaster in Atlanta, who in turn appointed an Atlanta University-qualified Black man who worked alongside a White woman in an Atlanta post office. All hell broke loose. The *Constitution* opined that "the appointment is the only one in the entire office in which the appointee was brought into intimate and direct association with a young White lady." Grady did not write the editorial, but the coarse coverage by the *Constitution* was his responsibility. Mobs assembled. Although the *Constitution* deplored the angry gatherings, Grady could not distance himself from it. His reputation was at stake. The postmaster instinctively disavowed any belief in social equality, but the damage was done.[42]

Then in East Point, south and west of Atlanta, named for the Atlanta and West Point Railroad's eastern-most terminus, an incident occurred that smacked of the radical racism to come. A Black man, Warren Powell, was lynched for the alleged rape of a White girl. A rampage followed with White marauders beating and flogging Blacks, even into their homes, with impunity. One of Grady's employees was involved in the rampage, and the horror was enough to convince Grady to fire him.

---

[41] Ibid., 151.

[42] Ibid., 153–54.

Although Grady would soon go to Boston to exalt the charity between the races once more, defending events in the South was getting harder. As Clarence Cason observed in 1935, "Southerners of a certain type like to imagine that special bonds exist between them and the Negro descendants of the plantation economy. But this bond, it must be admitted, is largely a sentimental one, for it does not always prove to be effective when the Negro needs it most."[43] Only days before Grady's death, he had tasted the future, and it was bitter. Without time left to change his message or his views, Grady died at the moment radical racism in the South asserted itself completely.

Lynchings in Georgia and the South became more frequent in the 1880s. In 1883 Georgia had only three, but by the end of the decade it had a total of fifty-one, with most of those in the last three years of the decade and most of those in South Georgia.[44] Grady could not have failed to notice the scourge of the South gaining momentum in his last years. Perhaps he continued romanticizing relations between the races, whistling in the dark, so to speak, *because* of the increasing frequency of lynchings. But as Grady prepared to board the train for Washington and on to Boston, he had some reason to believe his world was as he had imagined it before all those appreciative and adoring crowds. The world was not as he imagined it, though, and in the 1890s, lynchings more than doubled and continued at that same level over the first two decades of the twentieth century.

Grady's invitation to the Boston Merchants Association Banquet came from his friend Patrick Andrew Collins, a former Democratic congressman and soon to be mayor of Boston. Collins and Grady got to know each other by their participation in the Democratic Conventions of 1880, 1884, and 1888 (Collins presiding). Both were strong for Cleveland, and the former and future president and Grady were to be the featured speakers at the banquet. The *Washington Post* declared, "The coincidences which couple these illustrious names are of the sort that are carefully thought over a long time in advance." Grady once told Collins that Atlanta was becoming so famous that he received a card from Europe addressed simply to "Henry Grady, Atlanta," no state or

[43] Cason, *90 Degrees in the Shade*, 121.

[44] Brundage, *Lynching in the New South*, appendixes **[specific pages?]**.

country designated. To which Collins replied, "But why Atlanta? That was superfluous."[45] The Vendome Hotel was the only facility in Boston with a hall large enough for the four hundred ticketed guests who filed in on the evening of December 12, 1889.

Grady was in no condition to make the trip, much less stand the demands of a near-hour-long speech. Still, he locked himself in his home and did what he seldom did: he wrote out a complete draft. He allowed a next-door neighbor to read it, and later looking in on her, saw her teary-eyed, a sure sign he was hitting the mark.[46]

To reach Boston he commissioned a "car" from the Louisville and Nashville Railroad, and its president, Milton H. Smith, was on board. Others in his entourage were Howell and Hemphill from the *Constitution*; Rufus Bullock, the reconstructed Reconstruction governor; Samuel and John Inman; his old classmate Marion Verdery; Patrick Calhoun, railroad baron and grandson of John C. Calhoun; and a *Constitution* reporter, among others. In all, there were fourteen making the trip to Boston.

Grady was not well. He had fainted only days before as a cold grew worse. His wife and a homeopathic doctor urged him not to go, but they relented to his ebullient spirit. The message was too important. He and Collins had agreed it would be the "Negro Problem in the South." President Benjamin Harrison's administration at the urging of Boston's own Henry Cabot Lodge was agitating for voting rights with what Southerners called a "Force Bill" to oversee elections in the South. It reverted to a theme Grady addressed often, and he was headed to the home of abolition to put it to rest. In the end the Lodge bill made no difference to Blacks' voting rights. Southern states used grandfather clauses, literacy tests, and poll taxes to eliminate Black voters—ele-

---

[45] Nixon, *Henry W. Grady*, 316.

[46] The neighbor, Lucy Peel and her husband, William Lawson Peel, a prominent banker, would dominate Atlanta's music scene. One writer, observing Enrico Caruso holding court at the Georgian Terrace hotel in 1918, said, "... there it was that the ebullient tenor languished beside the one person in Atlanta who overshadowed him, Mrs. William Lawson Peel" (Williford, *Peachtree Street Atlanta*, 122).

ments all present in Mississippi's 1890 constitution, which the Supreme Court upheld in *Williams v. Mississippi*, 1898.[47]

On the train, Grady proved he could not resist being his garrulous self. Despite promising to stay quiet and recuperate, he met with former governor George S. Boutwell of Massachusetts in Washington and felt he had made progress in convincing him of the South's good intentions. He went on to New York where he was entertained, confiding to Julia that "I have been so sick I haven't had the heart to write.... I am so *tired*. That's just the feeling. If I don't brace up in Boston, I'll 'bust.'"[48] He arrived then in Boston where much was expected. He refused only one or two invitations in order to gather his strength, but he was declining rapidly. The cold, cough, and fever were intensifying, but he assembled himself for a huge reception and banquet at the Vendome. How could he manage it? How could he even speak? But he did with spectacular results.

One more time he was at his oracular best. The words flowed; the pitch was perfect. The audience burst into twenty-nine ovations. The dais was weighted with the most impressive cast, Cleveland the heaviest on one side of the president of the association, Grady on the other. Others included the governor of Massachusetts, Oliver Ames; Grady's friend Patrick Collins; Leverett Saltonstall; William E. Russell; Andrew Carnegie; John Lowell; and others, all reeking of New England rectitude. President Jonathan Lane read a letter from James Russell Lowell, who expressed his regrets at being unable to attend "a dinner where distinctions of party are sunk in the common interest of patriotism which we all share together."[49] The sickly Grady rose to the occasion. Ovations interrupted his stentorian speech. Still he kept reaching

[47] A Southern White Democrat would later settle the issue. On March 15, 1965, President Lyndon Johnson entered the House of Representatives for his most important civil rights speech. In it he said, "There is no Negro problem. There is no Southern problem. There is no Northern problem. There is only an American problem. And we are met here tonight as Americans—not as Democrats or Republicans—we are met here as Americans to solve that problem." See R. White, *Republic*, 635.

[48] Grady to Julia from New York and Boston, December 10 and 12, H. W. Grady Papers, Rose Library, Emory; Nixon, *Henry W. Grady*, 318.

[49] Nixon, *Henry W. Grady*, 319.

deeper into his rhetorical reserves. He swept all before him, a spectacular last performance. Eleven days remained.

Death is often foreshadowed by premonition. Earlier that fall Grady had made a jocular reference about subscriptions to the weekly *Constitution*, saying that when they "began to flow in at the rate of two thousand a day, he wanted to die." On the return trip from Boston, Grady received a telegraph from his business manager, saying, "more than two thousand subscribers had been received the day before."[50]

A night after the Boston speech, he was at Plymouth Rock to absorb the nation's history. Hatless, he teetered between the cold winds and a fevered brow. He was plunging into pneumonia from which he would not recover. Arriving in Atlanta on Tuesday, December 17, he could not walk and was assisted from the platform. Six days remained. Not until Sunday, December 22, did Atlantans begin to realize his illness might prove fatal. On that Sunday morning, Mrs. William Lawson Peel, the woman who had teared up on reading his manuscript for the Boston speech, now read to him from Bishop Haygood's oration for Jefferson Davis's memorial service. (Davis died two weeks before, December 6.) When she reached Haygood's closing words, "And the little children cried in the streets," Grady wept softly then repeated the phrase "And the little children cried in the streets." They were his last words.[51] Grady lapsed into a coma and died the next morning at 3:40. Services were on Christmas Day, his favorite day of the year. His body was placed in a mausoleum at Oakland, later to be removed to West View where the memorable of his generation would find their resting places, most much later.

The Boston speech provided a punctuation mark for Grady's legacy. He had said it all before, but the occasion in the city of Channing, Phillips, and Garrison gave it added moment. He was back to the "you're as bad as we are" argument, if a bit more artfully. The Red Man had been exterminated; the Yellow Man put under forced contracts with no future. Yet the South, saddled with six million Blacks with an arbitrary decree that they be equal in all respects, despite their savage

---

[50] Joel Chandler Harris, *Life of Henry W. Grady*, 66.

[51] Mrs. Peel in *Constitution*, May 24, 1921 (Grady's seventy-first birthday); Nixon, *Henry W. Grady*, 329–30.

and cannibalistic beginnings. "The slave-ships of the Republic sailed from your ports—the slaves worked in our fields." "You will not defend the traffic, nor I the institution." The races in the South, almost equal in numbers (not close but substantial, almost two to one White, except in states like Mississippi and South Carolina where Blacks were a majority), "but terribly unequal in intelligence and responsibility," Grady honed in on the audience's prejudices against all immigrants and the politics they generated—ward heelers in Brooklyn and New York, the Tammany regime. "It matters not that no two races, however similar, have lived anywhere at any time on the same soil with equal rights in peace!" Moreover, the North brooked "no delay—a rigor that accepts no excuse—and a suspicion that discourages frankness and sincerity." All assembled knew their own suspicions about "others" and aliens. Grady knew his audience.

Grady then turned to the South's reemergence:

> We give to the world this year a crop of 7,500,000 bales of cotton [near his prediction of 8 million by 1890, which it achieved], worth $45,000,000, and its cash equivalent in grain grasses and fruit. This enormous crop could not have come from the hands of sullen and discontented labor.... For every Afro-American agitator, stirring the strife in which he alone prospers, I can show you a thousand negroes, happy in their cabin homes, tilling their own land by day, and at night taking from the lips of their children the helpful message their State sends them from the schoolhouse door.

He waxed on about schools, however hollow the promise. He even defended the penitentiary system, saying "60 percent of prosecutors [*sic*; likely meaning "offenders"] are negroes, and in every court the negro criminal strikes the colored juror, that white men may judge his case." What fevered brow could conjure such a case! His numbers, however generated, in no way sustained the truth of reality, a cruel and unusual system of incarceration and punishment. No wonder New England newspapers picked at faults in his arguments, despite general acclamation.

Then Grady moved to his traditional "mote in the eye" theme, the argument *tu quoque*, that the North was just as bad. "Lawless men may ravage a county in Iowa and it is accepted as an incident—in the South a drunken row is declared to be the fixed habit of the community," he said. "We might as well claim that the union was ungrateful to the colored soldiers who followed its flag, because the Grand Army post in Connecticut closed its doors to a negro veteran, as for you to give racial significance to every incident in the South." These sentiments were not likely to have drawn ovations, whatever the number claimed, except as Grady may have extemporized lines beyond his text. But Grady turned back to meat and text for his elevated audience, asking "when will the black cast a free ballot? When ignorance anywhere is not dominated by the will of the intelligent…." Grady then declared that voting in the South, far from being suppressed exceeded that of New England states, even Massachusetts. What the South considered an eligible vote might well have skewed his numbers. The South was well-known for suppressing Black votes through such methods as the "eight-ballot box law" in South Carolina and similar measures in other states. South Carolina created one district, the seventh on the coast, to assure that all six other congressional districts went "White," with that state's majority Black population crammed into one, the seventh. (Gerrymandering continues on today in the South and in certain other rogue states like Pennsylvania and Wisconsin albeit under the Republican banner with the courts only recently calling a halt to some of it.)

Finally, Grady returned to romanticizing the relationship between Blacks and Whites in the South. "The love we feel for that race you cannot measure nor comprehend," he claimed. He then used his own father's death to describe the loyalty of slave to master.

> I see a slave, scuffling through the smoke [of Petersburg] winding his black arms about the fallen form, reckless of the hurtling death…. Then finally his father speaks from the grave, saying, "Follow him! Put your arms about him in his need, even as he puts his about me. Be his friend as he was mine." And out of this new world—strange to me as to him, dazzling, bewildering both—I follow! And may God forget my people—when they forget them!

To Grady's credit, he never identified the fallen soldier as his father. He could have with effect, but Grady was also a man of uncommon judgment, eschewing an opportunity for self-aggrandizement to make a larger point.

Nothing has been more despicable than how Whites almost universally regarded Blacks in the nineteenth century. Whites asserted themselves as charitable, even kindly, while "willing to destroy assertive Blacks as they had exterminated the Red Man."[52] Neither people of color nor immigrants of various stock (largely Irish and Italian, often not considered White) were granted protections. This attitude now reaches into the current presidential administration's preference of Nordic immigrants over, as Donald Trump says, immigrants from "shithole" African nations.[53] Color of skin and place of origin historically have driven feelings of alienation and antagonism despite the mitigating success of the mid-twentieth-century civil rights movement.

Following classical allusions to Hamilcar and Hannibal, Grady closed with five requests: The first three were patience, confidence, and sympathy. The fourth request was to "give us your sons as hostages. When you plant your capital in millions, send your sons that they may help know how true our hearts are and may help to swell the Anglo-Saxon current until it can carry without danger this black infusion." The fifth request was loyalty: "This hour little needs the loyalty that is loyal to one section and yet holds the other in enduring suspicion and estrangement. Give us the broad and perfect loyalty that loves and trusts Georgia alike with Massachusetts—that knows no south, no north, no east, no west; but endears with equal and patriotic love every foot of our soil, every State in our Union." The last line would appear on the statue erected in his honor two years later.

Only Cable among the progressives, perhaps two in all, but no more, would demur. Cable wrote seven stanzas, two of which are summative:

> There wasn't a line, good sirs, bless ye,
> Of all that he chose to address ye,
> That touched the one point
> Where *his* South's out of joint
> For it wasn't his wish to distress ye….

---

[52] Ayers, *Thin Line of Freedom*, 437–37**[check page range]**.

[53] Josh Dawsey, "Trump derides protections for immigrants from 'shithole' countries," *Washington Post*, January 12, 2018; Alan Fram and Jonathan Lemire, "Trump: Why allow immigrants from 'shithole countries'?" APNews.com, January 11, 2018.

There's a day coming fast to the light, man,
When the Law shall appraise each upright man
Not by skin nor by birth
Nor by custom, but *worth*
And assure him the rights of a white man.[54]

The Years Out

Events and Grady's successors do not define him, but they do measure the temper of his times and how he sought to influence the future. In order, the Cotton States and International Exposition of 1895, the Atlanta race riot of 1906, the Leo Frank case 1913–1915, the revival of the Ku Klux Klan, and the combustible race riots that spread across the nation in 1919—each reflects the radical elements of racism that overwhelmed a central theme of Grady's New South—that left to its own charitable devices, the White South would resolve race relations to mutual satisfaction. Instead White nationalism trumped reason and radicalized rather than rationalized. He had glimpsed it in the East Point lynching and riot, but historians agree the 1890s were the advent of a White nationalism with a "savage ideal" that looked to the reduction, subjugation, and subsequent elimination of African Americans.

Into these circumstances stepped Booker T. Washington, who used Grady's platform to stop, in Wall Street terminology, a "free-fall" in race relations by establishing a "floor" from which Blacks could rebuild. The occasion would be the Cotton States and International Exposition. Piedmont Park was the obvious location, but having the expo at the park would be costly. Because a federal subvention would be essential, a delegation appeared before "Uncle" Joe Cannon, chairman of the House committee that would hear the appeal for funding. The cranky Cannon asked how many states produced cotton. When the answer came back "ten or twelve," the speaker asked why then must the whole nation support it? Atlanta's congressman, Leonidas F. Livingston, proved nimble. "Mr. Chairman," he said, "this exposition is for the benefit of all those who grow cotton and all those who wear cotton." Cannon had his answer, but another congressman, General William

[54] Turner, *George W. Cable*, 247–48.

Cogswell of Massachusetts, who led the first contingent of Sherman's army to reach the center of Atlanta, said, "If I stand alone, there is one voice and one vote that will give Atlanta any reasonable assistance from the General Government. And so, all hail to her in her grand and what I believe will be successful exposition."[55]

One other appearance before the committee cinched it. The 1893 Columbian Exposition in Chicago had no Negro exhibition hall, and the South in general and now Atlanta in particular had some convincing to do. So the delegation put out a call for two African Methodist Episcopal bishops and one Black educator, Booker T. Washington, to testify. Summoned hastily by telegram, they went before the committee with only fifteen minutes' notice. Their excellent presentations had the desired effect, and accordingly Congress approved $200,000 for a government building on the exposition grounds. This was in mid-May 1894.

Soon five hundred crew members, including Fulton County convicts, were preparing the grounds—grading, planting, and expanding a pond that would become Lake Clara Meer, where youngsters would "shoot the chutes" with miniature railcars plunging into the waters below to their delight. The main entrance to the exposition would be on 14th Street. Soon the park began to take on the configuration it maintains in large measure today. The Piedmont Driving Club was already a going concern, but transformation lay ahead. The buildings were to be of gray wood and glass topped by soft green shingles. The committee established that buildings would not have galleries and would thereby have straight-line uniformity. The midway featured popular attractions: Rocky Mountain ponies, monkey paradise, ostrich farm, Indian village, Rolstair's illusions as living pictures (for the first time visitors would see pictures in motion), Chinese village, beauty show, German village, Vaudeville, animal arena, and the water chutes. States and industries built exhibit halls.

The Negro Building was just off the Jackson Street entrance. Although the organizers had offered Booker Washington complete authority over it, he delegated it to others. A Negro contractor from La

---

[55] Garrett, *Atlanta and Environs*, 2:319–21.

Grange, Georgia, built it and featured, as Washington wished, the accomplishments of African Americans from 1865 to 1895. On President's Day, Grover Cleveland made special purpose to visit the exhibit, as did numerous other dignitaries. Architect Elsie Mercer, of Pittsburgh, Pennsylvania, designed the Women's Building, an impressive structure and the center of much planning and attention from White Atlanta women, who raised $35,000 to build it. Just across from the Japanese Village, the Women's Building was designed in the Colonial Renaissance style. It contained departments representing almost every art and industry in which women engaged. It also featured women speakers from across the country. The Fine Arts Building, in which Grady had taken a personal interest and commissioned his friend Horace Bradley to direct, contained sculptures and paintings by leading artists. Henry Ossawa Tanner, African American artist formerly of Atlanta and then Paris, exhibited his painting in the Negro Building.[56]

Opening Day, September 18, was spectacular, including spectacularly hot. It began with the longest military parade in memory, interspersed by carriages filled with governors, diplomats, and dignitaries. Victor Herbert composed "Salute to Atlanta" for the occasion, and his orchestra performed it. The crowd roared on hearing the band strike up the "Star Spangled Banner," roared even louder when it moved to "Dixie," but there was only a whisper for "Yankee Doodle." Fortunately, platform proceedings began at sundown with President Cleveland setting off a thunderous cannonade with the press of a key from his Gray Gables library at Buzzard's Bay, Massachusetts. When the platform party entered, the tall and handsome Booker T. Washington had a front row seat. In all 25,000 sweltering but joyful people turned full attention to the speakers. Youngsters had their minds on other things like "shooting the chutes" at Lake Clara Mere.

The master of ceremonies was the Reconstruction governor Rufus Bullock, who was indeed master of the occasion. Washington rose with grace to his impressive height, and as one New York reporter wrote, "There was a remarkable figure, tall, bony, straight as a Sioux chief,

---

[56] Tanner still has three paintings in today's High Museum with a special room to salute his contributions to art. In it are his famous *Entables Fisher Folk*, *The Destruction of Sodom and Gomorrah*, and *Fez*.

high forehead, straight nose, heavy jaws and strong determined mouth, with big white teeth, piercing eyes and a commanding manner."[57] His voice was deeper than Grady's, but, like Grady's, it carried to all quarters. He had worked on the speech over the summer. When he was done, listeners might have thought Grady had written it. Washington thought four Southern Whites had the Negroes' interests at heart: George Washington Cable, Bishop Atticus Haygood, Jabez Lamar Monroe Curry, and Henry Grady. With Cable in exile and Grady gone, now there were two. He praised the "symbolic message of wisdom and kindness in Joel Chandler Harris's Uncle Remus stories."[58] So perhaps three remained. Washington had not accurately assessed the four men, but, like Grady, he acquiesced to appearances, which amounted to hope against hope.

He then proceeded to say that enfranchisement was premature because Blacks were not ready for the vote. This perspective played into the hands of White Nationalists, who had believed from the beginning that Blacks weren't equipped to vote. Grady had shared that belief; though he had said in the early days that the South could live with Black enfranchisement, he later retreated. In his metaphor of the "hand," Washington abandoned social equality, saying that in all social aspects, White and Black could be as the fingers on the hand, separate but equal, but in all things related to economic advancement for both races like the "hand," fist and all. Washington, now distanced from the aspirations and advances of Reconstruction, was conceding the emerging doctrine of "separate but equal." In his other famous (or infamous) metaphor, he said that Blacks and Whites should "drop down their buckets" where they were, Blacks to build from their emancipation purchase as freedmen in the South, Whites to embrace Southern Blacks as part of the economic fabric. Though it sounded calm and reasoned, his message was desperate. Washington called opening day of the Exposition "one for which William Lloyd Garrison, Frederick Douglas, and Henry Grady all had prayed."[59] But was it? It certainly would not play out that way.

---

[57] Norrell, *Up from History*, 123.

[58] Ibid., 86–87.

[59] Ibid., 127.

The applause for Washington was uniform and enormous. Governor Bullock hurried across the platform and shook his hand enthusiastically. The fairest White women in Georgia threw flowers. Washington's message was what Whites of the Grady class wanted to hear. Clark Howell, Grady's successor as editor, leapt to the podium and proclaimed "the beginning of a moral revolution in America." It was a platform, he said, on which "whites and blacks can stand with full justice to each other." But as with a receding tide, the sands were washing away. Grady's immediate successors, if only as chimera, did not share his sympathies. Their racial feelings were coarser, certainly less optimistic. They too headed toward radical conclusions. Washington himself had become delusional. In the next day's *New York World*, "he [Booker T. Washington] invoked Henry Grady, a symbol of the white South's acceptance of Blacks as well as the North's acceptance of white authority over southern race relations, a reminder that some whites rejected the White nationalists' racial antipathy."[60] Although Washington won the plaudits of his soon-to-be enemies in the Black community—even W. E. B. Du Bois applauded his accomplishment in Atlanta. The praise would not last long, but for now Washington was still leader of the Black nation. Moreover, Blacks knew that nothing would change the fact that walls were closing in on them. Reality invited acquiescence.

In 1899, the White citizens of Richmond County, Augusta, Georgia, decided they could not afford three high schools: one for White boys, one for White girls, and one for Blacks. So they collapsed the Black high school into a grade school for all Black children. Black parents appealed all the way to the Supreme Court under the "separate but equal doctrine." In *Cumming v. Richmond County*, the court ruled that it was a matter of local appropriations and therefore a "local" matter. John Marshall Harlan, who had entered the eloquent dissent against *Plessy v. Ferguson,* wrote the opinion. No justice dissented.[61] Freedom's promise was a voided check. Grady's promise, even if such it was at the end, was also nullified. White nationalists now had a free hand.

---

[60] Ibid.

[61] Kluger, *Simple Justice*, 83.

With Grady's demise, the *Constitution* itself had changed. Although Grady had earned for the most influential paper in the South "a reputation for sectional and racial enlightenment," the paper "now reflected the typical bigotry of white-owned southern newspapers in the 1890s." Clark Howell, Evan's son, who succeeded Grady, had a progressive spirit but was blind on race. Bill Arp, without Grady's restraining influence, reverted to crude racial depictions in his otherwise humorous columns. Joel Chandler Harris, who left the *Constitution* in 1900, remained thoughtful and creative. In a letter to Andrew Carnegie asking support for his *Uncle Remus Magazine*, Harris said, "I think its success will mean more to the whole south, white and black, than any work of purely local philanthropy." He pledged to dedicate his magazine to "gentle persuasion" and "the negro question, which is also the white man's question."[62] John Temple Graves, who would soon leave the *Constitution* for other opportunities (eventually the up-start Atlanta *Georgian* in 1906) remained hard-core on race. In August 1903, he even went to New York's Chautauqua and advocated openly for lynching.[63] The *Constitution* drifted with the South's acknowledgement and acceptance of Reconstruction's total surrender, embracing crude depictions of African Americans and inured to their suffering.

Not that instinctive racism required "thinking," but Social Darwinism and a blossoming eugenics movement buoyed it and provided scientific pretext, not that the South needed a pretext for its "savage ideal," which held that so-called inferior races were doomed to extinction—the sooner the better. No regard need be given to their education, much less betterment. Nor was the animus limited to Blacks. The famed American anthropologist Daniel Garrison Brinton described the Celts in 1890 as having adverse mental traits: they were "turbulent, boastful, alert, courageous, but deficient in caution, persistence and self-control. They never have succeeded in forming an independent state, and are a dangerous element in the body politic of a free country." The Irish were thus characterized by race even though DNA evidence

---

[62] November 2, 1907, delivered by hand from son Julian, reel 4, Joel Chandler Harris Papers, Rose Library, Emory.

[63] *New York Times*, 1903; *The Chautauquan* 38 (September 1903–February 1904): 184; see also pg. 12 (catalog.hathitrust.org/Record/000541248).

now proves Ireland was never settled by Celts. This noxious view confirmed turn-of-the-century conclusions about the unfitness of Irish for democracy.[64] Brinton, educated at Yale and at the Philadelphia College of Medicine, advanced theories of scientific racism, observing that the characteristics of "races, nations, tribes…supply the only sure foundations for legislation, not *a priori* notions of the rights of man."

Nathaniel Southgate Shaler at Harvard, following his mentor Louis Aggassiz, supported "polygenism," a theory of human origins often used to support racial discrimination. In 1884, Shaler wrote on "The Negro Problem" for the *Atlantic Monthly*, claiming that Black people freed from slavery were "like children lost in the wood, needing the old protection of the strong mastering hand." In its absence, he argued, Blacks would revert to their "animal nature." American slavery, he concluded, was "infinitely the mildest and most decent system of slavery that ever existed."[65] No Old South advocate could have put it more concisely. Not even the most progressive thinkers of the nineteenth century slipped the surly bonds of "science," although from their own personal observations some got close.[66]

The equivocal Grady had a softer message for his audiences in New York and Boston. No doubt aware of claims that the Negro was a brute and, without masters, headed for extinction, he never said it himself. He walked to the edge of the idea with the notion that culture was a blood inheritance. Instead, he won his Northern audiences by affirming that the South was better without slavery and that the promise of a rising tide of prosperity would lift all boats, if separately. He was unapologetic in those appearances about White supremacy, and his audiences were of the same mind. He had little difficulty in assuring them of a charitable adjustment for Blacks if left to White Southerners. However, stern reality was that in the decade between Grady's speech in New York and Booker T. Washington's in Atlanta, mobs lynched over a thousand Blacks and some two hundred Whites.[67] The violent were bearing it away, and in another ten years Atlanta would experience an eruption.

---

[64] *Atlanta Journal Constitution*, March 20, 2016.

[65] Shaler, "The Negro Problem," 697–98.

[66] See also Gutman, *Black Family*, 531–44.

[67] Egerton, *Speak Now Against the Day*, 38–39.

Charles Darwin

Room must be made here for Darwin. As retrograde and racialist as was thinking of the nineteenth century, one man stood out. In the same years that Sherman learned soldiering, 1836–1842, Darwin evolved his notion of the origin of species. His return from the *Beagle*'s second voyage, 1836, led him to six years of fructifying thought, and thus *Origin*, which would not be first published until 1859. Darwin detested slavery, and his observations of the four Fuegian "savages" on his journey to Tierra del Fuego convinced him that the term "savage" belied the common human structure of the brain. The brain was not condemned by race or ethnicity to what Europeans called savagery but rather was shaped by environmental circumstances. The Fuegian was as capable by brain structure to be European as the European to savagery, as so defined. Thus, comparable humanity for all in the species.

It was a remarkable insight for the nineteenth century, shared by virtually no one until the twentieth century stumbled upon cultural relativism, and even then, there was heated religious resistance. Darwin was in the process of overthrowing nineteenth-century Anglican conservatism that had dominated England and the Anglo-American world. Gladstonian liberalism was picking up from it, but not fully there. Perhaps John Stuart and Harriet Taylor Mill were zeroing in, but it was Charles Darwin's scientific observations that made it possible for the revolution to come.

Darwin was not alone. It was simmering. His grandfather Erasmus's poem prefigured the future:

> Organic Life beneath the shoreless wave.
> Was born, and nurs'd in Oceans pearly caves;
> First forms minute, unseen by spheric glass,
> Move on the mud, or pierce the watery mass;
> These, as successive generations bloom,
> New powers acquire, and larger limbs assume;
> Whence countless groups of vegetation spring,
> And breathing realms of fin, and feet, and wing.[68]

---

[68] R. W. Clark, *Survival of Charles Darwin*, 25.

The future cometh, and others moved toward it. He was not alone, but he would be singular in his early scientific expression of common origins.

Others prefigured it too, but Darwin perfected it. Although Darwin had essentially arrived at his theory by 1842, he would not publish it until 1859, prompted in part by Alfred Russel Wallace's coming to similar conclusions by 1858. Both credited the other, but Wallace conceded that Darwin had done the hard science and deserved the pedestal—a rare concession in intellectual history. From 1859 on Darwin would revise the work virtually every year until 1864. When *Origin* and the theory of natural selection finally appeared, both would change the world forever. Darwin had feared the religious pushback, which may have contributed to the anxiety of his long battle with bad health, possibly Chagas disease, caused by parasites picked up in South America.

In 1838, he married his cousin Emma Wedgewood, daughter of Josiah Wedgewood II and heir to her family's fortune. Given Darwin's father's financial well-being, the couple lived comfortably for the rest of their lives. It was a loving marriage, and they had seven children and lived the country life in Down House, just southeast of London for the remainder of their days. Before his death he was honored as one of the world's greatest scientists and was buried in Westminster Abbey.

Social Darwinism would come back to stalk Darwin in his last years. A phrase first used by Herbert Spencer in 1851, "survival of the fittest" was then used by industrial and financial titans to justify their success, especially in America. Darwin's prestige attached the phrase to his name as it became shorthand for capitalism's justification that to the financially successful goes the title of "fittest." William Graham Sumner would become a Social Darwinist, but he was by no means the only apostle. Although it is not clear whether Darwin endorsed the social applications of survival of the fittest, he at least leaned in the direction by never completely abandoning Victorian notions of elitism. For example, he believed that the Caucasian races of Europe would inevitably defeat the lesser Turks. What this belief may indicate is that Darwin was not able to "think through into human terms the exploitation of the natural laws [the social application] that he believed to be self-evident." "The second," noted by a biographer, "which Darwin stressed more fully elsewhere, was that 'the fittest' were not necessarily the strongest or the most brutal but those who were able to adapt to new circumstances."[69] Indeed, by the end of the century, evolutionists were beginning to think that community rather than conflict most influenced the survival of the fittest. In the twentieth century, E. O. Wilson would elaborate its cooperative side in his theory of sociobiology.[70]

Grady railed against atheism but never mentioned Darwin.[71]

1906, the Fire Next Time

On January 1, 1906, a county in Georgia was named for Henry W. Grady. A year later, one in Oklahoma would bear his name. Otherwise, 1906 was an awful year. It began with a spectacular fire in Piedmont Park, where ten years before Atlanta's great exposition cast the city in radiance. By the time a Fulton County employee who lived nearby discovered the fire, the New York Building was completely engulfed, and the Fine Arts Building, of which Grady's friend Horace Bradley had made a showcase, was going up in flames. The nearby Piedmont Driving Club was so damaged by water and fire that it had to be completely rebuilt. Then in April news spread quickly about a disastrous earthquake in San Francisco. These events were but harbingers of how terrible 1906 was going to be.

Whatever their rivalries, Atlanta's editors were peas from the same pod. "The Clark Howells and James Grays, the Hoke Smiths and Joseph Browns—all the men who ran the Atlanta newspapers—were, if not brothers in blood, brothers in the same larger faith." They attended the University of Georgia before it had a journalism school, dated girls from the Lucy Cobb Institute, on whose "ornately carved verandas many a romance had bloomed," then proceeded to marry "each other's sisters and cousins" and bury "each other's fathers." Although they "might spar in print and hate for life," it rarely threatened their "rigidly ordered world." They were "sons of the true South."[72]

Trouble began with a gubernatorial campaign that centered on

[69] Ibid., 207.

[70] Wilson, *Naturalist.*

[71] *Constitution*, 1881; Joel Chandler Harris, *Life of Henry W. Grady*, 230–37.

[72] Oney, *And the Dead Shall Rise*, 41.

disfranchising African American voters. The candidates were Hoke Smith, former owner and editor of the *Atlanta Journal*, and Clark Howell, editor of the *Constitution*. Despite a lineage that linked them both to the New South, it turned into a vicious campaign of sound and fury over the Negro vote. Howell thought a constitutional amendment eliminating Blacks' right to vote, which Smith favored, was unnecessary and would only invite outside censure. However, the *Constitution*'s editor was no less vociferous in opposition to the Negro vote. Howell said that Smith's measure would draw Blacks "out of the cotton patch and into the negro colleges," where they would become "bow-legged with the burden of carrying their books to school." He warned that "whenever the nigger learns his [hic], haec, hoc, he right away forgets all about gee-whoa-buck."[73] (Whether Howell intended a pun with the Latin "hoc"—pronounced *hoke*—is not known, but probable.)

With Tom Watson's support, Smith won by a comfortable margin, but the campaign generated rhetorical outrage aimed directly at Atlanta's African American community. Smith had grown up in Chapel Hill, North Carolina, where his father was a professor of modern languages, so he likely got Howell's pun on "hoc." He took most of his education from his father and moved to Atlanta in 1872 at age seventeen, passing the bar examination in 1873. He became a highly successful personal injury lawyer, taking cases mostly from railway workers, which encouraged his lean toward Populism, but for the most part he was a solid New South citizen, presiding over county and state Democratic conventions. He acquired the *Journal* in 1887. A big Grover Cleveland supporter, he served during Cleveland's second term (1893–1897) as secretary of the interior. Being a Gold Democrat, he swallowed hard to support William Jennings Bryan and his Populist running mate Tom Watson in 1896. Now he was in lock-step with Watson for the gubernatorial campaign, aiming to corral up-country Georgia independent Democrats and rural votes more generally.

The hated press and politics were not solely responsible for Atlanta's race riot. White feminist reformers also saw Black men as roadblocks to reform. Rebecca Felton had long charged that the few White men who supported Blacks at the polls encouraged them to think of

[73] Norrell, *Up from History*, 338.

themselves as equals elsewhere. Also in lock-step with Tom Watson, she believed that disfranchisement and Prohibition would spare women the threat of Black beasts. Simultaneously a huge Prohibition campaign was being waged yet again in Atlanta with its principal target Decatur Street where bars, called dives, catered to Black men. These dives were reputed to have pictures of naked White women (likely true), which was thought to further encourage bestial instincts. Moreover, Black males arriving from Georgia farms found themselves vastly underemployed, with the best manufacturing and skilled jobs going to arriving Whites. Thus, African Americans developed a street culture and they acquired some mobility with Atlanta's streetcars where their presence made White passengers uncomfortable. Historian Glenda Gilmore found that upper crust Blacks viewed young Blacks as "corner loafers" and "street dudes."[74] African American females more often found domestic employment that led to "toting," the ability to bring food home from where they worked, which helped confirm the stereotype held by Whites that Black men were "shiftless."

Rebecca Felton was not alone. Frances Willard of the Women's Christian Temperance Union, "connected reform with Anglo-Saxons and white evangelical Protestants and corruption with liquor, blacks, Mormons, and immigrants." She considered Blacks "ignorant" and "voters who were tools of the liquor interests." She urged them to go back to Africa. She was equally vehement against women's suffrage.[75] Even Susan B. Anthony and Elizabeth Cady Stanton of the National Woman's Suffrage Association agreed "that suffrage for black men ensured the rape and abuse of white women."[76]

Another point of offense for Atlanta's Whites was that some African Americans were achieving notable success. Entrepreneur Alonzo Herndon and others plied various trades from barbering to barkeeping; there were a handful of African American physicians as well as other professionals such as college faculty members at Atlanta University, Clark College, Atlanta Baptist Female Seminary, and Atlanta Baptist College; thus an upper strata of Black professionals evolved that Whites

---

[74] Gilmore, *Gender and Jim Crow*, 76.

[75] R. White, *Republic*, 629; see also Gilmore, *Gender and Jim Crow*, 49.

[76] Newman, *White Women's Rights*, 56–63.

did not like either. In addition to his three barber shops, Herndon would found and eventually head the Atlanta Life Insurance Company, thereby earning a true fortune.

The tinder was set. The spark came on Saturday, September 22, 1906—eleven years and a week after Booker T. Washington's Atlanta speech. Farmers who filled the wagon-yards in the city were coming to shop for their weekly provisions—and, likely, to drink. The day was hot and sultry, when at about five o'clock newsboys ran through the streets reporting an attempted assault on a White woman. Within another four hours, three more assaults were reported, each resulting in lurid headlines. (Papers cranked out new editions with each alleged assault.) White men and boys started gathering for harangues that urged action, and a violent rampage soon started. Blacks were chased, surrounded, beaten, and slashed, often to death. Two barbers (not in one of Herndon's three barbershops as some accounts have it) did not defend themselves and were brutally murdered, their bodies tossed at the foot of Grady's statue at Marietta and Forsyth; another body was dumped there later. No one has determined the motive for placing the bodies at Grady's feet, whether it was purely symbolic or merely convenient is unknown. The statue was near the barbershop, and some accounts have the bodies placed "within the shadow of Grady's statue." It was certainly a prominent spot.[77]

At the height of the violence on Saturday night, Atlanta mayor James G. Woodward mounted a box at the corner of Decatur and Pryor, where it had all started, and begged the crowd to go to their homes quietly. "I beseech you," he said, "not to cause this blot on the fair name of our most beautiful city. What you may do in a few minutes of recklessness will take Atlanta many years to recover from." Besides, the mayor's own reputation for drunkenness was well known. While they appeared to listen with respect, they paid no heed and resumed their deadly purpose. On Tuesday the president of the Chamber of Commerce, Samuel D. Jones, exclaimed "for God's sake, let us be men! Here in one night the reputation of our fair city has been blasted and we are held up to the scorn of the world by the brutal murders committed by a cowardly mob. If we allow the helpless and dependent race

[77] Much of what is drawn is from Garrett, *Atlanta and Environs*, 2:195–205.

to be slaughtered before our eyes we cannot face God in judgment!" That last thought is exactly how Grady would have put it. Jones headed a relief committee to cover funeral expenses, wages lost to injury, and other needs of Atlanta's cowed and grieving Black community. He also went to Black churches. It seemed that all Atlanta's leaders recoiled at the wreckage caused by years of hateful speech and sensationalized accounts of Black bestiality.[78]

Alonzo Herndon did lose a bootblack, a disabled boy who was chased, caught, and beaten to death. The mob tired in the wee hours of Sunday morning but resumed late Monday, September 24, by attacking the Brownsville section, just south of the Black colleges. Another four were killed and numerous others seriously injured. By then some 3,000 troops had been called up from nearby armories to quell the violence, but instead some joined the rampaging gangs. By Tuesday things quieted down. The precise death toll is unknown, but it was probably between twenty-five and forty. Some accounts put it much higher, perhaps a hundred. The number of injured ran much higher, with no accurate way of determining because most were cared for in homes and churches, with only some in hospitals. Atlanta would be long in recovering. Shock set in among conservative Whites as did joy and elation among radicals. Not only had they defiled Grady's statue, but the image of Atlanta as capital of the New South, which he had brilliantly articulated twenty years before at Delmonico's in New York, would not rise again for at least two generations.

Blacks gathered in churches and homes to arm themselves and prepare for their defense. Authorities, who learned of such a meeting in Brownsville on the evening of Monday, September 24, formed a posse of seven county police and three citizens to break it up. While in route back to midtown, they were fired upon, and officer James M. Heard was shot from his horse and instantly killed. Several others were wounded. The only other White fatality was a woman who apparently had a heart attack. Even if armed, most Blacks simply took cover; no evidence exists of later retaliation. W. E. B. Du Bois was away at the time of the riot, but upon return he armed himself, determined to defend his family if disturbances threatened again. Ironically, none of the

[78] See also Merritt, *Herndons*, 83–100.

four women alleged to have been attacked were sexually molested—two were supposedly knocked to the ground, the other two allegedly peeped upon. Notwithstanding, the newspapers were wildly inflammatory.

Of interest, Black ministers decried the "dives" and seemed to attribute some of the cause to their presence. "The dives must go," declared Hugh Proctor, Alonzo Herndon's minister at First Congregational Church, saying they "are foul nests where evil birds lay their poisonous eggs which hatch out into loafers, thieves, thugs, murderers and rapists." Benjamin Davis, editor of the Black newspaper *Atlanta Independent*, avowed, "While there is no excuse for mob law, it cannot be denied that criminal idleness lies at the bottom of all the chaos and disorder." However, Du Bois may have put it best, "Whenever an aristocracy allows the mob to rule, the fault is not with the mob."[79]

Five nights after the riot ended another spectacular fire drew Atlantans to the center of the city. On a drizzly, cloudy Monday, October 1, the Western and Atlantic Railroad roundhouse and shops, dating back to the 1860s, went up in flames. Crowds gathered on the Forsyth Street bridge to watch the display. The *Constitution* described it "as one of the most picturesque fires that ever occurred in Atlanta." "The sky was overcast with clouds and the reflection from the flames lit up the entire city. Leaden clouds that had hung black and threatening over the town suddenly turned into lurid banners that rolled like banks of red fire as far as the eye could reach." The picture of Atlanta burning once more may well serve as metaphor for what it had done to its soul.

1915

Joel Williamson perceptively traced a transmutation of radical hatred. With African Americans now cowed by the conclusive determination of Whites to manifest their supreme destiny, White nationalists needed other "hidden" enemies. If the Black rapist became increasingly unavailable, other aliens became essential. Fear is the only thing that can call up rage, and who has rage without it? So an Atlanta incident in 1913 would affirm a new reality by 1915. The name Leo Frank would be its agency.[80] Born in Brooklyn, educated in engineering at Cornell,

---

[79] Ibid.

[80] Williamson, *Crucible of Race*, 222–23, 468–72; R. White, *Republic*, 629.

his moving to Atlanta in 1907 was precisely the model Grady called for when he told the Boston merchants "give us your sons as hostages." Essential to a New South was not only Yankee money but also Yankee ingenuity. The tragedy that follows defies any decent understanding of humanity. Populists, ordinary people who included those in high places at the Southern gate, robbed the region of any claim to decency.[81]

At age twenty-six, the diminutive Frank, at five feet, six inches tall, 110 pounds, with big eyes and a square jaw, looked different. He came South to head up his uncle's pencil manufacturing company. (Money anywhere in capitalism's commodity markets depended on how many needed a product, no matter how small the instrument, and lots of folks needed pencils. Henry David Thoreau's family also owned a pencil factory, which made his solitude at Walden Pond affordably comfortable.) Leo Frank did well. He was Jewish and married the daughter of a well-to-do Atlanta Jewish family. He made good money and got involved in the Jewish community, becoming head of B'nai B'rith. His future was bright until a Saturday in May 1913, when Mary Phagan, two weeks shy of fourteen, came by to pick up her wages. At twelve cents an hour, her pay was $1.20 for her last ten hours. She had dressed for Confederate Memorial Day, where two hundred veterans would march in review for the widow of Stonewall Jackson.

She was the daughter of a tenant farmer who could not make it in the cotton-crash of the early 'teens and who had moved the family first to Marietta, then to Atlanta for jobs in cotton manufacturing. Southern textile mills liked to hire rural White families, especially those with teenage daughters and even smaller children.[82] Mary wound up at the pencil factory. She was charming in every way, only recently having performed the role of the "beautiful princess" in a school play. Frank gave her the money around noon then returned to his Saturday bookkeeping until heading home for lunch. Frank spent every Saturday keeping the books. Sometime around 12:30 p.m., Mary was murdered. The night watchman who found her was first to be accused, and two days later the finger pointed to Frank. Authorities arrested him. He

---

[81] Steve Oney provides the most thorough and detailed account of the tragedy in *And the Dead Shall Rise*. See also Dinnerstein, *Leo Frank Case*.

[82] R. White, *Republic*, 418.

would not see hearth and kin again before his death two years later.

The Phagan family was the cheap labor the New South advertised, and the child labor that Asa Griggs Candler of Coca-Cola fortune and fame touted, saying, "The most beautiful sight that we see is the child at labor; as early as he may get at labor the more beautiful, the more useful does his life get to be."[83] Again, an earlier echo is found in Alexander Hamilton, who observed in his *Report on Manufactures*, "It is worthy of particular remark that, in general, women and children are rendered more useful, by manufacturing establishments than they would otherwise be."[84] The Phagan family did not see it differently and were glad the National Pencil Co. had 170 employees, mostly teenage girls, as with cotton manufacturing. "Little Mary Phagan" as she came to be known was a valued contributor to the family. Indeed, she could take care of her own entertainment that special day. Instead, the precious girl was murdered.

In a sweltering courtroom that summer, on the strength of testimony from an admitted liar, Black security man Jim Conley, twelve White men were persuaded that Frank did it. Conley himself was almost certainly the murderer, but transference was taking place in the South. The enemy was from within, looking White, but not White—a Jew. Thus, for the first time in the South, a jury took an admittedly lying Black man's testimony over a White man's, albeit a Jew. They convicted Frank and sentenced him to hang. Then, the governor, John Slaton, a distinguished Atlanta lawyer, a partner of whom helped in Frank's defense, commuted the sentence to life in prison. Slaton and his elegant wife were certain of his duty. After death threats and hostile demonstrations at the state house and at the governor's mansion, they would go into exile for the next months.

The court remanded Frank to the state prison in Milledgeville where one prisoner slashed his throat, nearly killing him. Meanwhile, twenty-five men of Marietta plotted to kill him. All twenty-five were among the foremost citizens of Mary Phagan's temporary hometown—a former governor, Joseph M. Brown, who succeeded Hoke Smith and

---

[83] Oney, *And the Dead Shall Rise*, 15–16. See also Freeman, *Behemoth*, passim. Freeman details the use of cheap young female labor in manufacturing throughout his magnum opus on the factory in American life. It continues.

[84] Chernow, *Alexander Hamilton*, 376.

preceded Governor Slaton, two judges, a minister or two, and *Constitution* editor Clark Howell's cousin, Robert E. Lee Howell, who would commit abominations on Frank's body, crushing in his face with his boot. The conspirators arranged a spectacular penitentiary break, using state officials to effect it, and grabbed Frank on the night of August 16, 1915, to drive him by cavalcade to Frey's gin in Marietta, near the site of Mary Phagan's home there. Because the kidnappers took a circuitous route to avoid detection, the midnight ride took seven hours. Frank reportedly said nothing on the journey to his execution although his captors taunted him and dangled the rope in front of him. He was dead and almost certainly knew it. The hanging was gruesome and the depredations on his body grotesque. What remained of his body was eventually sent back to his family in New Jersey where they finally laid him to rest. The "good and true" men of Marietta were satisfied; the nation horrified.

Governor Slaton, who commuted the death sentence, was in California, where the next morning, August 17, he learned of the horrific event of the day before. In an address that day before the San Francisco Center of the California Civic League, he opened with a curious remark, "I would prefer Frank to be lynched by a mob rather that he be hanged by judicial mistake." This circumlocution was his way of defending his controversial (in Georgia) decision to commute, but it no doubt caused considerable head-scratching among his California audience. Then he got to the point. He called the lynching "a consummate outrage" and said, "I believe the governor of Georgia will use all the power of the state to punish the malefactors who disgraced the state of Georgia."[85]

There would be no punishment. The Atlanta newspapers knew every conspirator involved, but their editors were themselves all "Sons of the true South." No one was identified. Silence was the true weapon for eliminating the different, the alien, the Jew, the Catholic, the Communist, as already it had silenced the Black presence. Tom Watson became the arch villain in demonizing the "different," but he had suffered a brain infarction from his early days of Black/White cooperation through the Farmers Alliance. Now he outrageously went after the Jew

[85] *Atlanta Constitution*, August 18, 1915.

Frank. By the end, it was all vitriol, which the Talmadges, Gene and Herman, would carry forward in Georgia politics, with Watson's statue guarding the entrance to the state capitol. (It has since been removed for understandable reasons, but reasons lost in the shroud of history on the Republican base of Georgia politics, the old solid South, and thus there was no protest.)

Tom Watson did earn the rebuke of one New South journalist, Tom W. Loyless. Born in Dawson in southwest Georgia in 1871, he went into journalism in the early nineties. In 1915 he was editor of the *Augusta Chronicle* and completely fed up with Tom Watson's vitriol against Catholics, Jews, and Negroes. In a three-columned editorial, reprinted in full the next day by *The New York Times*, September 13, Loyless said that Watson "has but four passions—bitterness, born of political disappointment; hate engendered by his attitude toward the world and the world's attitude toward him; exaggerated ego, causing him to seek notoriety in any and every way possible; and avarice, money to him being the greatest god of all."

Loyless was something of a hothead. He had gotten into a near duel with H. C. Hanson, of the *Macon Morning Telegraph* in 1897. Now Loyless stood with Governor Slaton and begged that the lynchers be identified and prosecuted. He named a host of distinguished Georgians who believed as he did, one of whom was the Grand Dame of the UDC, Miss Millie Rutherford. Loyless, a converted Catholic like Joel Chandler Harris, also went after Watson's rabid anti-Catholicism. Loyless attacked the Klan and began to lose support for his stands, eventually winding up as part-owner and managing editor of the *Columbus Inquirer-Sun*. He would be joined there by Joel Harris's son Julian, who took over editorial direction and by 1922 bought out Loyless, who then became general manager of the Warm Springs Inn. There he became a great pal of Franklin Roosevelt, whom in spring 1925 Harris convinced to write a half-dozen columns for the *Macon Telegraph*, where Loyless had continued as a columnist. The columns foreshadowed FDR's New Deal. Loyless died of cancer in 1926, the year Roosevelt purchased Warm Springs.[86]

---

[86] Bill Kirby, "The 30-Years War: *Augusta Chronicle* vs. Tom Watson," *Augusta Chronicle*, October 26, 2013. See also Rawlings, *Invisible Empire*, 162–64.

Only the craven haters in today's far right wing can identify with the reification and ossification of what race radicals accomplished in the early twentieth century. They also think that deep down all "right" thinking people agree with their racial beliefs. The South was marching on, finding new groups to marginalize and abuse: Jews (Leo Frank), Catholics, and immigrants generally. When *The Birth of a Nation* showed up in theaters in fall 1915, dancing visions of the enemy and a revived Ku Klux Klan merged. A cross flared on top of Stone Mountain, signaling that robed Klansmen were once again rescuing White women. The revived Klan did have a different agenda; no longer simply anti-Black, they became defenders of so-called family values as well. They went after wife-abusers, drunkards, and generally derelict fathers—actions admirable in their own way—except their leaders wound up with corruption and sex charges in the twenties more damning than today's worst revelations about wrong-doers in public office.

Edward Young "E. Y." Clarke Jr., son of the *Constitution's* second editor of the same name, became the revived Klan's prime mover. He too had been with the *Constitution* for seven years after dabbling with thoughts of the ministry but moved on to establish the Southern Publicity Association (SPA). His partner and assumed lover was Elizabeth "Bessie" Tyler, a woman of questionable reputation but with a business mind par excellence. When the revived Klan's founder, William J. Simmons, foundered (attracting only 4000 members in the first five years), Clarke, Tyler, and SPA came to the rescue. Clarke had a business plan that exploded with Klan growth not only in the South but nationally. With Clarke getting eight of every ten dollars from membership fees in the South with a different formula nationally (ostensibly for SPA expenses), the Klan grew from a meagre few to as many as five million nationwide. Effectively, Clarke and Tyler became millionaires. Chicago hosted the largest Klan rally, and Indiana had its largest per capita membership, equaled only by Oregon.

Even an exposé by Pulitzer's *New York World* in September 1921, later followed by Hearst's *New York American*, could not derail the Klan's momentum. The Atlanta papers, except Hearst's *Georgian*, did not report on the exposé, and then the *Georgian* used the *World's* report. Clarke instinctively knew that even bad publicity could be good, and by

1923 Atlanta's elite were on board. The mayor, sheriff, governor, congressman, and both U.S. senators supported the Klan. Senator Walter F. George backed off later in 1923 because the Klan financed a fellow senator in Texas, and George believed he might be called to testify. So it was sensitive. Moreover, the Klan was pouring money into Atlanta through its operations, "a new million-dollar industry within your gates" was what one reporter called it.[87] A friend of Julian Harris, Jonathan A. Manget, an Atlanta cotton merchant, wrote him in 1923, saying Atlanta's most influential citizens were in the Klan. He noted specifically the "governor-elect," the "United States senator-elect," the "congressman from the largest district in the Southeast," "several judges on the Georgia bench," the "mayor," indeed a "majority of county office holders throughout Georgia." From this Manget concluded that the only thing needed was to strip them of their masks and hoods and all would be right.[88] Whatever discomfort the Klan caused by its reputation, city fathers could afford to look the other way.

Julian Harris expressed surprise in his Columbus paper that the Atlanta press could remain silent on the KKK. In a letter to him, a woman exclaimed disappointment at his surprise, because "I was under the impression that you had an analytical mind and that you could see under the surface." She described the Atlanta papers as "ambitious" and so full of the vaunted "Atlanta spirit" that they wish to see the city as "the 'Krown Kourt' of America. They feel that it is a distinction to have the seat of Invisible Government in their city—to have an 'Emperor' with his imperial staff, and a 'Wizard' with his staff and court attaches." Noting all the dollars that were pouring into Atlanta, she found that "Clarke was now one of the largest real estate owners in Atlanta." Concluding that the above was what kept the newspapers quiet, she signed the letter "Kamelia," an uncommon female name and variant of the spelling of the camellia flower directly referring to the "kamelia" as used by Grand Wizard William Joseph Simmons and Hiram Evans in 1923 as an organizing symbol for a women's auxiliary within the Klan (which

---

[87] Scott M. Cutlip, a former dean of the Grady College, covers the rise of Clarke and Tyler in *The Unseen Power*, see especially 404.

[88] Jonathan A. Manget to Julian Larose Harris, February 21, 1923, Julian and Julia Harris Papers, box 1, folder 4, Rose Library, Emory.

became the Women's Ku Klux Klan or WKKK). The Klan often converted c's into k's for their peculiar naming practice. The original Klan also had the Knights of the White Camellia, which was a particularly virulent Klan group originating in Louisiana in the 1870s. As late as the 1930s, the Knights of the White Camellia was politically active in West Virginia, as the Klan transmogrified into militant anti-Jewish groups.[89]

The reality was that the revived Klan became even more insidious than the original group because its function and reach broadened. The original Klan stood against Blacks, but, as the new group spread nationwide, targets included any non-White population in the United States: Japanese, Chinese, and Mexicans on its Pacific rim, and redundantly Blacks also, who had already been barred from Oregon with its exclusion laws. The new Klan also functioned more like a social club than the old Klan, which primarily had formed White avenging gangs against Blacks (although in the South they remained that way also, if somewhat less so). In Indiana and Oregon, Klan members almost assumed super-majority status for the populist right.[90] They did so because they professed to be "victims" of all those to whom they were putatively superior. Their victimization came from modernism, science, urbanism, and education; i.e., liberals. Yet as "superior" (and "real") Americans, they determined to maintain all that was rightfully theirs against inferiors who would take it away. It was an irresolvable paradox, but they did not deal in paradoxes, only certainties.

E. Y. Clarke's messaging promoted the Klan's "moral leadership" as a fraternal order, endorsing what today is known as "family values." Indeed, the Klan way intended to return national virtues through a nation made great by and for Protestant Whites. The Imperial Klud (chaplain), Caleb Ridley, pastor of Atlanta's Central Baptist Church, preached that the "melting pot" was a "bastard theory" and that no

---

[89] Kamelia to Julian L. Harris, April 4, 1923, ibid. See Gordon, *Second Coming of the KKK*, 112, 118. Gordon attributes Kamelia more to Hiram Evans's effort to build the Women's KKK in 1923. See also Lichtman, *White Protestant Nation*, 76.

[90] Gordon and Lichtman offer the best overview of the revived Klan's cultural, racial, social, and religious roots and sensitivities.

right-minded Christian should subscribe to it.[91] By 1922, Clarke had become the Klan's titular head as Imperial Wizard pro tem, but in early 1923, because of personal misconduct that included sexual and financial transgressions, he had created enough opposition that the emerging leader, Hiram Evans, ousted him. Clarke attempted to establish yet another Klan, but despite one large rally in Muncie, Indiana, numbering perhaps 50,000, Clarke drifted out of sight, but not without a trail of lawsuits and prison terms for crimes that ranged from violation of the Mann Act to swindling.[92]

Later Clarke established the Monarch Publishing Company, a third-rate outfit that in 1939 published Thomas Dixon's reprise of three novels touting the early Klan and its continuing attempts to cleanse America.[93] *The Flaming Sword* centers on the 1930s and creates a frightful specter of Communists and Blacks threatening to take over. It was not a success. However, it was topical, for in the 1930s the Communist Party was perhaps the only friend Blacks had. Through its International Labor Defense, the Communist Party provided Blacks their only meaningful legal representation, as for example the Scottsboro boys and four cases in Tuscaloosa in 1933 that tragically ended in the lynching of all four Black men. Clarke's partner, Bessie Tyler, remarried, moved to California with an estimated $700,000 and died there in 1924. Clarke is thought to have died in 1949, but where and how remain unknown.[94]

---

[91] Cutlip, *Unseen Power*, 393.

[92] It made much larger claims; the Klan always touted huge numbers for its rallies (and occasionally got them), much like President Trump today.

[93] Thomas Dixon Jr., after graduating from Wake Forest, began a graduate program in political science at Johns Hopkins, where he befriended Woodrow Wilson; thus an entrée to Wilson's White House for the 1915 showing of D. W. Griffith's *The Birth of a Nation*, based on Dixon's *The Clansman* (1905). Upon seeing the film, Wilson distanced himself from its racist depictions, demurring that "Its exhibition at the White House was a courtesy extended to an old acquaintance." Dixon died in 1946 and is still listed by Wake Forest as among its most distinguished graduates.

[94] Cutlip, *Unseen Power*, 393. See ch. 14, "Clarke and Tyler: Builders of the Ku Klux Klan," and Rawlings, *Invisible Empire*, passim. Emory's Rose Library has a large collection on the revived Klan and Clarke. See also Meacham, *Soul of America*, 109.

The Klan of the 1920s, like the Tea Party of today, played to White grievances and was staunchly anti-immigrant. A former governor of Georgia and Phi Beta Kappa graduate of its university, Clifford Walker, proclaimed before a 1924 Klonvocation in Kansas City, "I would build a wall of steel, a wall as high as Heaven, against the admission of a single one of those Southern Europeans who never thought the thoughts or spoke the language of a democracy in their lives."[95] The Klan was also jobs driven because connections through Klaverns "could lead to jobs, customers, investment opportunities." As Sinclair Lewis put it in *Elmer Gantry*, the new Ku Klux Klan was an organization "of the fathers, younger brothers and employees of the men who had succeeded and became Rotarians."[96] Thus was the racism of the moment normalized. No one other than radicals or kooks could or would justify integration. After Lincoln and Grant, no American president broached the subject of equality in a serious way until Harry Truman, except perhaps, ironically, Warren G. Harding.

In 1921 Harding accepted an invitation to address a large gathering on October 26 in Birmingham, Alabama, then a city of 178,000.[97] Harding traveled by train through Charlottesville and then on to Atlanta before arriving at his destination. He was greeted there by his senatorial friend Oscar Underwood. What Harding said on that occasion left the White multitude assembled in recently re-named Woodrow Wilson Park thunderstruck. He called for educational and political equality for Blacks.

In education he was not calling for "amalgamation" (integration) but for truly equal schools and a curriculum that "would mean equality proportional to the honest capacities and deserts of the individual." In politics he said, "I would say let the black man vote when he is fit to vote and prohibit the white man voting when he is unfit to vote." He applauded Birmingham for its industrial growth but said it should lead to economic opportunity for all. The mortified Whites fell silent; the

---

[95] Meacham, *Soul of America*, 120.

[96] Gordon, *Second Coming of the KKK*, 182.

[97] Birmingham stayed close to Atlanta in population until the 1950s, when Atlanta took off as the transportation hub of the South, including airlines, and adding commerce and finance, thereby overwhelming Birmingham's industrial economy.

smaller Black contingent erupted in a joyful noise. Although nothing would come of it in the short time remaining to his presidency, he at least had reached into the heart of the segregationist South and said what they did not want to hear. He opened with a promise to speak "frankly, like it or not," and they did not. W. E. B. Du Bois praised it, with reservations only about its segregationist tone; Marcus Garvey praised it without exception. The *Birmingham Post* called it an "untimely and ill-considered intrusion."[98]

Red Summer, 1919

World War I contributed to the intense nativism and nationalism of the emerging twenties.[99] Returning Black veterans may have had a new sense of themselves, but they could not escape the racism that thrived at home, both the tortured view of the White lower classes and the discrimination of higher class Whites, who thought that because unprejudiced French women had "ruined" them, the returning veterans were a threat to White women. Moreover, the success of the Bolshevik revolution in 1917 meant the evil would be insidious, unseen but always there. The moral capital generated by war—in this case the woman's suffrage and Prohibition amendments were the dividends. African Americans would pay for it. In 1919, the "Red Summer" saw more African Americans killed in race riots than at any time to that point in the nation's history. The Tulsa riot in 1921 topped it, with numbers ranging from near forty to more than two hundred. The "Red Summer"

---

[98] Dean, *Warren G. Harding*, 125–26. Harding's opponent for the presidency was another Ohioan, Progressive Democrat James Middleton Cox, a journalist who in the 1930s would come to own the *Atlanta Georgian*. He closed it when he acquired the *Atlanta Journal* soon after. In 1950, he acquired the *Constitution* and WSB television. The *Atlanta Journal-Constitution* and WSB remain in the Cox family. Cox's running mate in 1920 was Franklin Delano Roosevelt, soon to be a part-time Georgia resident.

[99] Coincidentally, Atlanta's arguably worst fire occurred one week after the U.S. entry into WWI when on May 21, 1917, fires raced up the 4th Ward and destroyed most of the city. The *Constitution*'s May 22 headlines declared, "OVER 50 BLOCKS DESTROYED BY FLAMES / FIRE DAMAGE IS ESTIMATED AT $5,000,000."

(James Weldon Johnson's term for the 1919 riots) began in Charleston's navy yard and spread through Georgia's smaller towns and counties, reaching to Washington D.C. and Chicago. It would end in the small Arkansas county of Elaine. Only in D.C. would more Whites (five) be killed than African Americans (three). Rampaging Whites killed hundreds of Blacks in most savage ways, and although fighting back in some instances, Blacks killed fewer than twenty Whites.[100]

That summer, an African American was born on a plantation in the southern part of Grady County, just south of Cairo (pronounced Kay-row), Georgia, its county seat, and twenty miles from the afore-noted Barrow plantation in the Blowing Cave District. His name was Jack Roosevelt Robinson. In another year, he, his mother Mallie, along with three older brothers and a sister, would be on their way to Pasadena, California, joining the great migration that depopulated the South of its most valuable labor force and helped fuel the Red Summer. Police in Cairo hassled them and other relatives before allowing them to board the train. The journey took twelve days. History was made, although Jackie Robinson never found Southern California to be as hospitable with respect to race relations as his uncle promised. Still, it was not South Georgia, and he could be warmed by other suns.[101] The sad truth is that had Robinson grown up in or near my hometown of Cairo, there would have been no "Jackie Robinson."

Just a hundred miles north and over the line in Alabama, George Corley Wallace was born in the same year. He would go on to stand in the schoolhouse door at the University of Alabama in 1963, revive the American Independent Party (AIP, the Know Nothings of the 1850s), then rip working-class Democrats from the Democratic Party in the Midwest and West, especially in California where the AIP was formed in 1967. The AIP changed its name to the American Party in 1969 after Wallace had run under its banner in 1968. Wallace took some Eastern states too, eventually transforming the Republican Party by

---

[100] Tindall, *Emergence of the New South*, 151–53; Kluger, *Simple Justice*, 10–13.

[101] Rampersad, *Jackie Robinson*, 16–17 (and passim) on race relations; Wilkerson, *Warmth of Other Suns*. Title from Richard Wright's unrestored edition of *Black Boy* and used by permission.

Nixon's and Reagan's Southern strategy of garnering Wallace Democrats. Jon Meacham would say, "It was not a bad starting point for a subsequent populist candidate (Trump) who would tell voters that walls and tariffs would bring back the America they thought they had once known."[102] In Wallace country, the clerical collar also drew suspicion because it appeared all too often in civil rights marches. One vivid example is what happened to Jonathan Daniels, an Episcopal seminarian murdered in Hayneville, Alabama, while shielding fellow activist Ruby Sales.[103] Like its predecessors, Wallace's was a White Protestant movement and echoes to this day under the Trump banner.

After 1919's Red Summer, hatred entered a sub rosa zone and would wind its way out with still more brutal lynchings up to the Moore's Bridge occurrence in Walton County, Georgia, in 1946. Another forty people would be killed in the civil rights movement from Emmett Till's death in 1955 to 1968 (a third of those White sympathizers), followed by Martin Luther King Jr. and Robert Kennedy two months later, June 6, 1968. The Red Summer (1919) and the Tulsa riot of 1921 may have been the last paroxysms of mob violence against Blacks in the United States until Watts in 1965. The urban riots of the sixties arose from Black protests over conditions in their ghettos, with police and military force used to suppress them with substantial loss of life among African Americans. Although 1967 can be emphasized both for number of riots and the Detroit riot that left forty-three dead, America has experienced historically memorable years of riot-induced change: 1765, 1834, 1877, 1919, 1931, and 1965–1968 all come readily to mind.

Where does that leave Grady and the New South as progenitors of the Jim Crow era? Certainly all the elements of White supremacy and segregation were built into his new order, but it also included paternalism and charity for those African Americans he believed to have demonstrated loyalty and charity toward their masters both before and through the Civil War. Perhaps only a small question exists between

---

[102] Meacham, *Soul of America*, 249.

[103] See Mary Frances Schjonberg, "Remembering Jonathan Daniels 50 years after his martyrdom," Episcopal News Service, August 13, 2015 (www.episcopalnewsservice.org/2015/08/13/remembering-jonathan-daniels-50-years-after-his-martyrdom/).

mastery and a debt owed, but the nine thousand slaves who followed Sherman's march demonstrated a desperate preference for freedom. Human relations, built by whatever system, may create relationships that nurture. As a young boy, Grady had one servant named Isaac, whom he always called "Brother Isaac." When an elder told him he could not do that, he wailed.[104] Some systems, like slavery, are not benign, but they too disguise the day-to-day interactions and interpersonal relationships. Blacks are not to be faulted for their compromises; Whites can be faulted for their blame. Slavery was never right by system nor excused by whatever human kindness owners showed the enslaved. The modus vivendi of the New South never rectified slavery by segregation, even as it built a bridge to the future of race relations that effectively reified the harm of it.

One should remember here Sherman's remarks to Louisiana's assembled leadership before departing that state to defend the Union. To a question about his own stand on slavery, he replied that from observation he found house slaves to be treated much better than field slaves and felt that all slaves should be treated as if part of a household. He also advised that education would only improve the value of any slave. Although Sherman would not renounce slavery where it already existed and defended charges of abolitionism as lodged against his brother, he had a point, although a small one, about varying treatment of slaves. Still, the truth was that all slaves were subject to the whims and cruelties of their masters. Even in Reconstruction and after they were condemned to second class citizenship and subject to lynchings, rape, and other violence as marauding Whites strutted their White nationalism, rendering moot the promise of the three Civil War amendments.

The Myth

So why did liberals in the civil rights movement cling to Grady's New South ideology, even as emerging scholars denounced him for enlarging the improbable and promising the impossible New South. As a recent and respected scholar of Grady noted: "Though he was invoked by mid-twentieth century Southern white liberals, Grady sounded

[104] Joel Chandler Harris, *Life of Henry W. Grady*, 16.

more like Alexander Stephens"—the Confederacy's seemingly moderate vice president.[105] Fair enough, but who did Grady inspire? The truth is, his vision transcended him.

Grady appealed to whatever the nation wanted beyond the emerging radical racism in the South. His successor, Clark Howell, 1863–1936, who would become a loyal New Deal Democrat, was a stuck-in-the-mud racist. The *Constitution*'s coarsening racial views played a role in Joel Chandler Harris's resignation in 1900.[106] Harris, like Grady, never dismissed the possibility for African Americans to succeed. He was even more forward-thinking than Grady in believing them capable of higher education. Grady favored "practical education" as later advocated by Booker Washington, but he was content to leave higher education in the hands of Bishop Haygood, his favorite Methodist bishop.[107]

Joe Harris obviously influenced Grady. If Grady did not personally condemn lynchings in the pages of the *Constitution*, Harris did. Prompted by a national report of seventy-four lynchings in the decade of the eighteen-seventies, four in Georgia, he wrote, "These figures are a disgrace to the country. Judge Lynch should have no more excuse to show his head in Georgia." Harris called it "a demoralizing and dangerous form of barbarism."[108] Harris, like Grady, believed that Reconstruction created "the Negro problem." In *The Saturday Evening Post*, January 30, 1904, he wrote "the responsibility of the negro was no more than that of the child who had wandered, by accident, into the halls of legislation, and remained, pleased at the novelty of the situation, and yet wondering what it was all about." What Harris abhorred most was

---

[105] Cobb, *Away Down South*, 71.

[106] Alcoholism, which also fueled his kindness, may have been part of his reason for resigning, but Harris could not stand the *Constitution*'s new directions. Another contributing fact may have been pay. In a letter to Evan P. Howell, December 10, 1896, pledging undying fealty for his twenty years with Howell at the *Constitution*, Harris threw in a line about salary. "I have not remained at the Constitution on account of the salary attached," he wrote, "for I could have doubled my income any day during the past ten years by devoting myself wholly to literary work" (Joel Chandler Harris to Evan P. Howell, December 10, 1896, Evan Park Howell Papers, Atlanta History Center).

[107] H. Davis, *Henry Grady's New South*, 162.

[108] Julia Harris, *Joel Chandler Harris*, 102.

violence against Blacks. Following the horrific Atlanta race riot, Harris has his fictitious character, the Country Philosopher of Shady Dale (a small community just east of Eatonton, Georgia), Uncle Billy Sanders, say in his *Uncle Remus Magazine*, September 1907, "The riot has give me a whole lot of trouble." It felt like his true love "had fetched me a swipe in the face wi' a cold an' rancid mackerel.... [W]hen you-all up here let a lot of thirty-cent loafers whirl in and kill innocent niggers, [it neither] looked nor smelt like Southern chivalry."[109]

Harris died in 1908 at age sixty from complications of acute phrenitis and cirrhosis. Of his and Essie's nine children (seven born at the Wren's Nest), six lived to adulthood. He was a wonderful father and grandfather. But what he learned as a bastard child, Irish, and redheaded on the Turnwold plantation in Putnam County, made him the writer he became. His Irish paternity and flaming red hair may have made him the butt of jokes later at the *Macon Telegraph*, but it also made him most comfortable among African American workers at Turnwold. Their speech became his literary outpouring. He listened. Their language became his, and his "Uncle Remus" stories became a blueprint for children's literature from Beatrix Potter to A. H. Milne. In recent times Alice Walker, also from Putnam County, writes that he "stole a good part of my heritage," and made it "a white man's publishing commodity."[110] Toni Morrison denies that her "Tar Baby" owes anything to him, but James Weldon Johnson, Mark Twain, and a long list credit Joel Chandler Harris for listening and "getting it."

At a recent presentation in Eatonton by Julie Hedgepath Williams on her book about *Three Not-So-Ordinary Joes: A Plantation Newspaperman, a Printer's Devil, an English Wit, and the Founding of Southern Literature* (Montgomery: NewSouth Books, 2018), an African American woman stood to comment about her grandmother. The commentator said that as a child her grandmother told her all the Uncle Remus stories. As the speaker was finishing high school, she learned that Joel Chandler Harris was the author. When she told her grandmother, she

---

[109] *Uncle Remus Magazine*, September 1907, Rose Library, Emory.

[110] Walker, "Uncle Remus, No Friend of Mine," 637; Arlinda Smith Broady, "Harris became a voice of the South, not beloved by all," *Atlanta Journal Constitution*, September 23, 2016.

realized her grandmother had learned the tales from relatives in Putnam County, who had been telling those stories for years, not from the pages of Harris. The point being that Joel Chandler Harris had heard the same stories on the Turnwold plantation where he was a printer's devil for Joseph Addison Turner, editor and publisher of *The Countryman*; thus, as Harris always maintained, when it came to Uncle Remus, he was amanuensis, not author.

One should not dismiss local color writers like Cable, Twain, and Harris. They sought to listen to the language of "others." Getting the "negro patois" that infiltrated Creole was important to Cable as was Georgia coastal Black speech to Harris. They corresponded about it. In a humorous exchange between Harris and Cable in 1883, Harris insisted that it was not the "banjo" but the "fiddle" that preponderated among Blacks. Eventually Cable agreed. It was important to get details of local culture right among these authors—and their music too. Authenticity about Creole language and Black coastal language in Georgia was paramount for Cable and Harris, and thus the survivability of their literature was dependent on it. Otherwise, James Weldon Johnson would not have saluted Harris in such an effusive way. Besides, the "banjo" had become the staple of minstrelsy with all its blackface caricatures, thereby making authenticity all the more important.[111]

Julian Harris had an interesting take on his father's legendary characters. In a letter to a Philadelphia publisher seeking an adaptation he had made for publication as a play, Julian described them thusly: "Uncle Remus typifies the dependence and almost helplessness of the negro after freedom"; "Brer Fox is more or less the spirit of emancipation and commercialism"; and the "Little Boy" is the "workman, and as the New South is filled with the spirit of aggressiveness and adventure, so was the Little Boy."[112] Joel Chandler Harris would have seen it as his son did.

When Teddy Roosevelt arrived in Atlanta on October 20, 1905, in part to visit his mother's home in Roswell, his second wife, Edith,

---

[111] George Washington Cable to Joel Chandler Harris, July 28, 1884 and Cable to Julia Harris, August 5, 1917, Joel Chandler Harris Papers, Rose Library, Emory.

[112] Julian Larose Harris to Willis Sweatman, February 5, 1910, Julian and Julia Harris Papers, Rose Library, Emory.

insisted on seeing "Uncle Remus." But first there came the most touching moment of the trip. On approaching Bulloch Hall, his mother Martha "Mittie" Bulloch's home, they found gathered on the veranda the old family servants, among them a stooped Negro woman who had slowly made her way to the event. "And this," said one of the ladies, "is Auntie Grace." "Mom Grace" insisted the president, and, turning to the old woman, asked, "Isn't that true?" And Grace Wing said, "Yes sah, dis am Mom Grace, Miss Mittie's nus, and is you Miss Mittie's son?" He assured her he was and so happy to see her. Soon there was also produced "Daddy William," who could barely speak, but assured the president that he too was glad to see him.[113]

The president and first lady's visit with "Uncle Remus" happened, but how it came about is disputed. One version has Joel Chandler Harris at the reception for the president's wife at the Governor's Mansion while Roosevelt spoke at a luncheon at the Piedmont Driving Club,[114] but the other account reports that the visit took place at the president's hotel Roosevelt five days later, October 25, visited Booker T. Washington in Tuskegee. (Only four years before, Roosevelt hosted Washington at a dinner at the White House, an event that shocked the sensibilities of White Southerners—and an occasion Roosevelt later regretted. By 1905 Washington knew Roosevelt to be as racially bigoted as any White nationalist. Indeed, Teddy Roosevelt mirrored Sherman's views on the incapacity of Black soldiers, believing that none should serve as officers and that most would flee the field in battle. On returning from his 1905 tour of the South, he declared to industrialist and historian James Ford Rhodes that Negroes of the Yazoo Delta were "two hundred thousand years behind" White folks. When Rhodes said more like "a million," Roosevelt agreed and openly doubted the wisdom of the 15th Amendment, which secured voting rights for African Americans.[115]

When invited to visit the White House in 1907, Harris accepted and apparently had a good time of it. Roosevelt famously said, "Presidents may come and presidents may go, but Uncle Remus stays put.

---

[113] Garrett, *Atlanta and Environs*, 2:486

[114] Ibid., 488.

[115] Morris, *Theodore Rex*, 425; see also Norrell, *Up from History*, 240–41.

Georgia has done a great many good things for the Union, but she has never done more than when she gave Mr. Joel Chandler Harris to American literature...."[116] In May 1905, Harris was inducted into the recently formed National Institute of Arts and Letters, an induction list that included among others William James and Henry James (although William refused because his little brother Henry was invited at the same time).[117] Also among the inductees were William Dean Howells, Mark Twain, and George Washington Cable. Eventually the honorees numbered only fifty. (It is now the American Academy of Arts and Letters and honors over seventy composers, artists, architects, and writers a year.)

Perhaps the best way to understand "Joe Harris," as he signed editorials in the *Constitution,* is to look at the career of the local colorist Bill Arp after Grady's death and after Harris had stepped away from the paper in 1890 (though not completely until 1900). As noted previously, Grady was a restraining influence on Arp with his insistence on the reconciliation theme. Booker T. Washington's biographer, Jeff Norrell, noted that "Washington considered the *Atlanta Constitution* the most influential newspaper in the South. Whereas it had earned a reputation for sectional and racial enlightenment under Henry Grady in the 1880s, it reflected the typical bigotry of white-owned Southern newspapers in the 1890s." Arp wrote in 1890 that the "universal sentiment in the South is that the Negro shall not rule us" and that the South "was suffering under an explosion of black crime." Norrell also noted that Arp inspired imitators, columnists at big newspapers "retailing pernicious black stereotypes that underpinned White cultural antipathy."[118]

The era became even more crass. *Van Norden Magazine* published in March 1907 what it purported to be the intelligentsia of the South,

---

[116] Bickley, *Joel Chandler Harris*, 58–59.

[117] Of three reasons the father of American pragmatism offered for non-admission, this is the third: "I am the more encouraged to this course by the fact that my younger and shallower and vainer brother is already in the Academy [Henry on the second ballot, William on fourth] and that if I were there too, the other families represented might think the James influence too rank and strong" (Edel, *Henry James*, 615).

[118] Norrell, *Up from History*, 118–19, 317.

twelve college presidents and a few bankers. The subject was Blacks. The president of Randolph-Macon College in Virginia said the Negro does not work regularly, needs but three dollars a week and when he gets it "quits work to spend it." His solution was "reduce their wages so that they shall have to work all the time to make a living and become better workmen or disappear into the struggle for existence...." The president of Howard College in Marion, Alabama (now Samford University in Birmingham), said "My deliberate opinion is that the days of the Negro as a fair, and honest laborer are numbered and few at that." The president of the bank at Lexington, North Carolina, declared it a mistake to grant rights of citizenship to the Negro and that education was a curse to him. As late as 1923, President Calvin Coolidge "lectured a black audience that while he admired 'their progress,' they should recall 'that the Anglo-Saxon race has been centuries in reaching its present position and that the Negro could not and must not expect to bridge the chasm in a century.'"[119] How bewildering.

In the same issue of *Van Norden*, Booker T. Washington wrote (not in reply), that Negroes owned 23,383 square miles of territory, "an area nearly as large as Holland and Belgium combined, and that in the single county of Glouster, Virginia, Negroes were paying taxes on land valued at 88 million dollars and on buildings assessed at 80 million—all on the land they had previously worked as slaves—and that representing only a quarter of the land they worked." As noted earlier it is difficult to know how much plantation land escheated to White and Black small farmers, but Booker Washington was confident in his assessment.

All indicating a bewildering picture of what was taking place.

[119] I am indebted to Cleophus "Cleo" Thomas Jr. for this reference to *Van Norden Magazine*. He was the first (and until recently, the only) African American student body president at the University of Alabama (1976–1977); he was also the first African American member of the Board of Trustees. He is a Harvard Law graduate and art collector extraordinaire, and he lives in Anniston, Alabama. See also Greenberg, *Calvin Coolidge*, 87.

Who Succeeded Grady?

One might begin with Julian and Julia Collier Harris. Julian was Joel's first son, born in Savannah, and Julia was the daughter of Charles Augustus Collier, who served as president of the Piedmont Exposition in 1887, and president and director-general of the Cotton States and International Exposition of 1895. He was elected mayor of Atlanta in 1897, the year Julian and Julia married (they became engaged on March 13, 1896, but did not announce until 1897), and Collier served as mayor pro tem in 1899.

It was Collier who invited Booker T. Washington to serve as chief commissioner for Alabama and to oversee exhibits for the Negro Building. Collier's son and Julia's brother, John Collier Sr., would become commissioner for Indian affairs from 1933–1945 and is said to have brought about a New Deal for Indians through a reformed Bureau of Indian Affairs. Charles Collier's life ended suddenly and tragically on the night of September 28, 1900, when, thinking a burglar was in their yard, he proceeded to investigate and died from an accidental discharge of his firearm. Julia believed the official account suspicious, and the question of suicide lingered. Poignantly, Joel Harris had written of Collier's first grandchild and namesake, Charles Collier Harris, that the mayor believed his grandson "is the only baby in Atlanta."[120] This grandson would die in 1901 after his namesake grandfather in 1900, followed by another grandson Pierre LaRose Harris, who was born in 1901 and died in 1905 also of typhoid. Julia and Julian would have no other children, a reminder of how sadly challenging parenthood could be at the turn of the last century.

Julian started on the *Constitution* as a cub reporter in 1890 at age sixteen. In 1900 he rose to managing editor just weeks before turning twenty-six, a position he served with rave reviews, but he resigned four years later, having had it with administrative duties. He also had had enough with Clark Howell, editor and part-owner. In later years he confessed, "I grew tired of the politics-ridden, milk-and-water policy of the Constitution."[121] He moved over to the *Atlanta News* as news

---

[120] Joel Chandler Harris to Tommus, December 10, 1899, Joel Chandler Harris Papers, Rose Library, Emory.

[121] Lisby and Muggleston, *Someone Had to Be Hated*, 48–49.

editor and part-owner. Its editor-in-chief was John Temple Graves, an even worse racist than Howell, and Harris stayed a little over a year before going back to the *Constitution* for another brief stint before joining his father on his *Uncle Remus's Home Magazine* in 1908.

Following his father's death shortly thereafter, Julian struggled on with the magazine for another five years before its collapse although it maintained a fine reputation. An Oklahoma journalist wrote more than a decade later that the magazine stood "unequivocally, from its first issue, for science and progress."[122] With the demise of the magazine, the Harrises went to New York, where Julian was hired by James Gordon Bennett's *New York Herald*. Following stateside service in World War I as a military attaché (he had volunteered for trench warfare but at age forty-three it was not to be), Julian took a position with Bennett's *Paris Herald* that put him in proximity with the mercurial and capricious expatriate Bennett. Julian got along with him well enough and even improved the always-struggling *Paris Herald*'s fortunes.

Julia and Julian loved their time in Europe. They observed firsthand the signing of the Paris Peace Accords and the Treaty of Versailles. (They did not have a good opinion of Woodrow Wilson, but that may have owed to their continuing affection for Teddy Roosevelt, a relationship that began with Julian's father and continued with the son. It was also the year of Roosevelt's death.) Julia was fluent in French and wrote copiously and published in the language. On their return stateside in late 1920, the Harrises purchased an interest in the *Columbus Enquirer-Sun*, later acquiring controlling interest. There they joined Tom Loyless, formerly of the Macon and Augusta newspapers where he was a strong progressive and attacked Tom Watson relentlessly. When the *New York World* launched its exposé on the Klan in 1921, Rowland Thomas of its staff wrote Julian, "I want to say here that the courage and guts displayed by you and Mr. Loyless are for me one of the brightest spots...of the whole job."[123] The *Enquirer-Sun* ran the entire *World* series. Only the Hearst *Georgian* ran it in Atlanta.

In Columbus, Julian and Julia hit their stride as strong advocates

---

[122] John Mason, Atoken, OK, to Julian Harris, September 1, 1925, Julian and Julia Harris Papers, Rose Library, Emory.

[123] Thomas to Julian Harris, October 10, 1920, ibid., folder 4.

for progressive causes. With pioneering Atlanta journalist Mildred Seydell, Julia and Julian planned to cover the Scopes trial. (Mildred was named for her great aunt Mildred Lewis Rutherford, "Miss Millie" of earlier reference, and attended the Lucy Cobb Institute in Athens, which Miss Millie had superintended for so many years. Afterward, Seydell went to the Sorbonne for further study.) When the threesome attended the Scopes trial in 1925, they returned with great fervor for the cause that John Thomas Scopes and Clarence Darrow advocated. Julian and Julia wrote "very critically of the fundamentalist impulse behind the trial," and their editorial stands against Georgia attempting to ban the teaching of evolution and their attacks on the Ku Klux Klan won for them in 1926 the state's first Pulitzer Prize for public service—the year Roosevelt purchased Warm Springs and Tom Loyless died. Their friend Howard Odum, influential sociologist at the University of North Carolina, joined them in Dayton and sought to temper Julia's outrage at the "holy rollers" they had witnessed in a church service there. Odum would go on to publish both Julian and Julia several times in his ground-breaking *Journal of Social Forces*.

Their courageous stands against lynching and for truly equal educational opportunities for African Americans, albeit segregated, eventually forced them to sell the paper in 1929. (Also, Julian, like his father, never managed money all that well.) Deeply in debt, they refused to declare bankruptcy and eventually paid off their creditors. Following a brief sojourn in New York, Julian returned to the *Constitution* in 1930, and Julia published *Joel Chandler Harris: Editor and Essayist* the following year with the University of North Carolina Press. Julia always referred to Joel Harris as "Father," explaining to a correspondent, "I feel that I can speak as I do of Father because while not of his blood I was of his heart. Our friendship was very close and tender, and I have the viewpoint both of an outsider and of a daughter."[124] Julia and Julian continued in journalism and publishing until Julian retired in 1945 as Atlanta-based Southern correspondent for the *New York Times*. They were true Southern liberals in their day, with an abiding affection for Joel Chandler Harris and Henry W. Grady, both of whom they would have described as sectional and racial conciliators and progressives.

---

[124] Julia to Ms. McDowell, 1909, box 1, folder 2, ibid.

As "liberals," the Harrises never drifted far from their progenitors. Like his father, Julian had a sentimental attachment to the Old South and a patronizing view of Negroes in the New South. He believed in racial separation, even to denouncing the *Brown* ruling in 1954 and opposing the use of force in 1957 by the federal government in Little Rock.[125] He did modify his view of Negro inferiority by the late 1920s and was a strong advocate for equalizing (while still segregating) educational opportunities for African Americans. His sharp attacks on the Klan and his opposition to lynching and other acts of violence against Negroes earned his and Julia's reputations as liberals, as did their strong stances on evolution and against fundamentalism. Their later years were not easy. His biographers thought he had a dual, if not split personality that fueled his attacks on other newspapers and bedeviled his own employees. Julia suffered nervous breakdowns that kept her in sanitariums for long stretches.

Although their journey was not without its trials and tribulations, it also had its champions. Leading American progressives and intellectuals were their companions. Joseph Wood Krutch (*The Modern Temper*, 1929), then at Columbia University, wrote of his admiration for their being in Dayton for the Scopes trial and added his own satisfaction at William Jennings Bryan's death shortly thereafter. "In consideration of Bryan, I refuse to make any allowances for the fact that he is dead and I take satisfaction in the fact that his death was caused either by over eating (which would be most gratifying) or that by suppressed indignation at the people who are scoring hits against him."[126] The plaudits did come to them but also the critics, although the Harrises' "saved" correspondence did not include the complaints even as the local opposition they engendered may well have cost them their paper. Perhaps no one put it better than J. Sprole Lyons, pastor of Atlanta's First Presbyterian Church. With the Harrises in mind, he wrote, "I am thoroughly persuaded that someone will have to be thoroughly hated in order to serve Georgia to the fullest measure."[127]

---

[125] Lisby and Muggleston, *Someone Had to Be Hated*, 241.

[126] Krutch to Julian Harris, undated, c. 1926, Julian and Julia Harris Papers, Rose Library, Emory.

[127] Lyons to Julian Harris, January 20, 1926, ibid.

Even locally in Columbus they got some praise and not only regarding race and religion. Louis T. Chase, president of the Chase Conservatory of Music and Expression (Columbus has always had a remarkable position in the world of music, even to the present day at Columbus State University), wrote, "I feel like congratulating the people of Columbus upon having a man in charge of our morning paper who is so just and fearless in the treatment of poor and rich alike." The issue was whiskey and gambling at the elite Muscogee Club. Chase regretted the grief an exposé caused their families, "but there has been so much belief that the poor are down-trodden and that the rich escape, that it is a gratifying matter when we find in public print all treated alike." Chase concluded, "It makes us value the paper even yet more."[128] Earlier that year John Donald Wade, then of the University of Georgia's English Department and soon to be a Vanderbilt Agrarian, wrote George Foster Peabody, formerly of Columbus and influential trustee of the University of Georgia, defending the right of the *Georgia Cracker*, the student monthly magazine, to editorialize in the spirit of Julian Harris. One editorial named Senator Walter George as a member of the Klan. Although Harris himself was publicly skeptical of that charge, it is true that George was a member briefly but resigned the same year he joined, 1923.[129]

With their declining fortunes in 1929, Julian and Julia desperately sought rescue. One publishing friend inquired about help for them from the likes of Julius Rosenwald, Adolph Ochs, and Perry Straus without success.[130] Following their brief tour in New York, Harris sought a return to the *Constitution*, but Clark Howell, Sr. and Jr., were none too receptive although they understood the name recognition and accomplishments that would attach to a Harris return. Eventually they reached an agreement for Julian to come back as state news editor. Julian's intermediary was Edwin Camp, then editor and business manager of the *Atlanta Journal*, who assured the Howells that Julian had been "severely chastened in recent years" and "was quite sure [Julian] would

[128] Chase to Julian Harris, August 22, 1923, ibid.

[129] Wade to Peabody, June 3, 1923, folder 4, ibid.; Cutlip, *Unseen Power*, 404.

[130] Huebsch to Julian Harris, July 12, 1929, Julian and Julia Harris Papers, Rose Library, Emory.

never seek to impose [his] personal views against the opinion of the owners…."[131] It was humiliating. Howell Sr.'s offer lectured, "Your first duty would be to completely reorganize the state news department, and to make that a worthwhile feature. The column [editorial] of which you write, could come in incidentally. All this would depend upon developments."[132] In sum, no incendiary stuff. The *Constitution* after Grady was not going to stick its neck out. Julian stuck it out at the *Constitution* until 1935, when he joined the *Chattanooga Times*, then came back to Atlanta in 1942 as *New York Times* correspondent. Thus did Adolf Ochs come to his rescue after all, and his nephew, Julius Ochs Adler, would continue the relationship. Julian retired at age 70 in 1945. He and Julia remained jewels in the Southern liberal crown. He died in 1963, she died in 1967. By then Ralph McGill was successor-in-chief to Grady.

McGill and Patterson

As Grady legatee, McGill was the South's most influential newspaper editor of the twentieth century. Born in 1898, he grew up in a farming community about twenty miles from Chattanooga, Tennessee, and graduated from the McCallie School in that city. He attended Vanderbilt but did not graduate because he offended its administration by criticizing its failure to build a student center from proceeds of a gift that had stipulated one. He no doubt could have appealed and graduated, but by then he had become a sportswriter for the *Nashville Banner*. He joined the *Constitution* in 1929 as an assistant sports editor. He was migrating away from sports when he won a Rosenwald Fellowship for study in Europe during the first six months of 1938. There he covered Adolph Hitler's seizure of Austria, the Anschluss. He was soon made editorial-page editor, and over the next thirty years became the dominant voice of Southern liberalism as he rose to editor and finally publisher of the *Constitution*.[133] His daily column, appearing below his picture above the left column of page one, challenged Georgia to abandon its old ways and eventually to embrace integration. For his daring, many

---

[131] Camp to Julian Harris, November 3, 1929, folder 17, ibid.

[132] Howell Sr. to Julian Harris, November 22, 1929, ibid.

[133] Biographical details are from McGill, *South and the Southerner*, passim.

Georgians called him "Rastus" McGill, but they still read him as the state finally made its turn toward equality under law.

First, McGill had to deal with Governor Talmadge, "Ole Gene" as he was affectionately known among Georgia farmers. Elected first in 1932, he even had a brief run at the presidency in 1936 as a "slew of Liberty Leaguers backed his quixotic 1936 presidential campaign" for president, delighting in his racism. He was an FDR hater. He even got backing from a "shirt" movement in West Virginia (as in Brown Shirts and Black Shirts of Nazi infamy), styling itself as Knights of the White Camellia, a familiar Klan organization of the twenties that had then transmogrified into a militant anti-Jewish hate group in the thirties.[134]

McGill always thought he was in the tradition of Henry Grady. As Georgia neared the "materialization" of the New South in the fifties and sixties, he imagined Grady doing "an editorial jig." In another essay, he wrote of Lucy Randolph Mason, scion of the Old Dominion, petite, gray-haired, with charming manners, traveling the South in white gloves, spreading the gospel of the CIO (Congress of Industrial Organizations), i.e., labor unions that many thought Communist. Certainly most mill owners and industrialists thought so. McGill liked "Miss Lucy" personally. At the close, McGill wrote, "I like to imagine a scene in Heaven: Miss Lucy Mason, modest and neat, is giving Henry Grady a lecture, and Grady, always the courtly gentleman, with a weakness for Virginians, is listening patiently, albeit with a certain restless wish to reply. He (Grady) liked to say that he came by talking naturally because his father was Irish and his mother a woman." Then, McGill closed, "I hope they both peer over the balustrade when the New South at last arrives."[135] Spoken in affection, McGill never thought Grady was not pointed in the right direction, however blinkered by stern custom. McGill received his Pulitzer for commentary in 1959. Grady's biographer, Raymond Nixon, dedicated his 1943 biography of Grady to Ralph McGill.[136]

Also in 1943, McGill's later successor as dominant voice at the

---

[134] Lichtman, *White Protestant Nation*, 71, 76.

[135] Ibid., 208, 2012.

[136] See also L. R. Teal, "Ralph McGill (1898–1969)," *New Georgia Encyclopedia*, www.georgiaencyclopedia.org/articles/arts-culture/ralph-mcgill-1898-1969.

Constitution, Gene Patterson, graduated from the Grady School of Journalism at UGA. Having already received his stripes as a cavalryman in ROTC, he was immediately mustered in as a tank group commander under George Patton. Patterson was a true "first to Bastogne" in relief of the besieged American forces in the Battle of the Bulge. For his heroism, he won a Silver Star. Born twenty years earlier in Sparks, just outside Adel in South Georgia where he grew up, he too championed desegregation. His column, written the day of the bombing of the 16th Street Baptist Church in Birmingham, September 15, 1963, "A Flower for the Grave," cannot be read without weeping, painfully poetic and beautiful beyond measure. He received his Pulitzer in 1966 for defending the right of Julian Bond to a seat in the Georgia legislature to which he had been duly elected, as the Senate tried to deny him that seat for his opposition to the Vietnam War, but doubled-down because he was the first African American to be elected. Patterson supported Bond despite his own support for American intervention in Southeast Asia.[137] Patterson left the *Constitution* in 1968 and took a position at the *Washington Post* before eventually landing at the distinguished *St. Petersburgh Times* as its brilliant editor and publisher from 1972 until his retirement in 1988. He remained as board chairman of the Poynter Institute. Patterson died in 2013 and is buried at Arlington. My wife and I attended those services and walked behind the caisson that transported him to Arlington.

Fermentation

Howard Washington Odum was born on Grady's thirty-fourth birthday, May 24, 1884 in Bethlehem, Georgia, thirty miles west of Athens.

---

[137] Patterson told me that his support for the war owed most to his age, which allowed him to experience WW II and observe the Korean conflict through that lens. He said that "Pappy," his pet name for McGill, followed his lead out of respect for his wartime experience. Patterson told McGill that they would lose a rising generation of youth who opposed the war (letter from Patterson to author and epilogue of E. C. Clark, *Centennial*, published by Mercer University Press. MUP acquired the manuscript after UGA Press tore up copy of a contract with author over seven pages dealing with a recent university president whose new quarters are on site with the press. The way of all flesh.).

He graduated from Emory College while it was still in Oxford, Georgia. He completed a masters in classics at the University of Mississippi, where Thomas Pierce Bailey Jr. introduced him to the behavioral sciences and to a biological racism as thorough as ever articulated by an academic. Bailey's racism is interesting because of the journey Howard Odum would make away from it. From Ole Miss, Odum completed a Ph.D. in psychology at Clark University in Worcester, Massachusetts (1909) and another in sociology at Columbia (1910). Appointments at the University of Georgia and Emory eventually led him to Chapel Hill in 1920 as chair of the sociology department and dean of the School of Public Welfare, where his remarkable career flourished. Like Joel Chandler Harris, he was a student of Negro folklore.

A prolific scholar, Odum developed a regional sociology program that promised not only detailed scholarship but also uplift for the region's inhabitants. It attracted philanthropic support for himself and numerous students, especially from the various Rockefeller foundations and the Rosenwald Fund. His 1910 dissertation on "The Social and Mental Traits of the Negro" did not rise above prevailing racialist thought, but he took a keen interest in African American welfare, and his thinking evolved, even to publishing a trilogy (1928–1931) that followed the progress of a common Black laborer. He founded and edited the *Journal of Social Forces* and compiled and published the enormously influential and massive statistical portrait, *Southern Regions of the United States*. Odum presided over the Commission on Interracial Cooperation, progenitor of the Southern Regional Council that he also headed for a time. The CIC-*cum*-SRC was a moderating force for ameliorating the terms of segregation first and later for changing the system itself. As with most great scholars, a group of young intellectuals formed around him, including Guy Johnson, who studied Black folklore; Arthur F. Raper, whose examination of lynching along with a microscopic look at tenancy made his reputation; and Guion G. Johnson, the only female in the group, all of whom contributed importantly to Gunner Myrdal's magnum opus *An American Dilemma*. (Guion Johnson less so, not because she was a woman, but because Southern historical writing then was miniscule compared to the behemoth it was to become. Indeed, Myrdal's wife, Alva, was deeply involved in his work.)

Upon being commissioned by the Carnegie Foundation in 1937

to do a massive study of Black-White relations in America, the Swedish economist Myrdal turned first to Odum and his team. The personalities of the two could not have been more different. Odum always viewed the debonair Swede with gimlet-eyed suspicion. To him, Myrdal was another turf invader with more advanced, and accordingly more unrealistic, ideas on race. Odum, like most "liberals" of his generation, could not overcome completely the centripetal pull of region and race. His sociology, although more academic, could no more escape the "realism" of White supremacy than could Vanderbilt University's Agrarian mythology. As a result, Odum would go to his death in November 1954, the year of *Brown*, still uncertain that the better wisdom did not lie in separate but "truly" equal. (Odum's sons Howard T. Odum and Eugene Odum became acclaimed environmental ecologists at the universities of Florida and Georgia respectively.)

Myrdal steered away from the historical component of his study despite Guion Johnson's best efforts, because in part there was so little of it, but more importantly it still reflected the prevailing Southern mythos that little change in race relations could be expected. Where Myrdal wanted to go with his "value-driven" sociology required a more fluid state for both White and Black Southerners than history, as it was then known, was likely to cede. Myrdal saw the Enlightenment principle of equality, what he styled the American Creed, operating as a countervailing force to existing racial practice in the South. He believed that the resulting dilemma between practice and belief produced a creative tension that would ineluctably draw Southern Whites toward racial accommodation and ultimately equality. The beneficiaries would be Blacks, who with charitable support from Whites could become as American as any other group. Appearing in 1944, the drums of war drowned out the book, but by 1954 it had become the famous footnote 11 to *Brown v. Board of Education*, standing alone as proof that segregation was an inherent denial of equality and therefore constitutionally repugnant and injurious.

Myrdal's work had profound consequences for the Martin Luther King Jr.-led phase of the civil rights movement and for historians working amid profound professional change. His "determinism" offered an inspirational outcome to struggle, honestly waged. Had not Myrdal prefigured completely the Southern White response to desegregation, namely, its leaders would stand in one schoolhouse door after another only to retreat. Even though the "new history" of the thirties had chipped away at the determinism of earlier progressive historians, here was a new brand, shorn of impersonal economic forces and replaced by an exalting ideology. Coming off victory in Europe and Japan, American idealism could be taken at the flood.

William Terry Couch, editor of the University of North Carolina Press, published much of the research that was then fermenting and pointed out a pivotal aspect of the social transformation underway. Like so many of his generation, his view was Janus-faced but no less revealing. Couch offered three possible views of the African American: 1) that he is naturally inferior and left to his own devices produces no civilization; 2) that the Negro's condition is produced by a natural inferiority which can be overcome gradually and the prejudice resulting from it cured; or 3) that the Negro is not inferior, "that he only appears to be so, that his condition is wholly and completely the product of race prejudice and the consequent disabilities inflicted on the Negro by the white man."[138] The latter view he attributed to Myrdal and to Rayford Logan, an African American historian at Howard University, whom Couch had asked to compile a book titled *What the Negro Wants*. Appearing the same year as *Dilemma*, 1944, Logan further disturbed the equipoise of Couch and associates by saying forthrightly what the Negro wanted—complete equality. Despite Couch's remarkable record as a publisher, over 400 books with a UNC Press imprimatur, he adhered to the second view articulated above.

Couch was so disturbed by Logan's compilation that he wrote an editor's introduction to make clear his point of view. Logan, a Negro, could be forgiven if not understood, but Myrdal who, working with scholars like Logan, came to the same conclusions Couch could not. He was an outsider and White. Couch was quick to say that Myrdal's work was preceded by "numerous books, pamphlets, and articles presenting the same arguments" and that it was "exceptional only in that it was written under highly favorable and most reputable auspices, and is more comprehensive, more thorough, and more readable than the mass of material sharing its attitude." Couch was right in saying that

---

[138] Logan, *What the Negro Wants*, xi–xiv.

Myrdal did not invent his arguments from whole cloth, but what most offended Couch was the Myrdalian insistence on "cultural relativism." Couch said that those who believed in relativism could not believe in equality because they had rejected "universal values."[139] Without differentiation there could be no movement across the stations of life from low to high. His notion of equality involved a long process, lower cultures becoming equal to the better or indeed the best. He could not shake the Victorian link that equated culture with civilization, which he defined more generously than he intended as an "accumulation of universal values from various cultures."

More than the pleadings of any other person, Myrdal's *An American Dilemma* represents the end of a worldview that dominated the last thirty-five years of the nineteenth century and the first thirty-five of the twentieth—terms like conservatism and progressivism during this seventy-year period being but a continuum within a Victorian hierarchy of elitism. At its heart was a dim view of the African American's prospects. Myrdal shook things loose, and the younger generation of liberals would grab the ring. If Vanderbilt offered up Richard M. Weaver as progeny, Chapel Hill countered with C. Vann Woodward, whose lordly dominance of Southern historiography in the last half of the twentieth century had no equal. Ralph McGill and Gene Patterson took this cresting tide of Myrdalian scholarship, the Grady inheritance, and ushered in The New South.

Demurrer

Lillian Smith, whose Laurel Falls Camp for Girls in North Georgia became the base for her advocacy of human rights, foreshadowed the reputation that Grady would come to have. In her book *Killers of the Dream*, published sixty years after Grady's death, she observed correctly that newspapers in the South "had worked out a system of leaving out everything they thought might 'upset people,'" especially racial matters. She went on to concede in 1949 that Grady was rightly known as "the 'conciliator,' who talked a good kind of common sense that seemed lucid and statesmanlike in comparison with most, though he showed little awareness of the moral problems of human relations so completely

[139] Ibid., xv–xvi.

unsolved or the economic and social needs of the eighty percent of whites who were not in the dominant group."[140] The assessment was fair enough if a bit jaundiced, yet one must concede that Grady talked about all she said he ignored, even if he was blinkered by common assumptions of his times and its circumstances.

Smith even took a dislike to Ralph McGill's slow progress toward embracing the future of a fully integrated society. Few journalists and advocates were where Smith thought they ought to be before *Brown v. Board of Education*, but a reading of McGill's *The South and the Southerner* shows him taking the region and its leadership to task for its failures from the 1880s into the early 1960s. McGill himself died in 1969, three years after Lillian Smith's passing. Smith's splenetic side revealed itself in her correspondence with Ashley Montagu, who presided over the Anisfield-Wolf Award Committee that rewarded the best books on race relations. She whined considerably about the committee not getting to the meat of things and described McGill as "whitewashing Atlanta" and a "token liberal." When a racial incident erupted in Chapel Hill, she charged that Chapel Hill was getting a "pass" because "both Chapel Hill and Atlanta are supposed to be liberal."[141] Smith may have been right or just never happy, but her views from Grady to McGill may well have forecast conclusions of generations to come and bear reflection.

At some odds with these pronouncements, she also said that "what caused Atlanta's sudden change was dynamiting the [Hebrew Benevolent Congregation] Temple in 1958 with its echoes of the Frank case, which McGill was too young at the time to understand." Still, it caused McGill, the mayor, and a handful of businesspeople "to move and move fast."[142] Again she was right about the motivating force of the temple bombing, but at least a half bubble off plumb about McGill. He was seventeen at the time of the Frank lynching, and she eighteen, having just moved with her family to Clayton, Georgia, the year before the lynching. In *The South and the Southerner* and a chapter titled "The Twig is Bent," McGill dealt directly with White nationalism and the

---

[140] L. Smith, *Killers of the Dream*, 12, 67–68.

[141] Smith to Ashley Montagu, February 20, 1957 (quoted material) and continuing through 1966, Hargrett Library, UGA.

[142] Ibid., February 3, 1966.

radical racism revealed in the Frank case. Speaking of Tom Watson's "pathological" tangents and inflammatory appeal, McGill wrote, "God alone knows how many Negroes were lynched and murdered by his words. The Roman Catholic Church fought back. Men who sought to hold the sea wall against the tide of hate and helped defend Leo Frank in the circuslike trial and the lynching that followed were maligned and abused in Watson's paper, *The Jeffersonian*."[143] So whatever fault Smith found with McGill's accomplishments could not trace to any lack of awareness or motivation on his part.

Lillian Smith was born in 1897 in Jasper, Florida, just over the Georgia state line, where her father went bust in the turpentine business in 1915, an industry that had furnished fortunes for many in the piney woods of the South. The family moved to Clayton, in North Georgia, where they had a cabin, and her father started the Laurel Falls Camp for Girls. She took it over in 1925 when his health failed. In the meantime, she had studied a year at nearby Piedmont College. She followed that by four years as an aspiring pianist at the Peabody Music Conservatory in Baltimore. Then she had a five-year stint as a missionary in China. Upon her return, Smith ran the Laurel Falls Camp until 1949. Her first book, *Strange Fruit*, 1944, was her best and centered on interracial love, totally taboo in that time. The setting was obviously her native Jasper, Florida, with transparently autobiographical figures. Her second, *Killers of the Dream*, was a collection of didactic essays that included moral instruction for Southerners like Grady and indeed McGill, who was moving Southern liberalism front and center, if not fast enough for Smith. Still, she nudged the conversation, and her name is on the Southern Regional Council's book awards for fiction and nonfiction, even if in her day she had great reservations about the SRC itself and its leader, Howard Odum.

Although visible and consequential in the movement, like Joel Chandler Harris, she was painfully shy and certainly neurotic. She was helped greatly by her life partner, Paula Nettles, who added ballast and support. In the early sixties, she was torn between her distaste both for so-called White liberals and increasingly assertive Black nationalists. In a letter to one of her preferred editors, George B. Leonard of *Look*

[143] McGill, *South and the Southerner*, 125–26.

magazine, she complained about Leroi Jones (also known as Amiri Baraka) and James Baldwin, saying they were "too full of self-pity, too full of paranoid need to project on a whole mass of 'white people' the sins of the entire world." They were also "too full of their need for a simplistic scapegoat to add anything of richness to the picture." She reserved her praise for Martin Luther King Jr. and nonviolence, which she elaborated in a speech for the Montgomery Improvement Association (forerunner of the Southern Christian Leadership Conference) on the first anniversary of the Montgomery bus boycott. Because of her shyness, a professor from Atlanta University delivered the speech for her. By the mid-sixties, she resigned from the Congress of Racial Equality (CORE) because Floyd McKissick, then its leader, had also abandoned nonviolence.[144] Smith died of cancer in 1966, having made a name for herself in the annals of Southern literature and liberalism.

Dreamers

The reader now knows where Grady perched on all the subjects of his day and from his own words. Harold Davis said it best, when he noted an insensitivity on Grady's part to the great moral questions surrounding race relations in the South and that he died at the right time to avoid the worst of its radicalization. As T. S. Eliot wrote in the opening lines of "Burnt Norton," the first of his *Four Quartets*,

> Time present and time past
> Are both perhaps present in time future,
> And time future contained in time past.
> If all time is eternally present
> All time is unredeemable.[145]

T. S. Elliot's words can lead to a redemption of Grady's past and the moral imperatives of his day, however unsatisfying by present

[144] Smith to Leonard, September 12, 1965; interview with Leonard, *Look*, September 6, 1966; "In Praise of Non-violence," speech delivered for Smith by Hylan Lewis, Atlanta University, December 5, 1956 (first anniversary of Montgomery Bus Boycott), Lillian Eugenia Smith Papers, box 1, folders 1–3, Rose Library, Emory.

[145] Eliot, "Burnt Norton," 13.

lights.

Ta-Nehisi Coates and Lillian Smith have much in common, except perhaps in differing literary tone. Coates nudged and loved in a letter to his son. Smith was a Casandra with a full-throated jeremiad, but both came to same. Race suicide was the answer. Whites needed to abdicate rather than control the dialog. Coates weighed in against the "dreamers"—Martin Luther King Jr. and the like. Smith took on moderating progressives, labeling them as "killers of the dream," both saying a radical change in thought was the only solution. Each said the icons of change were the enemies of change. Coates and Smith needed to cleanse the soul, not cajole it. Smith called *Killers of the Dream* "the book that turned the South against me...blasted me out of existence.... Men like Hodding Carter and Ralph McGill and others on the [Atlanta] *Constitution* did a dirty job on me." It was a singular and self-centered view and did her no good.

They returned fire but with nuance. Carter described Smith's *Killers of the Dream* as a "dramatic little primer on racism." McGill was a bit more respectful, saying Smith was a courageous moralist who was "a bit dogmatic, or firmly naïve." To her insistence that leaders like McGill, Carter, Odum, and others should be held responsible for seeing that integration succeeded, McGill replied, "It isn't quite that simple."[146] Both Smith and Coates were right. Smith's adherence to Freudian psychology was only part of the equation. She was deeply imbued with Christian charity and humanity. Did anyone match up to Smith's exacting standards? In a letter to Montagu about the Anisfield-Wolf Award for 1957, she promoted Gilberto de Mello Freyre's *The Masters and the Slaves* for best book of the year on race and culture. It no doubt was, but she had to say it was superior to *An American Dilemma*, which changed America, saying "the Brazilian book is much richer in terms of symbolism, religion, psychology, grasp of the culture drives that made the Brazilian people what they are today, and with no undue stress on economics" (a shot at Myrdal whose book rolled out more than ten years before and cinched the sociological argument in *Brown v. Board of Education*). Freyre was clearly more sophisticated and nuanced about cultural forces but not as effective as Gunnar Myrdal with

[146] Hobson, *Tell about the South*, 317.

his expert compilation.[147] Smith's attempted comparison was so unnecessary.

As Fred Hobson said, "she was, like all radical truth-sayers, so devoted to her particular truth that she sometimes lost sight of all others."[148] Still, neither she nor Coates are less true for it. White supremacy was the root of all evil. If not rooted out, then evil would prevail.

---

147 Smith to Montagu, February 20, 1957, Hargrett Library, UGA.
148 Hobson, *Tell about the South*, 321.

Epilogue

When Charlottesville became a headline on August 12, 2017, the beautiful village that featured not only Monticello but also Jefferson's proud University of Virginia became a battleground for hate. It was the fulfillment of all the resentments White conservatives and nationalists harbored since the 1960s. They hated the "inclusive" impulses of liberalism's last turn—affirmative action, identity politics, globalization—all the things that would make America less White, or so they believed. So their warriors turned up to protest the removal of a statue of Robert E. Lee. They marched as neo-Nazis and nouveau Ku Klux Klan with torches, shouting "Jews will not replace us" and other harsh chants from another era of Nazism.

When greeted the next night by counter-protesters who opposed White supremacy and fascism, a melee erupted. The vicious "right" exacted the ultimate toll as a neo-Nazi rammed his car into the counter-protesters, killing Heather Heyer and injuring nineteen other people, five critically. But the denouement was not yet exacted. The president of the United States, whose sympathies are with the extreme right and who believes himself elected by them, stated to the media that the Nazis and KKK were morally equivalent in wrongdoing to protesters who supported liberal ideas of inclusiveness. He won the plaudits of alt-right conservatives and betrayed the better angels of American inclusiveness. In his own intentional, narcissistic way, he played to his White supremacist base, a popular minority that had gained him an electoral majority.

How could Donald J. Trump believe he was leader of or obligated to the alt-right? He could do so because the right had undermined liberal progressivism on the issues of inclusiveness. From Goldwater, to Nixon (with exceptions), to Reagan, to the Bushes (with other exceptions), the Republican Party's "dark money" has undermined the inclusive state, appealing to fear among some Whites about globalization, immigrants, and Black advancement. For these people, White America is the only America. The true majorities are not yet in, because of Republican gerrymandering, like that of Southern Democrats of old, but it is as plain as Trump's election over an opponent who won the popular vote by more than three million votes.

There is even thought as appeared in columns of the *Atlanta-Journal Constitution* (August 22, 2017) that we are on the verge of another Civil War, although perhaps more like the eruptions that emerged in American cities from Watts to Detroit. It is true that the promise I experienced in my days at Emory in the early 1960s has transmogrified. The moral arc of the universe may not be moving toward justice but to divisiveness driven by White nationalism and fear. There is hope that demographics will at last release the White supremacist grip on the throat of what remains of democracy, but "counting" has never substituted for "embracing."

In summer 2019 I walked the streets of Alexandria, Virginia, happy to be there for a wedding. I came across the Confederate statue, celebrating the day that Alexandrians marched off to war against the Union. The soldier depicted had a visage more somber than triumphant, no doubt acknowledging defeat. Alexandria was George Washington's village, next to Mount Vernon, and Robert E. Lee's childhood home. The monument bore two dates: May 24, 1861, the day Alexandrians marched off to join the Confederacy, and May 24, 1889, the day the monument was placed. Both dates were Henry Grady's eleventh and last birthdays.

History is both memorial and truth-seeking, neither compatible. The Northern monuments to generals and soldiers, who were as race-hating and abhorrent as any Southerners, are memorials to the same sentiments that continued to enslave our African American population, North and South. Years would pass until Martin Luther King Jr.'s rhetoric and revolution would advance both conciliatory rhetoric and power-sharing, not completely but better. Although in a better place, we are still far from the ideal. White supremacy remains the *bête noire* of American politics and sympathies.

Bibliography

PRIMARY SOURCES: SPECIAL COLLECTIONS AND ARCHIVES
Atlanta History Center
William Arnold Hemphill Papers
Evan Park Howell Papers
Samuel Martin Inman Scrapbook

Duke University Library, Durham, North Carolina
William Watts Ball Papers
Daniel Henry Chamberlain Papers
Francis Warrington Dawson, I and II Papers
Wade Hampton Papers
Hemphill Family Papers
Josephus Woodruff Diary (copy)

Georgia Historical Society
Thomas Spalding Family Papers

Hargrett Rare Books and Manuscript Library, University of Georgia
David Crenshaw Barrow Papers
Joseph Emerson Brown Papers
Alfred Holt Colquitt Papers
John Brown Gordon Papers
Henry Woodfin Grady Papers
Lillian Eugenia Smith Papers

Library of Congress
Thomas Francis Bayard Papers
Stephen Grover Cleveland Papers
Wade Hampton Papers (personal miscellaneous file)
Daniel S. Lamont Papers
Morrison Remick Waite Papers

Rose Manuscripts and Rare Books Library, Emory University
Henry W. Grady Papers
Joel Chandler Harris Papers
Julian and Julia Harris Papers
Lillian Eugenia Smith Papers

South Carolina Department of Archives, Columbia, South Carolina
Executive Files: Letterbooks of Governor Wade Hampton, et al.

South Carolina Historical Society, Charleston, South Carolina
Joseph Walker Barnwell typescript reminiscence
James Conner Papers
Report of the Examination of the Body of Francis Warrington Dawson, by Dr. William Middleton Michel (miscellaneous file)

South Carolinian Library, University of South Carolina, Columbia, SC
Milledge Luke Bonham Papers
Mathew Calbraith Butler Papers
William Ashmead Courtenay Papers
Robert Means Davis Papers
Francis Warrington Dawson Papers
Martin Witherspoon Gary Papers
Narciso Gener Gonzales Papers
Wade Hampton Papers
John Cheves Haskell Letter Book
Ellison Summerfield Keitt Papers
Benjamin Franklin Perry Papers
John S. Richardson Papers
William Dunlap Simpson Papers
Yates Snowden Papers
Hugh Smith Thompson Papers
Williams-Chestnut-Manning Papers

Southern Historical Collection, University of North Carolina
Francis Warrington Dawson Papers
Elliott-Gonzales Papers
William Lawrence Mauldin Diary
William Porcher Miles Diary
Francis Butler Simkins, notes on Benjamin Ryan Tillman
William Dunlap Simpson Papers
Daniel Augustus Tompkins Papers

Uncle Remus Museum, Eatonton, Georgia

SECONDARY SOURCES

Adams, Henry. *The Education of Henry Adams: An Autobiography*. Cambridge: Riverside Press, 1918.

Agee, James, and Walker Evans. *Let Us Now Praise Famous Men: Three Tenant Families*. Boston: Houghton Mifflin, 1941.

Alderman, Edwin Anderson, and Joel Chandler Harris, eds. *Library of Southern Literature*. 16 vols. Cambridge: The Martin and Hoyt Company, 1909.

Anderson, William. *The Wild Man from Sugar Creek: The Political Career of Eugene Talmadge*. Baton Rouge: Louisiana State University Press, 1975.

Andrew, Robert, Jr. *Wade Hampton: New South Warrior to Southern Redeemer*. Chapel Hill: University of North Carolina Press, 2008.

Applebome, Peter. *Dixie Rising: How the South Is Shaping American Values, Politics, and Culture*. New York: Random House, 1996.

Aune, James Arnt, and Enrique D. Rigsby, eds. *Civil Rights Rhetoric and the American Presidency*. College Station: Texas A & M University Press, 2005.

Ayers, Edward L. *In the Presence of Mine Enemies: War in the Heart of America, 1859–1863*. New York: W.W. Norton & Company, 2003.

———. *The Promise of the New South: Life After Reconstruction*. New York: Oxford University Press, 1992.

———. *The Thin Light of Freedom: Civil War and Emancipation in the Heart of America*. New York: W. W. Norton, 2017.

Bailyn, Bernard. *The Ideological Origins of the American Revolution*. Cambridge: Harvard University Press, 1967.

Baptist, Edward E. *The Half Has Never Been Told: Slavery and the Making of American Capitalism*. New York: Basic Books, 2014.

Barrow, D. C., Jr. "A Georgia Plantation." *Scribner's Monthly* 21/5 (March 1881): 830–36.

Battalora, Jaqueline. *Birth of a White Nation: The Invention of White People and Its Relevance Today*. Houston: Strategic Book Publishing and Rights Co., 2013.

Bauer, Marvin G. "Henry W. Grady: Spokesman of the New South." In vol. 1 of *A History and Criticism of American Public Address*, edited by W. N. Brigance, 387–406. New York: McGraw Hill, 1943.

Beckert, Sven. *Empire of Cotton: A Global History*. New York: Random House, 2014.

Bickley, R. Bruce. *Joel Chandler Harris: A Biography and Critical Study*. Athens: University of Georgia Press, 2008.

Black, Earl, and Merle Black. *The Rise of Southern Republicans*. Cambridge: Belknap Press of Harvard University Press, 2002.

Boney, F. N. *Pictorial History of the University of Georgia*. 2nd ed. Athens: University of Georgia Press, 2000.

Braden, Waldo W. *Oratory in the New South*. Baton Rouge: Louisiana State University Press, 1979.

Breitman, Richard, and Allan J. Lichtman. *FDR and the Jews*. Boston: Belknap of Harvard University Press, 2013.

Brown, Nikki L. M., and Barry M. Stentiford, eds. *The Jim Crow Encyclopedia*. Westport, CT: Greenwood Press, 2008.

Bruce, Marcus C. *Henry Ossawa Tanner*. New York: Crossroads Publishing Company, 2002.

Brundage, W. Fitzhugh. *Lynching in the New South: Georgia and Virginia, 1880–1930*. Urbana: University of Illinois Press, 1993.

Bulloch, Henry Allen. *A History of Negro Education in the South: From 1619 to the Present*. Cambridge: Harvard University Press, 1967.

Burns, Rebecca. "The Second Burning of Atlanta." *Atlanta* (February 2017): 86–89. Available online: www.atlantamagazine.com/great-reads/second-burning-atlanta/.

Carpenter, Ronald J. *History as Rhetoric: Style, Narrative and Persuasion*. Columbia: University of South Carolina Press, 1995.

Carter, Dan T. *The Politics of Rage: George Wallace, the Origins of the New Conservatism, and the Transformation of American Politics*. New York: Simon & Schuster, 1995.

———. *When the War Was Over: The Failure of Self-Reconstruction in the South, 1865–1867*. Baton Rouge: Louisiana State University Press, 1985.

Cason, Clarence. *90 Degrees in the Shade*. Chapel Hill: University of North Carolina Press, 1935.

Chernow, Ron. *Alexander Hamilton*. New York: Penguin, 2004.

———. *Grant*. New York: Penguin, 2017.

Clark, E. Culpepper. *Centennial: A History of the Henry W. Grady College of Journalism and Mass Communication at the University of Georgia*. Macon: Mercer University Press, 2015.

———. *Francis Warrington Dawson and the Politics of Restoration: South Carolina, 1874–1889*. Tuscaloosa: University of Alabama Press, 1980.

Clark, Ronald W. *The Survival of Charles Darwin: A Biography of a Man and an Idea*. New York: Random House, 1984.

Clark, Roy Peter, and Raymond Arsenault, eds. *The Changing South of Gene Patterson: Journalism and Civil Rights, 1960–1968*. In *Southern Dissent* series, edited by Stanley Harrold and Randall Miller. Gainesville: University of Florida Press, 2002.

Clark, Thomas Dionysius, ed. *The Postwar South, 1865–1900: An Era of Reconstruction and Readjustment*. Vol. 1 of *Travels in the New South: A Bibliography*. Norman: University of Oklahoma Press, 1962.

Cobb, James C. *Away Down South: A History of Southern Identity*. New York: Oxford University Press, 2005.

Cooper, Melissa L. *Making Gullah: A History of Sapelo Islanders, Race, and the American Imagination*. The John Hope Franklin Series in African American History and Culture, edited by Waldo E. Martin, Jr., and Patricia Sullivan. Chapel Hill: University of North Carolina Press, 2017.

Cooper, William James, Jr. *The* Conservative *Regime: South Carolina, 1877–1890.* Johns Hopkins University Studies in Historical and Political Science, series 86, no. 1. Baltimore: Johns Hopkins University Press, 1968.

Couch, William Terry, ed. *Culture in the South.* Chapel Hill: University of North Carolina Press, 1934.

Coulter, E. Merton. *Lost Generation: The Life and Death of James Barrow, CSA.* Confederate Centennial Studies, edited by W. Stanley Hoole. Tuscaloosa: Confederate Publishing Company, Inc., 1956.

Cox, Karen L. *Dixie's Daughters: The United Daughters of the Confederacy and the Preservation of Confederate Culture.* Gainesville: University of Florida Press, 2004.

———. *Dreaming of Dixie: How the South Was Created in American Popular Culture.* Chapel Hill: University of North Carolina Press, 2011.

Cutlip, Scott M. *The Unseen Power: Public Relations, A History.* Hillsdale, NJ: Lawrence Erlbaum, 1994.

Dabney, Virginius. *Liberalism in the South.* Chapel Hill: University of North Carolina Press, 1932.

Dadisman, Carrol. *Dear Old U-G-A: From* The Red & Black*: Student Life at the University of Georgia, 1893–2013.* Athens: Red and Black Publishing Company, 2013.

Daniels, Jonathan. *They Will Be Heard: America's Crusading Newspaper Editors.* New York: McGraw Hill Book Co., 1965.

Daniels, Josephus. *Tar Heel Editor.* Chapel Hill: University of North Carolina Press, 1938.

Davis, David Brion. *Inhuman Bondage: The Rise and Fall of Slavery in the New World.* New York: Oxford University Press, 2006.

Davis, Harold E. *Henry Grady's New South: Atlanta, a Brave & Beautiful City.* Tuscaloosa: University of Alabama Press, 1990.

Davis, Jingle. *Island Time: An Illustrated History of St. Simons Island, Georgia.* Athens: University of Georgia Press, 2013.

Dean, John W. *Warren G. Harding.* The American Presidents Series, edited by Arthur M. Schlesinger, Jr. New York: Henry Holt and Company, 2004.

Desmond, Adrian, and James Moore. *Darwin: The Life of a Tormented Evolutionist.* New York: W. W. Norton and Company, 1994.

Dinnerstein, Leonard. *The Leo Frank Case.* Rev. ed. Athens: University of Georgia Press, 2008.

Dixon, David T. "To Laugh in One Hand and Cry in the Other: W. B. Higginbotham and the Black Community in Civil War Rome." *Georgia Back Roads* 10/4 (Winter 2011): 14–19.

Dooley, Vincent Joseph, and Samuel Norman Thomas, Jr., eds. *The Legion's Fighting Bulldog: The Civil War Correspondence of William Gaston Delony,*

Lieutenant Colonel of Cobb's Georgia Legion Cavalry, and Rosa Delony, 1853–1863. Macon: Mercer University Press, 2017.

Dugat, Gentry. *Life of Henry W. Grady*. Edinburg, TX: Valley Printery, 1927.

Dunn, Lee C. *Cracking the Solid South: The Life of John Fletcher Hanson, Father of Georgia Tech*. Macon: Mercer University Press, 2016.

Dyer, Thomas G. *The University of Georgia: A Bicentennial History, 1785–1985*. Athens: University of Georgia Press, 1985.

Eckert, Ralph Lowell. *John Brown Gordon: Soldier, Southerner, American*. Southern Biography Series. Baton Rouge: Louisiana State University Press, 1993.

Edel, Leon. *Henry James: A Life*. New York: Harper & Row, 1985.

Egerton, John. *Speak Now Against the Day: The Generation before the Civil Rights Movement in the South*. New York: Alfred A. Knopf, 1994.

Eliot, T. S. "Burnt Norton." In *Four Quartets*. New York: Harcourt, Inc., 1943.

Elkins, Stanley M. *Slavery: A Problem in American Institutional & Intellectual Life*. Grosset's Universal Library. New York: Universal Library, 1963.

Ellis, Jerry. *Marching through Georgia: My Walk with Sherman*. New York: Delacorte Press, 1995.

Ellison, Ralph. *Juneteenth: A Novel*. Edited by John F. Callahan. New York: Random House, 1999.

Faust, Drew Gilpin. *This Republic of Suffering: Death and the American Civil War*. New York: Alfred A. Knopf, 2008.

Fawcett, Edmund. *Liberalism: The Life of an Idea*. Princeton: Princeton University Press, 2014.

Feldman, Glenn. *Politics, Society, and the Klan in Alabama, 1915–1949*. Tuscaloosa: University of Alabama Press, 1999.

Fogel, Robert William, and Stanley L. Engerman. *Time on the Cross: The Economics of American Negro Slavery*. Boston: Little, Brown and Company, 1974.

Foner, Eric. *Reconstruction: America's Unfinished Revolution, 1863–1877*. New York: Harper & Row, 1988.

———. *The Story of American Freedom*. New York: W.W. Norton, 1998.

Franklin, John Hope. *Mirror to America: The Autobiography of John Hope Franklin*. New York: Farrar, Straus and Giroux, 2005.

Frederickson, George M. *The Black Image in the White Mind: The Debate on Afro-American Character and Destiny, 1917–1914*. New York: Harper and Row, 1971.

Freeman, Joshua B. *Behemoth: A History of the Factory and the Making of the Modern World*. New York: W. W. Norton & Company, 2018.

Gaither, Gerald H. *Blacks and the Populist Revolt: Ballots and Bigotry in the New South*. Tuscaloosa: University of Alabama Press, 1977.

Garrett, Franklin M. *Atlanta and Environs*. 3 vols. Athens: University of Georgia Press, 1969.

Gaston, Paul M. *The New South Creed: A Study in Southern Mythmaking*. New York: Alfred A. Knopf, 1970.
Gates, Henry Louis, Jr. *Stony the Road: Reconstruction, White Supremacy, and the Rise of Jim Crow*. New York: Penguin Publishing Group, 2019.
Gilmore, Glenda E. *Defying Dixie: Radical Roots of Civil Rights, 1919–1950*. New York: W. W. Norton & Company, 2008.
———. *Gender and Jim Crow: Women and the Politics of White Supremacy in North Carolina*. Chapel Hill: University of North Carolina Press, 1996.
Glaab, Charles N. *The American City: A Documentary*. Homewood: The Dorsey Press, 1963.
Glatthaar, Joseph T. *General Lee's Army: From Victory to Collapse*. New York: Free Press, 2008.
Goldman, Eric Frederick. *Rendezvous with Destiny: A History of Modern America Reform*. New York: Alfred A. Knopf, 1952.
Goodwin, Doris Kearns. *The Bully Pulpit: Theodore Roosevelt, William Howard Taft, and the Golden Age of Journalism*. New York: Simon and Schuster, 2013.
Gordon-Reed, Annette. *Andrew Johnson*. The American Presidents, edited by Arthur M. Schlesinger Jr. and Sean Wilentz. New York: Times Books/Henry Holt, 2011.
Gordon, Linda. *The Second Coming of the KKK: The Ku Klux Klan of the 1920s and the American Political Tradition*. New York: Liveright Publishing Corporation, 2017.
Grant, Ulysses S. *Memoirs*.
Graves, John Temple, Jr. *The Fighting South*. Introduction by Fred Hobson. Tuscaloosa: University of Alabama Press, 1984.
Greenberg, David. *Calvin Coolidge*. The American Presidents. Edited by Arthur M. Schlesinger, Jr. New York: Times Books, 2007.
Greenstone, J. David. *The Lincoln Persuasion: Remaking American Liberalism*. Princeton: Princeton University Press, 1993.
Griffith, Louis T., and John E. Talmadge. *Georgia Journalism, 1733–1950*. Athens: University of Georgia Press, 1950.
Guelzo, Allen C. *Fateful Lightning: A New History of the Civil War*. New York: Oxford University Press, 2012.
Gutman, Herbert G. *The Black Family in Slavery & Freedom, 1750–1925*. New York: Pantheon Books, 1976.
Gwynne, S. C. *Empire of the Summer Moon: Quanah Parker and the Rise and Fall of the Comanches, the Most Powerful Indian Tribe in American History*. New York: Scribner, 2010.
Hain, Pamela Chase. *Murder in the State Capitol: The Biography of Lieutenant Colonel Robert Augustus Alston, 1832–1879*. Macon: Mercer University Press, 2013.
Halberstam, David. *The Fifties*. New York: Villard Books, 1993.

Harlan, Louis R. *Booker T. Washington: The Making of a Black Leader*. New York: Oxford University Press, 1972.

———. *Booker T. Washington: The Wizard of Tuskegee*. New York: Oxford University Press, 1983.

Harris, Joel Chandler, ed. *Life of Henry W. Grady, Including His Writings and Speeches. A Memorial Volume compiled by Mr. Henry W. Grady's co-workers on* "The Constitution." New York: Cassell Publishing Company, 1890.

Harris, Julia Collier. *Joel Chandler Harris: Editor and Essayist*. Chapel Hill: University of North Carolina Press, 1931.

———. *The Life and Letters of Joel Chandler Harris*. London: Constable, 1919.

Hendrick, Burton Jesse. *The Life and Letters of Walter H. Page*. Vol. 1. New York: Doubleday, Page and Co., 1922.

Hobson, Fred, ed. *South-watching: Selected Essays by Gerald W. Johnson*. Chapel Hill: University of North Carolina Press, 1983.

———. *Tell about the South: The Southern Rage to Explain*. Baton Rouge: Louisiana State University Press, 1983.

Hofstadter, Richard. *The Age of Reform: From Bryan to F. D. R.* New York: Alfred A. Knopf, 1955.

Holt, Thomas C. *Black over White: Negro Political Leadership in South Carolina during Reconstruction*. Blacks in the New World. Urbana: University of Illinois Press, 1977.

Hoogenboom, Ari. *Rutherford B. Hayes: Warrior and President*. Lawrence: University of Kansas Press, 1995.

Hornady, John R. *Atlanta: Yesterday, Today and Tomorrow*. American Cities Book Company, 1922.

Horwitz, Tony. *Spying on the South: An Odyssey across the American Divide*. New York: Penguin Press, 2019.

Hull, Augustus Longstreet. *Annals of Athens, Georgia, 1801–1901*. Introduction by Henry Hull. Athens: Banner Job Press, 1906.

Humphries, Robert L., ed. *The Journal of Archibald Carlisle McKinley*. Athens: University of Georgia Press, 1991.

Inscoe, John C. *Georgia in Black & White: Explorations in Race Relations of a Southern State, 1865–1950*. Athens: University of Georgia Press, 1994.

Isenberg, Nancy. *White Trash: The 400-Year Untold History of Class in America*. New York: Random House, 2016.

Isaacson, Walter. *Leonardo da Vinci*. New York: Simon & Schuster, 2017.

Johnson, Guion Griffis. "The Ideology of White Supremacy, 1876–1910." In *Essays in Southern History*, edited by Fletcher Melvin Green. Vol. 31 of The James Sprunt Studies in History and Political Science. Chapel Hill: University of North Carolina Press, 1949.

Jones, Jacqueline. *Saving Savannah: The City and the Civil War*. New York: Alfred A. Knopf, 2008.

Jordon, Winthrop D. *White over Black: American Attitudes toward the Negro,*

1550–1912. Baltimore: Penguin Books Inc., 1968.

Kantrowitz, Stephen. *Ben Tillman & the Reconstruction of White Supremacy*. The Fred W. Morrison Series in Southern Studies. Chapel Hill: University of North Carolina Press, 2000.

Kelley, Robert Lloyd. *The Transatlantic Persuasion: The Liberal-Democratic Mind in the Age of Gladstone*. New York: Alfred A. Knopf, 1969.

Kennett, Lee B. *Sherman: A Soldier's Life*. New York: HarperCollins, 2001.

Kirkland, Kirk. *Rhoda: A Story Based on the Life and Times of Rhoda Elizabeth Kilcrease Gibbes*. Bloomington: iUniverse Inc., 2013.

Klein, Maury. *The Great Richmond Terminal: A Study in Businessmen and Business Strategy*. Charlottesville: University Press of Virginia, 1970.

Kluger, Richard. *Simple Justice: The History of Brown v. Board of Education, the Epochal Supreme Court Decision that outlawed segregation, and of black America's century-long journey for equality under the law*. New York: Vintage Books, 1975.

Kraus, Michael. *The Writing of History*. Norman: University of Oklahoma Press, 1963.

Kruse, Kevin M. *White Flight: Atlanta and the Making of Modern Conservatism*. Princeton: Princeton University Press, 2005.

Laackman, Dale W. *For the Kingdom and the Power: The Big Money Swindle That Spread Hate Across America*. Chicago and Milwaukee: S. Woodhouse Books, 2014.

Lemann, Nicholas. *The Promised Land: The Great Black Migration and How It Changed America*. New York: Vintage Books, 1992.

Levine, Bruce C. *Fall of the House of Dixie: The Civil War and the Social Revolution that Transformed the South*. New York: Random House, 2013.

Lichtman, Allan J. *White Protestant Nation: The Rise of the American Conservative Movement*. New York: Grove-Atlantic Monthly Press, 2008.

———, and Joan R. Challinor, eds. *Kin and Communities: Families in America*. Smithsonian International Symposium Series. Washington D.C.: Smithsonian Institution, 1979.

Lisby, Gregory C., and William E. Muggleston. *Someone Had to Be Hated: Julian LaRose Harris, A Biography*. Durham: Carolina Academic Press, 2002.

Lofgren, Charles A. *The Plessy Case: A Legal-Historical Interpretation*. New York: Oxford University Press, 1998.

Logan, Rayford. *What the Negro Wants*. Chapel Hill: University of North Carolina Press, 1944.

Luxenberg, Steve. *Separate: The Story of* Plessy v. Ferguson, *and America's Journey from Slavery to Segregation*. New York: W. W. Norton & Company, 2019.

Lynch, John Roy. *The Facts of Reconstruction*. New York: Neale Publishing Company, 1913.

Magrath, C. Peter. *Morrison R. Waite: The Triumph of Character*. New York: McMillan Co., 1963.

Maharidge, Dale and Michael Williamson. *And Their Children After Them: The Legacy of* Let Us Now Praise Famous Men*: James Agee, Walker Evans, and the Rise and Fall of Cotton in the South*. New York: Pantheon Books, 1989.

Marshall, Charlotte Thomas. *Oconee Hill Cemetery of Athens Georgia*. Vol. 1. Athens, GA: Athens Historical Society, 2009.

Marszalek, John F. "Celebration in Dixie: Sherman Tours the South." *Georgia Historical Quarterly* 46 (Fall 1982): 368–83.

Martin, Harold H. *Ralph McGill: Reporter*. Boston: Little Brown, 1973.

Marzalek, John F. *Sherman: A Soldier's Passion for Order*. New York: The Free Press, 1993.

Mathews, Marcia. *Henry Ossawa Tanner: American Artist*. Chicago: University of Chicago Press, 1969.

Mayo, Marcia. "Stumbling into History: The Cotton States and International Exposition of 1895." *Georgia Back Roads* 11/4 (Winter 2012): 10–21.

McCaughey, Robert A. "The Usable Past: A Study of the Harvard College Rebellion of 1834." *William and Mary Law Review* 11/3 (March 1970): 587–610.

McCloskey, Robert Green. *American Conservatism in the Age of Enterprise, 1865–1910*. Cambridge: Harvard University Press, 1951.

McCullough, David. *The Great Bridge: The Epic Story of the Building of the Brooklyn Bridge*. New York: Simon & Schuster, 2012.

———. *Mornings on Horseback: The Story of an Extraordinary Family, A Vanished Way of Life, and the Unique Child Who Became Theodore Roosevelt*. New York: Simon & Schuster, 1981.

———. *The Path between the Seas: The Creation of the Panama Canal, 1870–1914*. New York: Simon & Schuster, 1977.

McGill, Ralph. *The South and the Southerner*. Boston: Little, Brown and Company, 1959.

McPherson, James M. *This Mighty Scourge: Perspectives on the Civil War*. New York: Oxford University Press, 2007.

Meacham, Jon. *The Soul of America: The Battle for Our Better Angels*. New York: Random House, 2018.

Merritt, Carole. *The Herndons: An Atlanta Family*. Athens: University of Georgia Press, 2002.

Miller, Perry Gilbert Eddy, ed. *American Thought: Civil War to World War I*. New York: Holt, Rinehart and Winston, 1954.

Mitchell, Broadus. *The Rise of the Cotton Mills in the South*. Baltimore: Johns Hopkins Press, 1921.

Morgan, H. Wayne. *From Hayes to McKinley: National Party Politics, 1877–1896*. Syracuse: Syracuse University Press, 1969.

Morris, Edmund. *Theodore Rex*. New York: Random House, 2001.

Muhammad, Khalil Gibran. *The Condemnation of Blackness: Race, Crime, and the making of Modern Urban America*. Cambridge: Harvard University Press,

2011.

Mumford, Lewis. *The City in History: Its Origins, Its Transformations, and Its Prospects*. New York: Harcourt, Brace & World, 1961.

Murry, Robert K. *The Harding Era: Warren G. Harding and His Administration*. Minneapolis: University of Minnesota Press, 1969.

Myrdal, Gunnar. *An American Dilemma: The Negro Problem and Modern Democracy*. New York: Harper and Brothers, 1944.

Nelson, Scott Reynolds. *Iron Confederacies: Southern Railways, Klan Violence, and Reconstruction*. Chapel Hill: University of North Carolina Press, 1999.

Nevins, Allan. *Grover Cleveland: A Study in Courage*. New York: Dodd, Mead and Company, 1933.

New Georgia Encyclopedia. https://www.georgiaencyclopedia.org. Athens: Georgia Humanities Council and the University of Georgia Press, c. 2004–.

Newman, Louise Michele. *White Women's Rights: The Racial Origins of Feminism in the United States*. New York: Oxford University Press, 1999.

Nixon, Raymond B. *Henry W. Grady: Spokesman of the New South*. New York: Alfred A. Knopf, 1943.

Norrell, Robert J. *Up from History: The Life of Booker T. Washington*. Cambridge: Harvard University Press, 2009.

O'Connell, Robert L. *Fierce Patriot: The Tangled Lives of William Tecumseh Sherman*. New York: Random House, 2014.

Oney, Steve. *And the Dead Shall Rise: The Murder of Mary Phagan and the Lynching of Leo Frank*. New York: Vintage, 2004.

Parker, David B. *Alias Bill Arp: Charles Henry Smith and the South's "Goodly Heritage."* Athens: University of Georgia Press, 1991.

Parks, Joseph H. *Joseph E. Brown of Georgia*. Southern Biography Series, edited by Fred C. Cole and Wendell H. Stephenson. Baton Rouge: Louisiana State University Press, 1977.

Patterson, James T. *Brown v. Board of Education: A Civil Rights Milestone and Its Troubled Legacy*. Pivotal Moments in American History, edited by David Hackett Fischer and James M. McPherson. New York: Oxford University Press, 2001.

Perret, Geoffrey. *Ulysses S. Grant: Soldier & President*. New York: Random House, 1997.

Pollack, Deborah C. *Visual Art and the Urban Evolution of the New South*. Columbia: University of South Carolina Press, 2015.

Rampersad, Arnold. *Jackie Robinson: A Biography*. New York: Alfred A. Knopf, 1997.

Ransom, John Crowe, et al. *I'll Take My Stand*. New York: Peter Smith, 1951.

Rawlings, William. *The Second Coming of the Invisible Empire: The Ku Klux Klan of the 1920s*. Macon: Mercer University Press, 2016.

Reed, Thomas Walter. *David Crenshaw Barrow*. Athens, GA: by author, 1935.

Reséndez, Andrés. *The Other Slavery: The Uncovered Story of Indian Enslavement*

in America. New York: Houghton Mifflin Harcourt, 2016.
Roberts, Eugene, and Hank Klibanoff. *The Race Beat: The Press, the Civil Rights Movement, and the Awakening of a Nation*. New York: Alfred A. Knopf, 2007.
Rose, Willie Lee. *Rehearsal for Reconstruction: The Port Royal Experiment*. Introduction by C. Vann Woodward. Indianapolis: Bobbs-Merrill Company, 1964.
Ross, Earle Dudley. *The Liberal Republican Movement*. New York: Henry Holt and Company, 1919.
Rubin, Louis D., Jr. *A Gallery of Southerners*. Baton Rouge: Louisiana State University Press, 1982.
Sanders, Lynn Moss. *Howard W. Odum's Folk Odyssey: Transformation to Tolerance through African American Folk Studies*. Athens: University of Georgia Press, 2003.
Sass, Herbert Ravenel. *Outspoken: 150 years of* The News and Courier. Columbia: University of South Carolina Press, 1953.
Scott, Anne Firor. *The Southern Lady: From Pedestal to Politics, 1830–1930*. Chicago: University of Chicago Press, 1970.
Segal, Ronald. *The Black Diaspora: Five Centuries of the Black Experience outside Africa*. New York: Farrar, Straus and Giroux, 1995.
Shaler, Nathaniel Southgate. "The Negro Problem." *Atlantic Monthly* 54 (November 1884): 696–709.
Sherman, William Tecumseh. *Memoirs of General William Sherman*. Vols. 1 and 2. 1891.
Singal, Daniel Joseph. *The War Within: From Victorian to Modernist Thought in the South, 1919–1945*. Fred W. Morrison Series in Southern Studies. Chapel Hill: University of North Carolina Press, 1982.
Smith, Henry Nash. *Virgin Land: The American West as Symbol and Myth*. New York: Vintage, 1957.
Smith, Lillian. *Killers of the Dream*. New York: W.W. Norton & Company, 1961.
Smith, William Rawson. *Villa Clare: The Purposeful Life and Timeless Art Collection of J. J. Haverty*. Macon: Mercer University Press, 2006.
Southern, David W. *Gunnar Myrdal and Black-White Relations: The Use and Abuse of An American Dilemma, 1944–1969*. Baton Rouge: Louisiana State University Press, 1987.
Sproat, John Gerald. *The Best Men: Liberal Reformers in the Gilded Age*. New York: Oxford University Press, 1968.
Stahr, Walter. *Stanton: Lincoln's War Secretary*. New York: Simon & Schuster, 2017.
Stover, John Ford. *The Railroads of the South, 1865–1900: A Study in Finance and Control*. Chapel Hill: University of North Carolina Press, 1955.
Sullivan, Buddy. *Early Days on the Georgia Tidewater: The Story of McIntosh*

County and Sapelo. Darien, GA: McIntosh Board of Commissioners, 1990.

Thurmond, Michael. *Freedom: Georgia's Antislavery Heritage, 1733–1865*. Atlanta: Longstreet Press, 2002.

Tindall, George Brown. "The Central Theme Revisited." In *The Southerner as American*, edited by Charles Grier Sellers, Jr. Chapel Hill: University of North Carolina Press, 1960.

———. *The Emergence of the New South, 1913–1945*. Vol. 10 of *A History of the South*, edited by Wendell Holmes Stephenson and E. Merton Coulter. Baton Rouge: Louisiana State University Press, 1967.

Trefousse, Hans L. *Andrew Johnson: A Biography*. New York: W.W. Norton & Company, 1997.

Trudeau, Noah Andre. *Southern Storm: Sherman's March to the Sea*. New York: HarperCollins, 2008.

Turner, Arlin. *George W. Cable: A Biography*. Durham: Duke University Press, 1956.

Tushnet, Mark V. *The NAACP's Legal Strategy against Segregated Education, 1925–1950*. Chapel Hill: University of North Carolina Press, 1987.

Varon, Elizabeth R. *Appomattox: Victory, Defeat and Freedom at the End of the Civil War*. New York: Oxford University Press, 2013.

Wade, Richard C. *Slavery in the Cities: The South 1820–1860*. New York: Oxford University Press, 1964.

———. *The Urban Frontier: The Rise of Western Cities, 1790–1830*. Cambridge: Harvard University Press, 1959.

Wade, Wyn Craig. *The Fiery Cross: The Ku Klux Klan in America*. New York: Simon & Schuster, 1987.

Waldorf, Gwendolyn Brock. *The Genesis of Grady County, Georgia*. Tallahassee: Sentry Press, 2006.

Walker, Alice. "Uncle Remus, No Friend of Mine." *The Georgia Review* 66/3 (Fall 2012): 635–37.

Wall, Joseph Frazier. *Henry Watterson: Reconstructed Rebel*. New York: Oxford University Press, 1956.

Wendling, Mike. *Alt-Right: From 4chan to the White House*. London: Pluto Press, 2018.

White, Dana F. *The Urbanists, 1865–1915*. Contributions in American Studies, No. 94. Edited by Robert H. Walker. Westport, CT: Greenwood Press, 1989.

White, Evelyn C. *Alice Walker: A Life*. New York: W.W. Norton & Company, 2004.

White, Richard. *The Republic for Which It Stands: The United States during Reconstruction and the Gilded Age, 1865–96*. New York: Oxford University Press, 2017.

———. *American Ulysses: A Life of Ulysses S. Grant*. New York: Random House, 2016.

Wiebe, Robert Huddleston. *The Search for Order, 1877–1920*. The Making of America. Edited by David Donald. New York: Hill and Wang, 1967.

Wienchek, Henry. *Master of the Mountain: Thomas Jefferson and His Slaves*. New York: Farrar, Straus and Giroux, 2012.

Wilkerson, Isabel. *The Warmth of Other Suns: The Epic Story of America's Great Migration*. New York: Random House, 2010.

Williams, Julie Hedgepeth. *Three Not-So-Ordinary Joes: A Plantation Newspaperman, a Printer's Devil, an English Wit, and the Founding of Southern Literature*. Montgomery, AL: NewSouth Books, 2018.

Williams, Susan Millar, and Stephen G. Hoffius. *Upheaval in Charleston: Earthquake and Murder on the Eve of Jim Crow*. Athens: University of Georgia Press, 2011.

Williamson, Joel. *After Slavery: The Negro in South Carolina During Reconstruction, 1861–1877*. Chapel Hill: University of North Carolina Press, 1965.

———. *The Crucible of Race: Black-White Relations in the American South since Emancipation*. New York: University of Oxford Press, 1984.

Williford, William Bailey. *Peachtree Street Atlanta*. Athens: University of Georgia Press, 2010.

Wilson, Edward O. *Naturalist*. Washington D.C.: Island Press, 1994.

Wineapple, Brenda. *Ecstatic Nation: Confidence, Crisis, and Compromise, 1848–1877*. New York: Harper Perennial, 2013.

Winkler, John K. *Tobacco Tycoon: James Buchanan Duke*. New York: Random House, 1942.

Woodward, C. Vann. *The Burden of Southern History*. Baton Rouge: Louisiana State University Press, 1960.

———. *The Future of the Past*. New York: Oxford University Press, 1989.

———, ed. *Mary Chestnut's Civil War*. New Haven: Yale University Press, 1981.

———. *Origins of the New South, 1877–1913*. Vol. 9 of *A History of the South*, edited by William Holmes Stephenson and E. Merton Coulter. Baton Rouge: Louisiana State University Press, 1951.

———. *Reunion and Reaction: The Compromise of 1877 and the end of Reconstruction*. Boston: 1951.

———. *The Strange Career of Jim Crow*. New York: Oxford University Press. 1974.

———. *Thinking Back: The Perils of Writing History*. Baton Rouge: Louisiana State University Press, 1986.

———. *Tom Watson: Agrarian Rebel*. New York: 1938.

Index